U.S. Arms
Sales Policy

U.S. Arms Sales Policy
Background and Issues

Roger P. Labrie
John G. Hutchins
Edwin W. A. Peura
With the Assistance of
Diana H. Richman

American Enterprise Institute for Public Policy Research
Washington and London

Roger P. Labrie is a research associate at the American Enterprise Institute. John G. Hutchins (Commander, U.S. Navy) and Edwin W. A. Peura (Lieutenant Colonel, U.S. Air Force) were visiting fellows at AEI at the time this study was written. Diana H. Richman is a research assistant at AEI.

ISBN 0-8447-3491-8

Library of Congress Catalog Card No. 82-72491

AEI Studies 359

Printed in the United States of America

Contents

Introduction

Arms transfers have been a major instrument of U.S. policy since the end of World War II. They were relatively noncontroversial at the height of the cold war, but over the last decade the growing global market for weapons became the object of concern for several members of Congress, government officials, and some segments of the general public. President Carter, on the one hand, tried to limit the sale of arms to the third world by adopting a series of unilateral restraints on American arms exports and by initiating negotiations with the Soviet Union. He believed that arms sales could contribute to regional instability and increase the risk of war. President Reagan, on the other hand, views arms sales as necessary to prevent the Soviet Union and its proxies from destabilizing the balance of power in various regions and threatening the security of America's friends and allies.

The recent change in American policy has renewed the debate over arms sales and the contribution they make to U.S. interests throughout the world. Do arms sales enhance the security of the United States and other friendly countries? What diplomatic advantages accrue to the United States from its arms exports? Are the economic benefits from selling arms to other countries worth the potential risks inherent in such sales? This monograph examines these questions, but arrives at no conclusion. Its purpose is to present the major arguments in the debate over U.S. arms sales policy. In doing so, it provides a framework for assessing the issues.

Chapter 1 presents an overview of U.S. arms transfer policy during the postwar period. It examines in detail the policy assumptions and objectives of the Carter and Reagan administrations and looks briefly at the arms transfer policies of other major arms suppliers: the Soviet Union, France, and Great Britain. Chapter 2 describes the decision-making process for U.S. arms sales. Chapter 3 presents the arguments favoring significant curtailment of U.S. arms sales, and chapter 4 outlines the case against curtailing sales. Although the authors do not agree with all of the viewpoints presented, they do believe that each one merits consideration.

This monograph has been written with several audiences in mind. It is hoped that academics, journalists, and the general public will find the study a useful introduction to a complex issue that bridges the foreign policy and defense policy arenas. In addition, U.S. arms sales policy has been chosen as the 1982–1983 national high school debate topic, and it is hoped that this monograph will be useful to those who take part in this debate.

We would like to thank several colleagues at AEI for their help in preparing this study. Marcus I. Hoffman wrote an early draft of chapter 2 and provided valuable assistance during the project. Robin Emery, Leslie Johnston, and Pamela Calvert performed a variety of administrative and secretarial functions with skill. Although two of the authors are active duty military officers, the views expressed in this study should not be construed as representing those of the Department of Defense.

Notes on Data and Terms

Various organizations compile statistics on arms transfers. The reader should be aware of differences in the use and presentation of data by these sources.

The U.S. Arms Control and Disarmament Agency (ACDA), for example, does not include the cost of military construction, training, and technical services in computations of the value of delivered arms transfers in its *World Military Expenditures and Arms Transfers 1970–1979* (March 1982). Although ACDA provides both current- and constant-dollar estimates, other sources often do not. The Department of Defense Security Assistance Agency's compilation *Foreign Military Sales, Foreign Military Construction Sales and Military Assistance Facts* (as of September 1981) differentiates between sales agreements and deliveries using current dollars.

The reader should also be alerted to the selective use of data to support an argument. One might, for example, select the 1975–1979 period to compare U.S. and Soviet arms sales rather than the 1970–1979 period. The former shows that Soviet transfers in the aggregate exceeded those of the United States; the latter shows the reverse. Trend analyses, in current or constant dollars, can also be misleading. Analysts do not always identify the source of their data and often fail to use data consistently. Data can be selected to support a bias.

Another aspect that should be considered is how the magnitude of arms transfers is presented. Most presentations, including this study, employ dollar values. Another measure used by some studies is the number of units transferred by type of equipment. The number of units may be more appropriate in some cases as a measure of actual military capability. Numbers of units, however, are not sufficient to evaluate relative military strength. The fact that the Soviet Union delivered almost twice as many tanks as the United States to third-world countries in the 1973–1979 period, for example, does not necessarily mean the Soviets supplied twice as much firepower or capability as the United States. The quality of the arms may not be the same, and some of the weapons may be replacements rather than

3

additions to the operational capabilities of recipient countries. (Data on numbers of tanks and other weapons delivered are in *Changing Perspectives on U.S. Arms Transfer Policy,* report prepared by the Congressional Research Service for the Committee on Foreign Affairs of the House of Representatives, September 25, 1981.)

Definitions of terms used in this study are as follows:

Commercial sales: sales made directly by private U.S. arms manufacturers to foreign governments. Examples of items transferred through commercial sales include spare parts, ammunition, small arms, and other equipment.

Foreign military sales (FMS): sales made with the U.S. government acting as the agent for U.S. manufacturers and foreign governments. The U.S. government buys the arms and resells them to foreign governments. Technical assistance and a variety of design, construction, training, management, and support services are often included in FMS sales. Credits (loans) are also made available to some foreign governments to purchase arms in the FMS program.

Grants: arms and other equipment given to foreign governments and paid for with funds appropriated by Congress under the Military Assistance Program (MAP).

1
U.S. Arms Transfer Policy since World War II

Arms transfers to other countries have been a major and continuing instrument of U.S. foreign policy since World War II. Arms exports have traditionally taken two forms: grant aid and weapons sales for credit or cash. From World War II until the mid-1960s, arms transfers were a noncontroversial component of U.S. national security policy. It was generally accepted that weapons exports not only were helpful to recipient countries but contributed to U.S. security as well. Providing weapons to allies and friends was justified by the perceived Soviet threat and constituted a key element of U.S. containment policy.

The situation began to change, however, in the late 1960s. Although arms transfers continued to play a prominent role in U.S. foreign policy, increasing reliance on weapons exports by successive administrations began to cause concern among members of Congress and segments of the American public. Not only was the volume of arms transfers rising steadily, but the weapons sold abroad were becoming more sophisticated. Whereas arms transfers had previously been directed almost exclusively toward European allies and other close friends of the United States, predominantly in the form of military assistance grants, more and more transfers in the 1970s were made to third-world countries through government-to-government sales.

By the mid-1970s Congress had begun to exercise greater control over U.S. arms transfers, although the primary responsibility for setting arms export policy still resided with the president. The Carter policy sought to limit unilaterally U.S. arms sales to the third world and to negotiate multilateral restraints with other major arms suppliers. The Reagan administration, however, appears to have abandoned a majority of the objectives of the Carter policy. It has instead emphasized what it sees as a global threat posed by the Soviet Union, a threat that requires the United States to supply arms to its friends and allies to ensure mutual security.

Early History

Before World War II the United States ranked third in arms exports behind France and Great Britain.[1] With the onset of the war, however, arms transfers became a major instrument of U.S. foreign policy. The initial step was the revision in 1939 of the Neutrality Act, which lifted the legal prohibition against the sale of arms to belligerents and permitted the "cash and carry" concept to prevail during wartime.[2]

As the war in Europe escalated, the United States expanded its role as a supplier of arms and defense services. After revision of the Neutrality Act, the U.S. government found additional ways to aid the Allies despite America's "neutral" status. After the German invasion of France in 1940, President Roosevelt made the destroyers-for-bases deal with Great Britain. This agreement, which many viewed as a flagrant violation of American neutrality, provided the British with fifty U.S. destroyers in exchange for ninety-nine-year leases on British bases in the Western hemisphere. In March 1941, Congress passed the Lend-Lease program, establishing the United States as the arms supplier for the Allied forces. Under Lend-Lease, arms worth tens of billions of dollars were transferred to the Allies between 1941 and 1945.[3]

The actions taken by the U.S. government during World War II marked a turn in weapons export policy. The United States had been a major arms supplier during World War I as well, but the volume of transfers had slackened during the interwar period. In the years immediately following World War II, however, arms transfer programs continued under the U.S. strategy of containing Communist expansion.

It had become clear that Soviet aspirations were in conflict with those of the United States and Western Europe. The Truman Doctrine, enunciated in 1947, was designed to provide American assistance to countries threatened by the Soviet Union, and it became the cornerstone of U.S. containment policy. The policy was initially a response to Communist guerrilla activity in Greece and Soviet pressure on Turkey to gain joint control over the Dardanelles. The enactment

---

1. Geoffrey Kemp, with Steven Miller, "The Arms Transfer Phenomenon," in Andrew J. Pierre, ed., *Arms Transfers and American Foreign Policy* (New York: New York University Press, 1979), p. 21.

2. Defense Institute of Security Assistance Management (DISAM), *The Management of Security Assistance* (Wright-Patterson AFB, Ohio: Defense Institute of Security Assistance Management, 1981), p. 1-22.

3. Ibid.

of Public Law 75, providing military aid to Greece and Turkey, marked the beginning of military assistance programs.[4]

With the formation of NATO in 1949 an increasing number of weapons were exported to America's European allies. That year Congress also passed the Mutual Defense Assistance Act, which formalized and expanded existing military aid commitments to the Philippines, Greece and Turkey, and the Republic of China.[5] The act was passed to demonstrate U.S. commitment to the newly formed NATO alliance and was designed to cover U.S. military assistance to NATO allies and other friends of the United States. It designated such assistance as "essential to enable the United States and other nations dedicated to the purposes and principles of the United Nations to participate effectively in arrangements for individual and collective security."[6]

Military assistance during this period consisted primarily of weapons transfers from stockpiles of surplus war materiel. The majority of U.S. arms transfers were made "free of charge" under what became known as the Military Assistance Program (MAP). Aid went mainly to NATO allies and other countries seen as threatened by communism. Of the $32 billion in military aid transferred in the immediate postwar years, France received $4.5 billion, Turkey $2.2 billion, Italy $2.3 billion, Greece $1.5 billion, and the United Kingdom $1.1 billion. The Netherlands and Belgium also received about $1 billion each.[7]

The use of weapons transfers as an instrument of American foreign policy thus began in response to perceived threats to the United States and its Western European allies. What emerged, according to one observer, was "a military strategy of deterrence; its foreign-policy counterpart was containment, and military assistance was to be the mortar of the NATO alliance."[8]

As the policy of containment expanded in the 1950s and early 1960s to include other geographic regions, so did U.S. military assistance policy. America's European allies were experiencing economic recovery sufficient to contribute to their own defense needs, and

4. Ibid., p. 1-25.

5. William H. Lewis, "Political Influence: The Diminished Capacity," in Stephanie G. Neuman and Robert E. Harkavy, eds., *Arms Transfers in the Modern World* (New York: Praeger, 1979), p. 188.

6. Quoted ibid.

7. *Debating the Direction of U.S. Foreign Policy: 1979-1980 High School Debate Analysis* (Washington, D.C.: American Enterprise Institute, 1979), p. 35.

8. Lewis, "Political Influence," p. 189.

events in the Middle East and the Far East were causing a reassessment of U.S. arms transfers policy. The outbreak of war in Korea in 1950, Egypt's turn to the Soviet bloc for arms in the mid-1950s, and increasing American involvement in Indochina toward the end of the decade resulted in a shift in the direction of weapons exports. U.S. foreign aid policy was broadened from support only for our allies to support for other nations as well. Thus from 1950 to 1965 the primary recipients of U.S. arms exports were France, West Germany, Italy, Turkey, Taiwan, and South Korea.[9]

The shift in arms transfers from traditional allies of the United States to third-world countries in Southeast Asia and the Middle East continued throughout the 1960s. The mid-1960s also saw a change in the form of U.S. arms exports. As the stock of surplus World War II military equipment diminished, U.S. security assistance changed from MAP grants to arms sales under foreign military sales (FMS) programs. In fiscal year 1961, military aid was twice as large as sales. By 1966, the sales figures were double those for military aid (excluding South Vietnam).[10]

In 1969 President Nixon, largely in response to the unsuccessful American military involvement in Vietnam, established new guidelines for U.S. security assistance policy. The Nixon Doctrine declared that the United States would respect its treaty commitments and continue to help its friends and allies through military and economic assistance, but it would "look to the nation directly threatened to assume the primary responsibility of providing the manpower for its defense."[11]

The use of grant military aid continued to decline in the 1970s. The number of countries receiving U.S. military assistance declined from fifty-eight in FY 1966 to forty-six in FY 1975. Meanwhile, the number of arms sales recipients increased. In fiscal year 1966, fifty-nine nations received FMS deliveries; by FY 1975 the number was seventy-four. Commercial deliveries also increased, from fifty-

9. Paul C. Warnke, with Edward C. Luck, "American Arms Transfers: Policy and Process in the Executive Branch," in Andrew J. Pierre, ed., *Arms Transfers and American Foreign Policy* (New York: New York University Press, 1979), p. 195.

10. Ibid., p. 197.

11. Congressional Research Service, *Changing Perspectives on U.S. Arms Transfer Policy*, Report to the Subcommittee on International Security and Scientific Affairs of the Committee on Foreign Affairs, U.S. House of Representatives, September 25, 1981, p. 5.

one countries receiving arms from U.S. companies in FY 1966 to seventy-seven in FY 1974.[12]

In the latter half of the 1960s, some members of Congress began to question U.S. arms transfer policy. With enactment in 1968 of the Foreign Military Sales Act, Congress required administrations to emphasize foreign policy considerations in their arms sales policies. The act prohibited arms sales to governments that engage in human rights violations or impede social progress.[13] The dollar value of arms transactions was rising dramatically, and the weapons sold by the United States were becoming increasingly sophisticated. These factors, combined with what was seen as an overcasual attitude on the part of U.S. policy makers toward arms sales, remained a source of concern among members of Congress and the public in the 1970s.

The Nixon and Ford administrations did not appear to have coherent arms sales policies. Many analysts thought that arms sales agreements were made haphazardly and without due consideration for long-term strategic interests. President Nixon in 1972 instructed the bureaucracy to honor virtually all requests from the government of Iran for conventional arms, thereby circumventing the formal review process. Similarly, President Ford decided during the 1976 presidential campaign to sell Israel military equipment that had previously been banned.[14] Arms sales appeared to have become a tool of politics rather than a policy for security, and the arms traffic appeared to be out of control.

In response, Congress asserted its power over individual transactions by enacting the Nelson amendment to the FY 1975 foreign aid authorization bill. The amendment required the president to report military sales of $25 million or more and gave Congress twenty days to veto them by passing a concurrent resolution of disapproval.[15] Congress had long exercised authority over grant aid,

12. As cited in Warnke, "American Arms Transfers: Policy and Process in the Executive Branch," pp. 198-99.

13. Congressional Research Service, *Changing Perspectives on U.S. Arms Transfer Policy*, p. 4.

14. U.S. Congress, Senate, Committee on Foreign Relations, *U.S. Military Sales to Iran*, Staff Report to the Subcommittee on Foreign Assistance, 94th Cong., 2d sess., July 1976, p. 41; and Andrew J. Pierre, *The Global Politics of Arms Sales* (Princeton, N.J.: Princeton University Press, 1982), p. 48.

15. Richard Whittle, "Controls on Arms Sales Lifted After Failure of Carter Policy to Reduce Flow of Weapons," *Congressional Quarterly Weekly Report*, April 10, 1982, p. 798.

which requires the appropriation of funds. With passage of the Nelson amendment, it secured veto power over major arms sales as well.

Other congressional initiatives in the area of U.S. arms sales culminated in 1976 in passage of the International Security Assistance and Arms Export Control Act. This measure was designed to shift the emphasis from selling arms to controlling the sales of arms, and it included specific congressional guidelines for U.S. arms sales policy. With the Arms Export Control Act, Congress retained the right to veto proposed arms sales and extended from twenty days to thirty days the period of time during which a proposed sale could be vetoed. Congress took several additional steps to control arms traffic.[16] A ceiling was placed on commercial arms sales: sales to non-NATO countries in excess of $25 million were required to occur on a government-to-government basis. Negotiations were encouraged to reduce and control international arms traffic. Information on arms transfers was disseminated to Congress and the public: the president was required to submit to members of Congress quarterly information on arms transactions. U.S. military assistance and advisory groups (MAAGs) in foreign countries were restricted; MAAGs were reduced in size and scope of action with regard to transfers of military equipment; and security assistance was withheld from countries whose governments engage in human rights violations.

The Carter Administration

The election of Jimmy Carter in 1976 represented an affirmation of the congressional initiatives to limit the sale of American arms overseas. On May 19, 1977, President Carter announced his arms sales policy, stating that conventional arms transfers would be viewed as an "exceptional foreign policy implement, to be used only in instances where it can be clearly demonstrated that the transfer contributes to our national security interests." The Carter policy established controls on transfers to all nations except member countries of NATO, Japan, Australia, and New Zealand. The controls were binding "unless extraordinary circumstances necessitate a Presidential exception, or where I determine that countries friendly to the United States must depend on advanced weaponry to offset quantitative and other disadvantages in order to maintain a regional balance."[17]

16. Congressional Research Service, *Changing Perspectives on U.S. Arms Transfer Policy*, pp. 6-9.

17. "President Carter Announces Policy on Transfers of Conventional Arms," *Department of State Bulletin*, June 13, 1977, p. 625.

Carter's basic guidelines, as expressed in his statement of May 1977, were as follows:

• The United States would reduce the dollar volume of new commitments. For fiscal year 1978, a ceiling was set at $8.4 billion, an 8 percent decrease from fiscal year 1977 in new commitments to nonexempt nations. Excluded from the ceiling were non-weapons-related services such as military construction and U.S. commercial arms transfers.

• The United States would not introduce newly developed advanced weapons systems into a region until they were operationally deployed with U.S. forces.

• An effort would be made to promote respect for human rights in recipient countries, and the economic impact of arms transfers to countries receiving U.S. economic assistance was to be considered.

• The United States would not permit development or significant modification of advanced weapons systems solely for export.

• The United States would not permit coproduction agreements for significant weapons, equipment, and major components.

• The United States would not permit the retransfer of American weapons to third countries. This stipulation was laid down to avoid "unnecessary bilateral friction caused by later denials."

• The "burden of persuasion" for a sale rested on proponents, not opponents, of an arms sale.

• An attempt would be made to remove the economic incentives for arms sales, such as lower per unit costs for Defense Department procurement of similar items.

• U.S. government employees were forbidden to help arms salesmen abroad without express authorization from Washington.

• An attempt would be made to reduce international arms traffic through multilateral negotiations.

In retrospect, the Carter policy of unilateral restraint met with mixed success. His guidelines did provide criteria to judge requests for arms, but in practice arms sales were not an "exceptional" implement of foreign policy, nor did the dollar ceiling result in reduced arms sales.[18] The conventional arms transfer talks, which were to complement the effort at unilateral restraint, also fell short of their objective of limiting the arms sales of the other major supplier nations.

18. Pierre, *The Global Politics of Arms Sales*, pp. 57-58. Seventeen exceptions were made to the guidelines by the Carter administration. See Congressional Research Service, *Changing Perspectives on U.S. Arms Transfer Policy*, pp. 25–26.

Conventional Arms Transfer Talks. One of the essential components of the Carter administration's arms transfer policy was its initiative for multilateral restraint among the major arms suppliers. Soon after the inauguration, administration officials were dispatched to major European capitals to discuss mutual cooperation in reducing arms transfers, including European agreement not to take advantage of American unilateral restraint by selling the arms the United States might refuse to sell. The reactions of the allies varied, but the Europeans made it clear that their support was dependent upon agreement on restraint by the Soviets.

Conventional arms transfers were discussed during the first visit to Moscow by Secretary of State Cyrus Vance in March 1977. The United States and the Soviet Union agreed to set up a bilateral working group to address this subject. The first session of the conventional arms transfer (CAT) talks was held in December 1977 in Washington. The American delegation explained the Carter administration's policy on arms transfers and outlined the idea of multilateral restraint. The Soviets viewed the session as exploratory and sought clarification of the Carter policy.[19]

The second round of negotiations was held in Helsinki five months later, in May 1978. The Soviet delegation agreed at this session that arms transfers were a serious problem that required further discussion. They also presented draft political-legal criteria for defining permissible and nonpermissible arms transfers. In a different vein, American officials suggested military and technical guidelines for weapons exports similar to the unilateral guidelines that the administration had adopted.[20]

Throughout the second session of the negotiations, the American delegation consistently linked CAT talks to the 1972 agreement on Basic Principles of Relations between the United States and the Soviet Union and the 1973 Agreement on the Prevention of Nuclear War. These documents had "sought to spell out rules necessary to sustain and promote cooperative relations between the superpowers and to avoid situations that might lead to nuclear war."[21] A joint communiqué issued at the end of the second session stated that "these meetings, being a component of the Soviet-American negotiations on cessation of the arms race, are held in accordance with the Basic Principles of Relations."[22]

19. Ibid., p. 287.
20. Ibid.
21. Barry M. Blechman, Janne E. Nolan, and Alan Platt, "Pushing Arms," *Foreign Policy*, no. 46 (Spring 1982), p. 142.
22. Ibid., p. 143.

It was evident after the second session that progress was possible, so a third round of talks was scheduled for July 1978. As the American delegation was preparing for the meeting, however, agreement within the government over the U.S. approach to the negotiations could not be achieved. The Arms Control and Disarmament Agency (ACDA) wanted to minimize the political aspects of the talks and instead emphasize technical issues. In lieu of dealing with foreign policy aspects of arms transfers, ACDA wanted to establish a list of weapons whose transfer could be limited or prohibited. According to this view "the objective of the talks would be to limit specific weapons worldwide, taking into account the differences between various regions, rather than to limit all weapons transfers to individual regions with exceptions for specific weapons."[23]

The State Department, however, viewed the political ramifications of the CAT talks as more important than the technical issues of arms transfer restraint. State Department officials hoped that one outcome of the negotiations would be a better mutual understanding of Soviet and American objectives in the third world as a basis for regulating their activities in that part of the world. It followed from this premise that the most effective strategy centered on limiting arms exports to specific regions or subregions of the globe rather than on controlling transfers of specific weapons systems worldwide.

President Carter eventually agreed to follow the political approach advocated by the State Department. During the third session of the CAT talks, the American delegation pressed the case for discussing arms transfers to specific regions of tension. The Soviet Union continued to emphasize the need to establish legal principles governing arms transfers. The United States also attempted to set military guidelines for weapons export. Both countries eventually agreed to attach equal importance to legal principles and to technical guidelines. The Soviet Union also agreed to discuss arms transfer restraints for particular regions. By the end of the third round of talks, both sides had agreed on a three-part framework for arms transfer restraint. Included in this framework were political-legal criteria by which to judge potential recipients, military-technical criteria limiting the export of certain weapons systems, and plans for implementing these guidelines in specific regions.[24]

In preparing for the fourth round of negotiations, scheduled for Mexico City in December 1978, American officials proposed that negotiations focus on two regions, Latin America and sub-Saharan

23. Ibid., p. 145.
24. Ibid., p. 147.

13

Africa. The Soviets agreed and suggested that negotiations also include a discussion of West Asia and East Asia. This presented a problem for American policy makers, because West Asia includes Iran and East Asia includes South Korea and China. Some American officials said that discussing arms transfer restraint in West Asia might further undermine the already unstable political situation in Iran. As for the Soviet proposal to discuss East Asia, American officials were reluctant to make U.S. arms sales to South Korea a subject for negotiations with the Soviets. Some American officials were also concerned that such discussions could interfere with the negotiations then under way to normalize relations with Peking. President Carter therefore instructed the American delegation to limit bargaining with the Soviets to Latin America and sub-Saharan Africa and to walk out of the negotiations if other regions were included.

The regional issue was not considered during the fourth round of talks. Legal and technical criteria were addressed, but the sessions did not end in agreement, and the CAT negotiations were over.

There are several reasons for the failure of the CAT talks, not the least of which was general deterioration of Soviet-American relations at the time. Some analysts said the greatest impediment to progress in the CAT talks was the unilateral restraint that the United States was applying to its arms transfers. The Soviets, for all intents and purposes, were negotiating in a "cost-free environment."[25] The administration's failure to reach agreement on restraints with the Europeans also circumscribed the U.S. bargaining leverage in the negotiations with the Soviets.

Dissension within the Carter administration and the resulting indecision on how to approach the question of multilateral restraints on arms transfers also contributed to the failure of CAT. The American strategy seemed to fluctuate between the technical arms control approach advocated by ACDA and the foreign policy approach preferred by the State Department. Once the president decided in favor of other diplomatic and strategic interests, such as normalization of relations with China and stability in Iran, the flexibility of the American negotiating strategy was severely limited. Several former Carter administration officials have provided the following explanation for the failure of the CAT talks: "In 1978 Carter made two contradictory decisions: first, that CAT should be a political rather than a technical negotiation; second, that the international political relations upon

25. Michael D. Salomon, David J. Louscher, and Paul Y. Hammond, "Lessons of the Carter Approach to Restraining Arms Transfers," *Survival* (September/ October 1981), p. 203.

which it would impinge were too sensitive to discuss with the Soviet Union. This contradiction, above all, assured the failure of CAT."[26]

The Reagan Administration

In contrast to the attempts by President Carter to control U.S. arms sales abroad, the emphasis under the Reagan administration has shifted to the use of arms sales as a key foreign policy instrument. Unlike the Carter statement on arms sales policy, President Reagan's first official statement on the matter, on July 8, 1981, underlined the need for flexibility in arms sales and focused on the use of arms sales to counter the Soviet global challenge.

According to the directive issued by President Reagan, the United States must "not only strengthen its own military capabilities, but be prepared to help its friends and allies to strengthen theirs through the transfer of conventional arms and other forms of security assistance." The Reagan administration views arms transfers as an "essential element of its global defense posture and an indispensable component of its foreign policy."[27] The goals of arms transfers are:

- to help deter aggression by enhancing preparedness of friends and allies
- to increase military effectiveness by improving America's ability in conjunction with its friends and allies "to project power in response to threats posed by mutual adversaries"
- to support efforts that "foster the ability of our forces to deploy and operate with those of our friends and allies," thereby strengthening our mutual security relationships
- to demonstrate the enduring interest that the United States has in its friends and allies "and that it will not allow them to be at a military disadvantage"
- to "foster regional and internal stability, thus encouraging peaceful resolution of disputes and evolutionary change"
- to help enhance United States defense production capabilities and efficiency

The Reagan policy contains no rigid guidelines; requests for U.S. arms will be evaluated "case-by-case" with "high priority" given to major alliance partners and to those countries with which the United States has cooperative security relationships. The Reagan

26. Blechman, Nolan, and Platt, "Pushing Arms," p. 148.
27. "Conventional Arms Transfer Policy," *Department of State Bulletin*, September 1981, p. 61.

15

directive concludes by asserting that the United States must pursue a "sober, responsible, and balanced arms transfer policy, a policy that will advance our national security interests and those of the free world." With respect to opportunities for restraint among major arms suppliers, the Reagan administration "retains a genuine interest in arms transfers restraint and remains prepared to consider specific proposals toward that end."

Although it is still too early to compare the impact of the Reagan arms sales policy with that of President Carter, the differences in rhetoric are clear.[28] The basic difference lies in the perception of American interests and the relationship that arms transfers have to those interests. President Carter seemed to accept the premise that arms sales are inherently bad and a potential threat to peace. It logically followed that the United States, then the world's largest arms exporter to developing countries, should pursue a policy of unilateral restraint to control the international arms traffic.

President Reagan, in contrast to President Carter, sees arms sales not as necessarily a cause of political instability but as a means by which governments can maintain peace and order within their countries and regional stability. The Reagan administration contends that the Soviet Union, not the United States, is the largest supplier of arms to the third world, that U.S. arms sales are necessary to counter the Soviet threat, and that pursuance of a policy of unilateral restraint would be harmful to U.S. interests. The current administration also views a "vital, viable, imaginative [arms] industry" as an integral part of American defense and foreign policy.[29]

In addition to the basic difference in the perceptions of the two administrations, there are more specific differences between the Carter and Reagan arms sales policies. An important one centers on the use of arms transfers as an instrument of foreign policy. The Carter policy stated that arms transfers were to be an "exceptional implement of foreign policy," but the Reagan administration views weapons transfers as "an essential element of its global defense posture and an indispensable component of its foreign policy."

One of the often disputed features of President Carter's policy directive was the unsuccessful annual ceiling on the dollar value of arms transfers. When the administration granted several major exceptions to the ceiling, the total value of U.S. arms sales continued

28. Congressional Research Service, *Changing Perspectives on U.S. Arms Transfer Policy*, pp. 35-39.

29. As cited in Whittle, "Controls on Arms Sales," p. 802.

to increase, from $12.8 billion in 1977 to $17.1 billion in 1980; only about half of these sales were covered by the ceiling.[30]

The Carter policy also included a number of qualitative restrictions on U.S. arms transfers. President Carter prohibited "the development or significant modification of advanced weapons systems solely for export"; the Reagan policy contains no such prohibition. (Carter, however, did eventually allow the development of the FX fighter specifically for export.) Unlike the Carter policy, the Reagan directive does not bar the United States from being the first to introduce new or more advanced weapons into a region. Another dissimilarity is that Carter prohibited the sale or coproduction of newly developed advanced weapons systems until they were "operationally deployed with U.S. forces." The two administrations also differed on coproduction agreements. The Carter policy prohibited coproduction agreements for "significant weapons, equipment, and major components" with exceptions confined to a "limited class of items." The Reagan policy states that requests for coproduction agreements will be given "special scrutiny," but does not prohibit them.

President Carter also sought to remove the incentive to use arms sales to lower per unit procurement costs to the Department of Defense. The Reagan directive states that arms sales can "help to enhance United States defense production capabilities and efficiency."

The Carter administration attempted to reduce commercial arms sales by discouraging American officials abroad from assisting U.S. arms salesmen. In a directive popularly named "the leprosy letter," U.S. government officials were barred from helping U.S. arms manufacturers abroad without express authorization from Washington. The Reagan administration has taken the opposite view: in April 1981 the Carter directive was rescinded, and U.S. officials overseas were instructed to extend the same courtesies to American firms selling arms as to other business representatives.

Another significant difference in the two approaches lies in the attitudes of the two administrations toward multilateral arms sales restraint. One of the cornerstones of the Carter policy was an effort to achieve multilateral restraint among other major arms suppliers. The administration's unilateral restraint was intended to set an example for other arms suppliers as it tried to initiate multilateral negotiations on the subject. Attempts at multilateral negotiations with America's NATO allies gave way to unsuccessful bilateral talks with the Soviet Union. In contrast to the Carter policy, the

30. Pierre, *The Global Politics of Arms Sales*, p. 57.

Reagan administration is willing to listen to the proposals of others, but says it is unwilling to jeopardize U.S. interests through a policy of unilateral restraint.

Finally, with regard to the issue of human rights, the Carter policy stated that in formulating security assistance programs consistent with its arms transfer policy the United States would continue efforts "to promote and advance respect for human rights in recipient countries." The Reagan policy directive does not make specific reference to human rights, and it appears that the linkage between human rights and the formulation of arms sales policy will be deemphasized.

Other Major Arms Suppliers

Aside from the United States, other major suppliers of arms to the third world include the Soviet Union, France, and Great Britain. Together, these four suppliers account for about 87 percent of all arms transfers to the third world.[31] West Germany, Italy, Sweden, and some East European countries are also suppliers. Moreover, several third-world countries, such as Israel, Brazil, Argentina, and South Africa, are developing indigenous arms industries and exporting weapons. This section will briefly examine the arms sales policies of the other three major arms suppliers. Unlike the United States, these exporters release little official information on their arms sales, and hence relatively little is known about their policies.

Soviet Union.[32] The Soviets have been providing military assistance to movements struggling to gain power in other countries and to friendly regimes since the time of the Bolsheviks. Soviet arms transfers and other forms of military assistance remained a relatively unimportant tool of Moscow's foreign policy until the post-Stalin years. Today, arms sales are perhaps the Soviets' most important instru-

---

31. Ibid., p. 42.

32. This section is based on the following sources: Pierre, *The Global Politics of Arms Sales*, pp. 73–82; Center for Defense Information, "Soviet Weapons Exports: Russian Roulette in the Third World," *The Defense Monitor*, January 1979; *The Military Balance 1981–1982* (London: International Institute for Strategic Studies, 1981); Edward L. Warner III, "The Defense Policy of the Soviet Union," in Douglas J. Murray and Paul R. Viotti, eds., *The Defense Policies of Nations: A Comparative Study* (Baltimore: Johns Hopkins University Press, 1982), chap. 3; and Congressional Research Service, *Changing Perspectives on U.S. Arms Transfer Policy*, p. 15. Dollar figures are in current dollars and include the value of weapons, spare parts, construction, and training.

ment to further their interests in the third world. The declining appeal of communist ideology and of the political and economic systems that Moscow has to offer the less-developed countries would seem to indicate that arms sales will continue to play a key role in Soviet foreign policy.

The Soviet Union was the second largest supplier of arms and other military services to the third world during the 1970s, after the United States. Measured by estimated current-dollar value (not cancelling out the effects of inflation), Soviet arms transfer deliveries to less-developed countries rose from $3.5 billion in 1973 to $6.7 billion in 1980. In the Middle East, Iraq, Syria, Libya, and (before 1973) Egypt have been the major recipients. Vietnam and India are the major recipients of Soviet arms in Asia; in sub-Saharan Africa, Ethiopia, Angola, Mozambique, Guinea, Nigeria, Somalia, and Uganda have received large quantities of weapons from Moscow during the last decade. Cuba, Peru, and Nicaragua are the principal recipients of Soviet arms in Latin America.

In recent years the Soviets have concentrated their arms exports on countries able to pay in cash, such as Libya, Iraq, and Algeria, and have also cut back on grant military aid and easy credit terms. Soviet motives for selling arms still remain the traditional ones—to gain political influence, to support ideologically compatible regimes, to gain access to overseas base facilities—but acquiring hard currency to finance Moscow's imports of food and technology from the West seems to have become an important motive in recent years. Yet when the Soviets have a keen interest in developing closer relations with a recipient, such as India, sales are still made on generous credit terms.

As Soviet arms transfers increasingly become cash sales, more buyers insist on receiving the best weapons for their money, a phenomenon that is also evident in the arms sales of the United States and other Western arms exporters. Whereas in the past the Soviet Union confined its transfers of modern weapons to its closest allies in Eastern Europe, in recent years it has sold some of its most sophisticated arms to select countries in the third world. MiG-23 and MiG-25 aircraft, for example, have been sold to Libya and Syria, and both countries have also received T-62 and T-72 tanks. The Soviets have also sold Scud missiles and medium bombers to developing countries.

Although Soviet arms sold to third-world countries tend to be somewhat less sophisticated and less expensive than American arms, the Soviets have demonstrated an ability in recent years to provide arms to recipients more quickly than the other major suppliers. At least two factors seem to account for this: considerable improvement of capacity to transport arms quickly by air and sea to distant countries and the production of surplus stocks of the latest weapons specifically earmarked for export. Production of Soviet arms outside the Warsaw Pact countries is rarely licensed by Moscow; production of MiG-21 fighters under license in India is an exception. In addition, the Soviets do not sell maintenance packages, but tend to replace weapons in kind rather than repair them. This also accounts for the larger number of arms transfered by the Soviets.

France.[33] French arms exports ranked third in dollar value of arms deliveries to the third world in recent years. Measured by estimated current-dollar value, deliveries rose from $620 million in 1973 to $2.5 billion in 1980.

The French government actively promotes arms sales to other countries. The nature of the French arms industry accounts for this aggressive sales policy. In 1980, about 40 percent of the arms manufactured in France were exported. More than 75 percent of the weapons produced in the aeronautics industry are sold overseas, and of the 280,000 workers employed in the French arms industry, at least 90,000 owe their jobs to sales to other countries. France's arms sales have become more than just a symbol of national independence in foreign affairs; arms exports have become indispensable to the economic viability of several sectors of French industry, in particular aeronautics. An independent arms industry is also viewed as a fundamental underpinning of an independent foreign and defense policy. France is largely self-sufficient today in military research and development and in weapons production. With the second largest defense industry in Western Europe (after Great Britain's), France is capable of producing the entire range of arms needed by its military forces.

The Délégation Générale pour l'Armement (DGA) is the government body responsible for overseeing the French arms industry. Within the DGA, a special office called the Direction des Affaires Internationales has the task of promoting arms sales to other countries. There are also four corporations owned jointly by the state and the

33. This section is based on the following sources: Pierre, *The Global Politics of Arms Sales*, pp. 83-99; Alan Ned Sabrosky, "The Defense Policy of France," in Murray and Viotti, *The Defense Policies of Nations*, chap. 5; Felix Kessler, "France Remains a Major Arms Dealer," *Wall Street Journal*, May 4, 1982; and Congressional Research Service, *Changing Perspectives on U.S. Arms Transfer Policy*, p. 15. Dollar figures are in current dollars and include the value of weapons, spare parts, construction, and training.

private sector that specialize in promoting arms sales. The French arms industry consists of three sectors: plants operated by the DGA, nationalized industries, and private enterprises. The French government maintains close ties with private arms producers, owning a percentage of some companies and influencing the appointment of their top executives.

Governmental decision making on arms sales is centralized in the Commission Interministérielle pour l'Etude des Exportations de Matériels de Guerre, which consists of representatives from the Ministries of Foreign Affairs, Defense, Finance, and Economy. The commission reviews all proposed sales case by case and determines which weapons are eligible for export. No formal policy guidelines have been announced by the government, but several general principles have been enunciated: no arms will be sold to belligerents or to countries in a war zone; caution is to be exercised when selling arms to regions of tension; and no arms will be sold that could be used for internal police action. These principles, however, have not always been observed. Until 1979, when arms sales were banned, France had been the largest supplier of arms to South Africa. France continued to sell arms to Iraq and Iran after they went to war in 1980.

France's policy on the types of arms sold and to whom is probably more permissive than that of any other major supplier. Some observers say that French weapons exports are guided more by politics than by profits. The recent trend in French arms sales resembles that of the United States. Before the 1970s, most of the arms that France exported were sold to other Western industrial countries. During the past decade, however, the focus of French arms sales shifted to the third world, in particular to the Middle East. In 1980, about 55 percent of French arms exports went to the Middle East.

France has been selling many of the weapons it produces to countries that supply it with oil, such as Saudi Arabia and Iraq. It is believed that such arms sales will help ensure oil deliveries in the future. Earnings from arms sold to the oil-producing countries in the Middle East have paid for about 20 percent of the cost of recent French oil imports.

French arms exports to countries outside NATO have been diverse, including Mirage F-1 fighters to Jordan; Mirage F-5s and Super Etendards to Argentina; Puma helicopters to Lebanon, Spain, and Argentina; AMX-30 and AMX-13 tanks to Iraq, Saudi Arabia, Lebanon, and Singapore; A69 frigates to Argentina; Exocet missiles to Argentina and Ecuador; and Milan and HOT antitank missiles to Syria. France is not a member of NATO's military structure; so it is somewhat at a disadvantage in selling arms to other countries in the alliance. Thus French arms sales are heavily concentrated in the third world.

Great Britain.[34] Britain ranks fourth among the major suppliers of arms to the third world. In 1973, British arms deliveries were valued at $360 million; by 1980 they had risen to $600 million, as measured in current dollars.

Arms are produced in Britain by both the public and the private sectors, with the private sector by far the larger producer. Although many of the economic motivations for French arms sales also apply to Great Britain, the British arms industry is not as dependent on exports as the French arms industry. Moreover, some of the economic benefits of French arms sales, such as lower unit costs, also apply to the British to a lesser degree.

Great Britain's Ministry of Defence accords a high priority to promoting arms sales to other countries. The Defence Sales Organization (DSO), located within the Ministry of Defence, is responsible for foreign military sales and has personnel stationed in embassies abroad. DSO sells directly to other countries arms manufactured by government-owned royal ordnance factories. In addition, DSO advises and supports overseas arms sales by the private sector and acts as a middleman between foreign governments and private arms manufacturers.

Most arms sales decisions of the British government are made by the Arms Working Party, which comprises representatives from various ministries. The views of the Foreign Ministry are very influential in the deliberations of the Arms Working Party. The cabinet-level Defence and Overseas Policy Committee passes judgment on the largest and most controversial sales.

Decisions to sell arms overseas are made case by case with no apparent policy guidelines to structure the government's deliberations. The official rationale for arms sales emphasizes foreign policy and strategic objectives. Embargoes were placed on sales to Chile and South Africa, and an informal embargo was placed on sales to Idi Amin's Uganda. The decision-making process is pragmatic, the presumption being that unless there are solid foreign policy reasons to the contrary, requests for British arms should be answered in the

---

34. This section is based on Pierre, *The Global Politics of Arms Sales*, pp. 100–108; and Congressional Research Service, *Changing Perspectives on U.S. Arms Transfer Policy*, p. 15. Dollar figures are in current dollars and include the value of weapons, spare parts, construction, and training.

affirmative. Although Parliament has no legal power to block a proposed sale, the prospect of hostile debate can deter controversial sales.

The British government makes public little information about its arms sales policy. Each year it releases an aggregate figure on the value of overseas sales that does not detail the number of arms sold, their types, or the identity of the purchasing countries. It is known, however, that most British arms sales are made to third-world countries. Like the United States, Britain sold Iran some weapons that were more sophisticated than those bought for the British military (a model of the Chieftain tank, for example). The shah had ordered 1,200 heavy tanks from Britain, more than the British had planned to buy for their own ground forces.

Current Trends.[35] The most recent data released by the U.S. Arms Control and Disarmament Agency (ACDA) show that the Soviet Union was the largest exporter of arms, as measured by cumulative current-dollar estimates, for the last half of the 1970s. Worldwide, the Soviets transferred approximately $33.5 billion worth of arms during 1975–1979, whereas the total for the United States was $29.4 billion. Of these totals, $27.7 billion (or 82.7 percent) of Soviet transfers went to developing countries, and $22.4 billion (or 76.2 percent) of U.S. transfers was received by the third world. French arms transfers to less-developed countries totaled $5.6 billion and British transfers $3.5 billion during 1975–1979.

For the decade of the 1970s as a whole, ACDA reports that the United States led the Soviet Union by a small margin in total arms transfers. The top four arms suppliers from 1970 to 1979 were the United States ($49.1 billion in current dollars, $60.4 billion in constant 1978 dollars), the Soviet Union ($48.9 billion in current dollars, $56.9 billion in constant dollars), France ($8.8 billion in current dollars, $10.2 billion in constant dollars), and Great Britain ($6.1 billion in current dollars, $7.1 billion in constant dollars).

The comparison of U.S. and Soviet arms transfers on an annual basis is also of interest. U.S. transfers averaged $6 billion per year (measured in constant 1978 dollars) during the 1970s. The value of transfers in 1979, $5.1 billion, was essentially the same as that in

---

35. Data in this section are from U.S. Arms Control and Disarmament Agency, *World Military Expenditures and Arms Transfers 1970-1979* (Washington, D.C.: ACDA, March 1982), tables II and III. Data compiled by ACDA include grant aid and cash or credit sales of ammunition, weapons systems, and support equipment delivered in a given year. Cost of military construction, training, and other technical services is not included.

1970, as measured in constant dollars. During the decade, arms transfers as a share of total U.S. exports fell from 7.2 percent to 3.1 percent. Caution should be exercised in using the available data, however. The entire period should be considered when analyzing trends to avoid being distracted by the peaks and valleys evident in yearly statistics.

The Soviet Union, meanwhile, almost quadrupled its arms transfers during the 1970s. Soviet transfers grew from $2.5 billion in 1970 to $9.6 billion in 1979, as measured in constant 1978 dollars. Arms transfers as a share of total Soviet exports grew from 11.7 percent to 16.0 percent during this period. The value of Soviet arms transfers surpassed that of the United States by 86 percent in 1979, accounting for approximately 44 percent of the entire world market for arms.

The Middle East continues to be the recipient of the largest shares of U.S. and Soviet arms transfers. Libya, Iraq, and Syria are the major recipients of Soviet arms in that area; Israel, Egypt, and Saudi Arabia are the major recipients of American arms. Algeria, Ethiopia, Vietnam, and India are the other major Soviet arms recipients outside the Warsaw Pact; South Korea is the only other major U.S. client outside NATO.

2

The Arms Sales Review Process

The previous chapter showed that arms transfers have been an important instrument of U.S. foreign policy throughout the post–World War II period. During the last decade, however, concerns have been expressed about the quantity and quality of arms exported to the third world by the United States and other major weapons suppliers. These concerns have encouraged a closer examination of policies, legislation, and other restrictions pertaining to U.S. arms transfers. This chapter examines how requests from other countries for American arms are reviewed by the executive and legislative branches and identifies some of the existing legal restrictions on arms sales.[1]

U.S. arms sales have been a subject of congressional legislation for almost thirty years, beginning with the Mutual Security Act of 1954. In 1961, Congress passed the Foreign Assistance Act, establishing a variety of restrictions and conditions for grant aid, foreign military sales (FMS), and other security assistance programs. FMS rules were later incorporated into the Foreign Military Sales Act of 1968. Commercial sales of military equipment remained under the purview of the Mutual Security Act until 1976 when, along with FMS, they were made subject to the International Security Assistance and Arms Export Control Act (hereafter referred to as the Arms Export Control Act, or AECA). Military grant aid and other security assistance programs continue to be regulated by the Foreign Assistance Act. The Arms Export Control Act has been amended annually since 1977, most recently by the International Security and Development Act of 1981.

U.S. arms exports take several forms, the major ones being grant aid and sales for cash or credits. The Military Assistance Program (MAP), which provides grant aid to other nations under the Foreign

---

1. In addition to the sources cited in other footnotes, information obtained during interviews with officials of the Department of State was used in preparing this chapter.

Assistance Act, was the primary vehicle for U.S. arms transfers in the 1950s and early 1960s. Arms sales have subsequently replaced grants as the primary arms transfer mechanism.

By 1981, MAP recipients included only four countries (Spain, Portugal, the Philippines, and Sudan). The Reagan administration in its fiscal year 1982 Congressional Presentation Document proposed that no new MAP material programs be initiated unless there were exceptional circumstances.[2] MAP recipients must comply with certain conditions to remain eligible for grant assistance: No assistance can be provided to Communist-controlled countries; the recipient must permit continuous observation of the use of U.S.-supplied military items by representatives of the United States; no assistance will be provided to a country that seizes, nationalizes, or expropriates U.S. property; and the recipient must refrain from engaging or preparing to engage in aggressive military action against the United States or other countries receiving American aid.[3]

The bulk of U.S. arms transfers today consists of sales. Each request from a foreign government to purchase American weapons must pass through a complex review process that can take from a few months to a few years to complete (figure 1). All arms sales requests are reviewed by officials in at least two major departments of the executive branch. All sales having a value of $14 million or more for major defense equipment, $50 million or more for all other defense articles and services, and $200 million or more for design and construction services must be reported to Congress, which has the power to veto them.

Executive Branch

The complex process of reviewing sales of U.S. military equipment and services involves numerous departments and agencies within the executive branch. The principal participants in the review process are the Department of Defense (DOD), the Department of State, the Arms Control and Disarmament Agency (ACDA), and the National Security Council (NSC) staff. The Central Intelligence Agency (CIA), the Agency for International Development (AID), the Office of Management and Budget (OMB), and the Treasury and Commerce departments may also become involved in reviewing specific cases. Many

2. Defense Institute of Security Assistance Management (DISAM), *The Management of Security Assistance* (Wright-Patterson AFB, Ohio: Defense Institute of Security Assistance Management, 1981), p. 24-2.

3. Ibid., p. 24-3.

FIGURE 1
Arms Sales Review Process

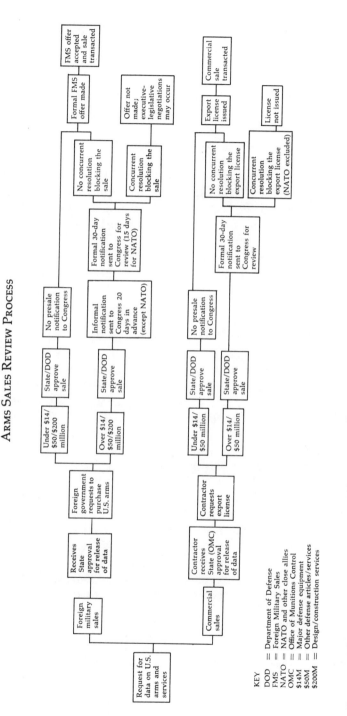

SOURCES: Adapted from Defense Institute of Security Assistance Management, *The Management of Security Assistance* (Wright-Patterson AFB, Ohio: Defense Institute of Security Assistance Management, 1981), p. 3-22; and interviews with officials in the Department of State.

KEY
DOD   = Department of Defense
FMS   = Foreign Military Sales
NATO   = NATO and other close allies
OMC   = Office of Munitions Control
$14M   = Major defense equipment
$50M   = Other defense articles/services
$200M = Design/construction services

officials within each of these organizations will frequently participate in the review process. Up to twenty signature clearances may be required on a single arms sale request before Congress is notified of a proposed sale.[4]

Each of the departments and agencies involved will have varied interests and viewpoints that will determine its position on a potential sale. Many concerns are inevitably addressed from these perspectives in the review process: for example, the security interests of the United States, it allies, and its close friends; U.S. financial, commercial, and resource interests; the strength of the relationship between the potential recipient and the United States; the recipient's role with respect to U.S. global objectives; and the importance of the sale to the overall bilateral relationship and to the military balance in the relevant region.[5]

Arms sales consist of two types: foreign military sales (FMS) and commercial sales. FMS are transactions between governments, the U.S. government buying items from American firms and transferring them to the recipient government for cash or credit. Commercial sales occur between American companies and foreign governments, the U.S. government either approving or disapproving requests for export licenses. Many foreign governments prefer the FMS type of sale for major weapons systems not only because the Department of Defense puts together a complete defense package (based on a thorough Pentagon study of the defense requirements of the purchasing countries) for each transaction, but also because FMS provide foreign governments the same legal protection as the DOD in contracting agreements with American companies.[6] FMS transactions currently constitute about 90 percent of all U.S. arms sales.

There are generally five basic steps in FMS transactions: (1) the request by a foreign government or international organization for data on a U.S. military item or service; (2) the initial review of the request by the State Department, DOD, and other agencies, followed by a decision to approve or deny release of the data; (3) the formal request initiated by the foreign government to purchase the equipment; (4) the formal review process within the executive branch and the acceptance or rejection of the request; (5) congressional

---

4. Jo L. Husbands, "How the United States Makes Foreign Military Sales," in Stephanie G. Neuman and Robert E. Harkavy, eds., *Arms Transfers in the Modern World* (New York: Praeger Publishers, 1979), p. 158.

5. Paul Y. Hammond, David J. Louscher, and Michael D. Salomon, "Controlling U.S. Arms Transfers: The Emerging System," *Orbis*, vol. 23, no. 2 (Summer 1979), p. 328.

6. DISAM, *The Management of Security Assistance*, pp. 11-1 and 11-2.

review, if required, and sale. In some instances, the foreign government may choose to bypass the first two steps.

Officials of foreign governments initially become interested in purchasing American arms and military services by attending air shows and weapons displays of American arms, by contacts with American manufacturers, sales representatives, or U.S. military advisers, or by a study conducted by a DOD survey team. The interest in acquiring American arms may also reflect satisfaction with earlier arms purchases or a desire to develop closer relations with the United States.

Foreign governments can obtain information about American arms by submitting to the State Department a Letter of Request (LOR) for planning and review data (P&R) and/or for price and availability data (P&A). P&R data consist of general information on the cost and capability of weapons. P&A data provide detailed information needed to submit a formal offer to buy. The release of P&R and P&A data by DOD can occur only with State Department approval after a review by officials in the Bureau of Politico-Military Affairs (PM), the concerned regional bureau in the Department of State, and ACDA, in coordination with DOD.

The decision to release the data is given careful consideration, because turning down a request for arms is easier at this point in the process than later when the request becomes formal. Accordingly, at this early stage participants in the review process must determine the requesting nation's eligibility for FMS purchases, confirm the availability of the military items or services for sale, and ensure that the prospective sale conforms to the policy guidelines of the current administration, the restrictions and controls in the Arms Export Control Act, and other pertinent legislation. The issuance of the data is often perceived by potential recipients as an indication that the United States is prepared to sell.

Requests for information on American arms are divided into three groups: first, major defense equipment (for example, tanks, aircraft, and ships); second, all other defense articles and some services (for example, ammunition, spare parts, and training); and third, design and construction services (for example, building airfields and other defense infrastructure). Foreign governments can make requests through several channels: directly to a U.S. ambassador or his political counselors, to the U.S. Military Assistance Advisory Group (MAAG) in the country or to defense attachés, to officials in Washington through their embassies, or to study teams and sales representatives of private companies. Foreign governments may sometimes make direct requests to the president or secretary of state.

Requests for information are directed to the State Department. The Bureau of Politico-Military Affairs solicits the views of the responsible offices within the State Department, DOD, and the ACDA. If there is any objection to the request within these offices, the decision is deferred to higher State Department and DOD officials or, in special cases, to the White House. If the request is approved, then the data are released.

If the foreign government finds the data satisfactory and decides to purchase U.S. military equipment through FMS, it must submit a second request for a Letter of Offer and Acceptance (LOA) from the U.S. government stating that the United States is willing to make the sale. The request for an LOA is processed through the same channels as the initial request for information noted above and represents a formal request to purchase military hardware. No LOA can be issued without State Department approval. The LOA is written by the relevant military service. In cases where equipment or services of all three military branches are involved, each one participates in drafting the LOA.

Requests to purchase American arms under FMS and commercial sales from NATO countries, Japan, Australia, and New Zealand are generally not controversial. Historically these countries have been the recipients of the majority of sales, although in recent years there have been exceptions. The State Department processes sales requests for defense items and services to these countries and also authorizes such sales. The initial review process may occur within the sales offices of the military services, and certain weapons requests are subjected to interagency review if other offices express interest. A further review is requested only occasionally.

Requests from all other foreign governments can be controversial because of the country involved, the equipment requested, or the amount of the proposed sale. All these factors contributed to controversy over the sale in 1981 of Airborne Warning and Control System (AWACS) aircraft and other defense items to Saudi Arabia. Requests from these countries usually receive a more extensive interagency review than those in the first category.

Requests for arms sales from countries in the second category are reported to PM and the office of International Security Affairs in DOD; these two offices act as primary managers and coordinators of the review within their departments. PM also serves as the coordinator of the interagency review within the executive branch.

The initial review is conducted by the relevant regional bureau of the State Department. Additional review and analysis may involve ACDA, the Defense Security Assistance Agency (DSAA), sales offices within the military services, the Defense Intelligence Agency, the CIA, the Joint Chiefs of Staff, and the office of the under secretary of state for security assistance, science, and technology. Each office has its own special interests and responds accordingly. The director of the Bureau of Politico-Military Affairs acts on behalf of the secretary of state in most arms sales decisions. More controversial cases are referred to the secretary of state and possibly to the National Security Council (NSC).

The Arms Transfer Management Group (ATMG) is an advisory body to the secretary of state concerned with the policies and procedures for all conventional arms transfers. The ATMG is chaired by the under secretary of state for security assistance and includes representatives of the State, Defense, and Treasury departments; the Joint Chiefs of Staff; ACDA; the National Security Council; the Agency for International Development; CIA; and the Office of Management and Budget. The ATMG may examine controversial sales.

The NSC's Senior Interdepartmental Group (SIG) dealing with foreign policy issues advises the National Security Council on arms sales. Arms sales requests rarely generate enough controversy to warrant a meeting of the SIG and the NSC. The chairman of the SIG is the deputy secretary of state, and its other members include the deputy secretary of defense, the president's national security adviser, the chairman of the Joint Chiefs of Staff, and the director of central intelligence. The director of ACDA participates in SIG meetings devoted to arms sales issues.

The president participates in the review process only for the most controversial sales. He may follow the recommendation of the NSC, the ATMG, or the secretary of state, or he may request a summary of the positions of the departments and agencies before making his decision.

Legislative Branch

All major defense-related sales must be reported to Congress. Major defense equipment valued at $14 million or over, other defense articles or services valued at $50 million or over, and design and construction services valued at $200 million or over are considered major sales subject to the provisions of the Nelson amendment in the Arms Export Control Act. That amendment permits Congress to block a major sale if it passes a concurrent resolution within thirty days (fifteen days for NATO and other close allies) after receiving formal notification of the intended sale from the executive branch. In practice, Congress receives informal notification of proposed sales twenty days in advance for countries other than members of NATO, Japan, Australia, and New Zealand. Congress also receives quarterly reports on all LOAs for major defense equipment valued at $1 million or more. The congressional review may be waived by the president if he declares that "an emergency exists which requires the proposed export in the national security interests of the United States."[7]

The legislative branch is notified of major arms sales through the House Foreign Affairs Committee and the Senate Foreign Relations Committee. These committees may hold hearings on the proposed sale if they conclude that such a review is warranted. Each committee then submits its recommendation to the full House or Senate. Congress has never passed a concurrent resolution to defeat a sale; the proposed sale of AWACS aircraft to Saudi Arabia in 1981, however, did attract considerable opposition. Although the House voted to block the sale, the Senate approved it by a vote of 52–48. Every administration since the passage of the Nelson amendment in 1974 (then part of the FY 1975 foreign aid authorization bill) has questioned the constitutionality of Congress's power to veto a proposed sale by concurrent resolution. The constitutionality of the legislative veto is now being considered in the courts. The Supreme Court has agreed to review a case unrelated to arms sales, but the outcome may affect the power of Congress to block arms sales by concurrent resolution.[8]

Past congressional opposition to proposed arms sales has usually been headed off through compromise with the executive branch. President Ford, for example, to win the approval of Congress, agreed to sell immobile rather than mobile Hawk missiles to Jordan in 1975 and to limit the number of Maverick missiles sold to Saudi Arabia in 1976. In some cases the executive branch has withdrawn formal notification of a sale rather than risk congressional rejection.

If the proposed arms sale survives the executive and legislative reviews, a formal LOA is issued to the purchasing country. The sale still may not be consummated, however, if too much time has elapsed between the initial request and final approval or if restrictions placed on the sale are unacceptable to the purchasing country. The sale is complete only after the LOA has been signed by U.S. officials and representatives of the foreign government.

7. *Arms Export Control Act*, as amended in 1981, Sec. 36(b)(1)(a).

8. A three-judge panel of the U.S. Circuit Court of Appeals in Washington, D.C., ruled in January 1982 that the legislative veto was unconstitutional in a case involving the pricing of natural gas. The Supreme Court has agreed to review a narrower but similar case involving a provision of an immigration law. See Laura A. Kiernan and Fred Barbash, "Court Declares Veto by Congress Unconstitutional," *Washington Post*, January 30, 1982.

Commercial Sales. Although commercial arms sales take place between arms manufacturers and foreign governments, they are reviewed by the U.S. government. The State Department's Office of Munitions Control (OMC) has primary responsibility for overseeing commercial sales. OMC must submit an advisory opinion before data on the arms or services requested are released. An export license must be issued for the actual sale. The appropriate regional bureau of the Department of State, its counterpart in DOD, PM, and ACDA are involved in reviewing proposed commercial sales. The National Aeronautics and Space Administration (NASA), the Federal Aviation Administration (FAA), the Department of Energy, and other government offices may be notified if the sale is of interest to them.

The OMC will disapprove a commercial sales request upon objection by PM, the regional bureau in State, ACDA, or DOD. OMC is responsible for seeking a resolution of the issue through the same interagency process followed for disputes over FMS. No export license is issued until all reservations are removed.

Congress must be notified of all proposed commercial sales of major defense equipment worth $14 million or more and of all other sales of military items and services valued at $50 million or more. Notifications must be sent to Congress thirty days before the issuance of an export license. The same procedures followed by the legislative branch in reviewing FMS are followed in reviewing a commercial sale. The license is issued only if Congress does not adopt a concurrent resolution within thirty days blocking the sale.

A dollar ceiling previously existed for commercial sales; all sales above it had to be FMS. The dollar ceiling was repealed in 1981, and some officials have speculated that the current mix of sales (about 10 percent are commercial) will change somewhat as an increasing number of transactions become commercial sales.

Major Legal Restrictions. Existing legislation places a number of major restrictions on foreign military sales. It covers the types of countries eligible to purchase American weapons and military services, the conditions under which sales are made, and the types of weapons that can be sold. Country-specific restrictions have occasionally been legislated.

Major restrictions in the Arms Export Control Act include the following:

• The president must determine that sales will strengthen the security of the United States and promote world peace before he can declare a country eligible to purchase American arms (sec. 3([a][1]).

- Arms sales are made only to enhance the internal security and self-defense capability of a recipient or to promote regional or collective defense arrangements consistent with the United Nations Charter (sec. 4).
- Arms sales cannot be made to less-developed countries that divert U.S. economic aid or their own resources to purchase arms to the extent that such military expenditures interfere with their development (sec. 35).
- Countries purchasing U.S. arms must agree not to transfer the arms to another country without the prior consent of the United States; such consent must be reported to Congress (secs. 3[a][2] and 3[b]).
- Export-Import Bank financing of U.S. arms sales to less-developed countries is prohibited (sec. 32).
- Consequences for arms control must be considered when evaluating all arms sales (sec. 42[a][3]).
- Congress must be advised before coproduction or licensed production agreements financed under this act are completed; the probable impact of such agreements on employment and production in the United States must be provided to Congress (sec. 42[b]).

3

The Case for Significantly Curtailing U.S. Arms Sales

This chapter presents the major arguments for significantly curtailing U.S. arms sales. It may be useful at the outset to state several assumptions. First, it is unlikely that the global market for arms can ever be closed completely. Even if the United States unilaterally stopped all foreign sales of arms, it is doubtful that other major arms suppliers would follow its example. Indeed, there are sound foreign policy and security rationales for continued arms sales by the United States. Arms sales can contribute to the collective security of the Western democracies, as they have since the end of World War II. They can also function as instruments of diplomacy to encourage the peaceful settlement of disputes by providing a foundation of security that enables disputing states to compromise their differences.

A second assumption of this chapter is that the debate over arms sales revolves around the adequacy of controls over their use as instruments of national policy. Few participants in the debate would argue that the sale of American weapons overseas should be unregulated, and few would argue that all sales should be prohibited. It is important to note, however, that the arms sales debate goes beyond the relative merits of proposed sets of restraints. Often at issue are different beliefs about the role the United States should play in the world and the best way to settle international disputes. Does the United States have vital interests throughout the world that necessitate the sale of arms to over one hundred countries in virtually every region of the globe? Do arms sales, rather than foster regional stability in areas like the Middle East and South Asia, actually exacerbate tensions and increase the chance of war?

Jimmy Carter came to office in 1977 believing that arms sales were out of control. He said that the "virtually unrestrained spread of conventional weaponry threatens stability in every region of the world" and that the United States was then the largest seller of arms, accounting for more than half of worldwide sales by the mid-1970s. Carter vowed that the United States would "henceforth view arms transfers as an *exceptional* foreign policy implement, to be used only in instances where it can be clearly demonstrated that the transfer contributes to our national security interests."[1] The Carter administration supplemented its unilateral policy of restraint with multilateral and bilateral efforts to negotiate limitations on the arms sales of other major supplier nations.

President Reagan's stated policy on arms sales differs sharply from that of his predecessor. "The United States . . . views the transfer of conventional arms and other defense articles and services as an *essential* element of its global defense posture and an *indispensable* component of its foreign policy," he said.[2] His administration identified the Soviet Union and its proxies, not arms sales, as the cause of regional instability. President Reagan also announced that his administration would not actively promote negotiated restraints among supplier nations. These and other differences in the Carter and Reagan policy statements ensure that arms sales will continue to be a topic of debate.

Why the Concern over Arms Sales?

Arms sales have become the subject of much controversy for several reasons. Critics of U.S. policy, for example, point to the increasing volume of sales during the past decade and argue that the United States was the largest supplier of arms to the world. Measured in current dollars, U.S. sales agreements grew from $1.1 billion in 1970 to $15.8 billion in 1975. American arms sales amounted to over $17 billion by 1980.[3] The exports of arms by each of the other major suppliers (Great Britain, France, and the Soviet Union) also registered sharp increases during the 1970s. The largest increases in sales have been to the third world, in particular to the Middle East. Since the 1973 Arab-Israeli war, the levels of arms in the region have more than doubled in some categories: there are now almost 17,000 tanks compared with 8,000 in 1973, and 220 surface-to-surface missile

1. "President Carter Announces Policy on Transfers of Conventional Arms," *Department of State Bulletin,* June 13, 1977, p. 625 (emphasis added).

2. "Conventional Arms Transfer Policy," *Department of State Bulletin,* September 1981, p. 61 (emphasis added).

3. Andrew J. Pierre, *The Global Politics of Arms Sales* (Princeton, N.J.: Princeton University Press, 1982), pp. 9-10; and Richard Whittle, "Reagan Policy Renews Arms Sales Debate," *Congressional Quarterly Weekly Report,* April 3, 1982, p. 721. Sales figures include the cost of weapons and equipment, training, and logistics assistance.

launchers compared with about 30. Inventories of combat aircraft have risen from 2,000 in 1973 to about 3,000 today.[4]

A second reason for the heightened concern about the global traffic in arms has been the increasing sophistication of the weapons being sold. Leslie Gelb, director of the Bureau of Politico-Military Affairs in Carter's State Department, told Congress in 1978 about the implications of this trend:

> Since 1970 Western and Eastern suppliers have made arms transfer commitments of about $140 billion to developing countries. Most of this equipment has not yet been delivered, much less absorbed. When these arms are delivered and when the recipients learn to use them, they will change the face of world politics. For the first time, many states throughout the world will have arms of much the same sophistication and quality as those of the few major powers.[5]

No longer are the United States and other suppliers exporting surplus stocks of aging weapons. Among the arms sold to third-world countries in the 1970s were "top-of-the-line" combat aircraft, such as the American F-14, F-15, and F-16, the Soviet MiG-23 and MiG-25, and the French Mirage F-1 and Mirage III fighters; advanced antitank and antiaircraft missiles; the most modern tanks and destroyers; and sophisticated Airborne Warning and Control System (AWACS) aircraft.

A third reason for the debate about arms sales has been the perception of some members of Congress and the public that American arms sales are out of control. The rising volume and quality of arms sold to third-world countries led many observers to question the arms sales policies of the Nixon and Ford administrations, and similar skepticism greeted many of the transfers proposed by the Carter administration as well.[6] Decisions to sell arms have often seemed to be governed less by long-term U.S. security interests than by short-run economic or diplomatic advantage. The prime example of such shortsighted policy was President Nixon's decision in 1972 to sell the shah of Iran virtually any conventional weapons without first having

---

4. Leslie H. Gelb, "The Mideast Arms Race: New Weapons, Old Fears," *New York Times*, January 24, 1982. States included are Israel, Egypt, Saudi Arabia, Jordan, Syria, Iraq, and Libya.

5. Quoted in Max Holland, "The Myth of Arms Restraint," *International Policy Report*, vol. 5, no. 1 (May 1979), p. 16.

6. See, for example, Nicole Ball and Milton Leitenberg, "The Foreign Arms Sales Policy of the Carter Administration," *Alternatives: A Journal of World Policy*, vol. 4, no. 4 (March 1979).

fully discussed it with the Pentagon and other interested agencies in Washington.[7] Seemingly unconstrained policies such as this one are seen as potentially contributing to regional arms races and increasing the chance of war. Other more benign foreign policy tools, such as diplomatic, economic, and technical assistance, have been de-emphasized as arms sales have become the main currency of American foreign policy transactions.

The fourth reason for the increased concern over arms sales centers on the several setbacks to American interests in the world that have been linked in part to such sales. In some cases, like the fall of the shah of Iran in 1979, many observers believed that excessive arms purchases diverted scarce resources from the social and economic development needs of the people and contributed to undermining the stability of friendly regimes.[8] In other cases, such as the competitive arms sales by the superpowers to the Middle East before the 1973 war, weapons transfers were seen as contributing to the outbreak of military conflict and to U.S.-Soviet confrontation. There have also been several instances where the diplomatic leverage presumed to accompany arms sales fell short of expectations.

Last, skepticism about the wisdom and utility of many arms sales transactions is a manifestation of deeper concerns about American foreign and defense policies since World War II. The experience in Vietnam—where a relatively low level of military assistance in the 1950s grew into a major American commitment of ground forces in the 1960s—together with the increasing awareness of the public about the human rights policies of many recipients of American arms, has contributed to the current debate on the wisdom of U.S. arms sales policy and the role Congress should play in formulating a new policy.

Arms Sales and U.S. Interests

Arms sales are often viewed as synonymous with U.S. national security interests. Friendly third-world countries need weapons to preserve their security and freedom and to maintain regional balances of power. Arms sales critics contend that even though these objectives are laudable, the security rationale for arms sales does not fully take

7. Barry Rubin, *Paved with Good Intentions: The American Experience and Iran* (New York: Penguin Books, 1981), pp. 134–35; and Tad Szulc, *Illusion of Peace: Foreign Policy in the Nixon Administration* (New York: The Viking Press, 1978), pp. 584-85.

8. See, for example, Theodore H. Moran, "Iranian Defense Expenditures and the Social Crisis," *International Security*, vol. 3, no. 3 (Winter 1978/1979), pp. 178-92; and Pierre, *The Global Politics of Arms Sales*, p. 151.

into account the ways in which such sales can conflict with American interests.

The first half of the 1970s saw two major occurrences that profoundly affected the global market in arms. First, the gradual withdrawal of American military forces from Southeast Asia was accompanied by enunciation in 1969 of the Nixon Doctrine, which called upon America's friends and allies to assume a larger share of the burden for their regional security. The United States would supply arms to those countries willing to provide the manpower for their own defense.

The second event contributing to the growth in arms sales was the 1973 Arab oil embargo and the skyrocketing of oil prices. The oil crisis resulted in a massive transfer of dollars into the coffers of oil-producing countries, and the United States and other arms suppliers were seen as eager to sell arms to the Middle East as a way of alleviating balance-of-payment problems resulting from the high cost of oil. In some cases, short-run economic and diplomatic advantages may have been achieved at the risk of long-term U.S. interests. The Nixon and Ford administrations, one observer said, viewed arms sales as "an unprecedented opportunity to win friends and influence events. But it is one thing to sell arms to buttress foreign policy goals and quite another to use them as a tactical device with little attention to their aftereffects on those goals."[9]

Security Interests. Critics contend that arms sales can undermine U.S. security in several ways. One way is by compromising the technology of American weapons. The United States, as noted earlier, has been exporting some of its most sophisticated conventional weapons to the third world for many years. The ruling regimes of some recipient countries are highly unstable because of domestic unrest or external threats (the case of Iran is instructive).

During the 1970s, the United States sold, or contracted to sell, F-4, F-5, F-14, and F-16 fighters, AWACS aircraft, and four Spruance-class destroyers more advanced than those the U.S. Navy was buying. Fortunately, not all of these weapons had been transferred by the time the shah was toppled by the Islamic revolution in 1979, but it is believed that some classified weapons technology has been compromised. The U.S. Navy, for example, assumes that the sophisticated Phoenix air-to-air missile system for the F-14 fighter may have been compromised; a new missile has been developed to replace it. It was not necessary for the Soviets to obtain one of the several hundred

9. Leslie H. Gelb, "Arms Sales," *Foreign Policy*, no. 25 (Winter 1976-1977), p. 4.

Phoenix missiles stockpiled in Iran—all they had to do was get the maintenance manual. Such an acquisition would benefit the Soviets not only because the technology could be adapted for their forces, but also because they can use it to develop countermeasures against Phoenix missiles deployed with U.S. forces.

Arms sold abroad can also be used directly against the United States or its allies. Once arms enter the arsenal of another country, the supplier has little control over their ultimate use, notwithstanding the prohibitions on their use for aggressive purposes or on retransfer to other nations that the United States includes in arms sales agreements. When South Vietnam fell in 1975, the North Vietnamese captured about $5 billion in American arms. Some of this equipment was probably used by the Vietnamese in fighting against Cambodia and the People's Republic of China in 1979. American arms sold to Iran have been used in the Iran-Iraq war; in fact, some M-60 tanks captured by Iraq have been passed on to Jordan. There are fears that F-15s sold to Saudi Arabia to cement a "strategic consensus" against Soviet encroachment in the Persian Gulf area could someday be used against Israel. Violations of U.S. arms transfer agreements may have occurred during the war between Ethiopia and Somalia over the Ogaden region of the Horn of Africa in 1977–1978. Egypt, Israel, Iran, Saudi Arabia, and Yugoslavia, each a recipient of U.S. arms, are reported either to have retransferred American weapons or spare parts to belligerents in the Ogaden dispute or to have relied on U.S. arms to replace other weapons sent to the Horn of Africa. Some of the retransfers were apparently made without American consent.[10]

Critics of arms sales argue that even America's closest allies have used U.S. arms in ways that run counter to our interests. Turkey, a NATO ally, used American arms to invade Cyprus in 1974. Israel may have violated an agreement prohibiting the use of U.S.-supplied military equipment for nondefensive purposes when it employed such equipment in an invasion of Lebanon in 1978. Three years later, Israel used American-supplied F-16 aircraft to bomb the Osirak nuclear reactor outside Baghdad. American A-4 fighter-bombers sold to Argentina were recently used against British ships in the war over the Falkland Islands.

It is also argued that the sale of sophisticated arms could limit U.S. policy options because American personnel are often stationed in the recipient country to service the equipment and train the local military. A 1976 report to the Senate Foreign Relations Committee noted that nearly 25,000 American technicians were in Iran to main-

---

10. Holland, "The Myth of Arms Restraint," p. 6.

tain American arms and to train Iranians in their use. So dependent were the Iranians on the continued presence of Americans, the report concluded, that "Iran could not go to war in the next five to ten years with its current and prospective inventory of sophisticated weapons . . . without U.S. support on a day-to-day basis."[11]

Iran, which is currently at war with Iraq without U.S. support, has not been able to make effective use of some of the sophisticated arms it bought from the United States because of the absence of American technicians. According to one observer, "If Iran had become involved in a war" before the 1979 revolution, "it would have been difficult to keep American personnel uninvolved." The American technicians, he said, "could physically become hostages at a moment of crisis."[12] The Senate report cited earlier foresaw this possibility and noted that "it is not clear *who really has influence over whom* in time of an ambiguous crisis situation."[13] Another report to the Senate Foreign Relations Committee in 1978 reached similar conclusions with regard to U.S. technicians in Saudi Arabia. That report said that "Saudi Arabia would be hard pressed to maintain its military strength for any length of time during hostilities without full U.S. logistic and maintenance support."[14]

America's policy options can be similarly circumscribed, according to critics, when the United States sells arms in return for base rights in another country. When the United States becomes dependent upon these bases, it may lose whatever leverage it might have gained from the original sale. Because of this reverse leverage, the United States may be reluctant to punish an arms recipient who violates the terms of a sale lest its access to bases be restricted. The events following Turkey's use of American arms to invade Cyprus in 1975 are often cited. When Congress punished Turkey by placing an embargo on arms, Turkey retaliated by restricting U.S. activities at its bases. The United States may also be reluctant to pressure the Philippines to improve its human rights record out of fear that the access of American forces to air and naval bases would be restricted.

Proponents of arms sales restraint also point out that some sales have reduced the readiness of U.S. forces by delaying the acquisition of some arms by the American military or by drawing down existing stocks of weapons. This problem is a logical consequence of selling

11. Quoted ibid.
12. Pierre, *The Global Politics of Arms Sales*, p. 18.
13. Quoted ibid.
14. Quoted in Dick Clark, "Needed: A Policy of Restraint for United States Arms Transfers," *AEI Defense Review*, vol. 2, no. 5 (1978), p. 8.

top-of-the-line weapons without adequately considering the needs of American forces. Large quantities of armor and other weapons earmarked for Western Europe were shipped to Israel during the 1973 Middle East war. The General Accounting Office (GAO) reported in 1977 that it took the U.S. Army four years to rebuild its stock of M-113 armored personnel carriers, which had been depleted during the 1973 war, in part because sales to Morocco and other countries were given priority. Deployment of antitank missiles with U.S. army units was likewise delayed because of sales to other countries. According to the GAO, "diversion and withdrawal of end-items and spare and repair parts have been made to the point where minimum essential quantities have been denied to the U.S. forces."[15] Congress subsequently passed legislation stipulating that arms transfers that adversely affect the combat readiness of U.S. forces should be kept to a minimum.

Overseas sales of sophisticated American weapons continue, however, and U.S. military stocks may again be drawn down or go unfilled to meet export demand. The United States is currently selling the F-16 fighter to South Korea, Israel, and Egypt and plans to sell it to Pakistan and Venezuela as well. The U.S. Air Force reportedly expressed concern about the adverse impact such sales could have on its own acquisition schedule for the F-16.[16] If the pace of arms sales accelerates, as is anticipated by most observers of the Reagan administration, U.S. military services may have to share more production lines for essential equipment with other countries. This could result in significantly delaying improvements in the readiness of U.S. forces.

Some critics contend that conventional arms sales can also interfere with another U.S. security interest, preventing the spread of nuclear weapons. Proponents of arms sales argue that such sales can help avert nuclear proliferation by allowing threatened countries to satisfy their security needs with conventional arms. It is also argued that such sales could raise the threshold on the use of nuclear weapons by states that already have them. Critics argue that sales of sophisticated arms could have the opposite effect by whetting the appetites of certain third-world countries for nuclear weapons, especially

15. General Accounting Office, *Foreign Military Sales—A Potential Drain on the U.S. Defense Posture* (Washington, D.C.: General Accounting Office, Report No. LCD-77-440, September 2, 1977), pp. 25, 27, 35.

16. Congressional Research Service, *Changing Perspectives on U.S. Arms Transfer Policy*, Report to the Subcommittee on International Security and Scientific Affairs of the Committee on Foreign Affairs, U.S. House of Representatives, September 25, 1981, pp. 48-49, 85.

if they are sold appropriate delivery vehicles.[17] Moreover, some states that decide to develop their own nuclear weapons may do so for reasons unrelated to perceived external threats. National prestige, emulation of neighboring states, and a desire to achieve dominance in a region are probable reasons for wanting a nuclear weapons capability. As one observer has noted, "conventional capabilities do not substitute for the political influence and prestige which are perceived to accrue to possessors of nuclear weapons."[18]

Some observers contend that it is entirely possible that countries have threatened to acquire nuclear weapons to secure the sale of conventional arms, which they really desire. This could also apply to Israel, a country already thought to possess nuclear weapons. Israel, by not publicly admitting to the possession of a nuclear arsenal, can expect to receive the conventional weapons it desires from the United States, which wants to keep the Israeli nuclear threshold high.[19]

The Carter administration decided not to permit the sale of A-7 combat aircraft to Pakistan in 1977 in part because of Pakistan's efforts to obtain technology that could be used to develop nuclear weapons. The Reagan administration, however, has proposed selling Pakistan the advanced F-16 fighter. Critics argue that this sale could adversely affect U.S. interests in South Asia. On the one hand, the sale of the F-16 could push Pakistan's arch-rival, India, to deploy nuclear weapons (India exploded a nuclear device in 1974). On the other hand, the sale could lead to another spiral in the conventional arms race with India. Either alternative not only would be detrimental to the U.S. interest in regional stability, but also could encourage Pakistan to develop nuclear weapons. Opposing further loosening of controls on conventional arms sales, proponents of arms sales restraint propose instead to stop the spread of nuclear weapons by persuading all suppliers of nuclear technology to agree on strict export controls. Strengthening the provisions of the Nonproliferation Treaty, in particular those relating to multilateral inspection of nuclear facilities, is seen as another way of averting the spread of nuclear weapons.

Last, arms sales are seen as undermining the prestige and influence that the United States enjoys throughout the world as a staunch

17. Clark, "Needed: A Policy of Restraint," p. 12; and Pierre, *The Global Politics of Arms Sales*, p. 31.

18. Steven J. Baker, "Arms Transfers and Nuclear Proliferation," in William H. Kincade and Jeffrey D. Porro, eds., *Negotiating Security: An Arms Control Reader* (Washington, D.C.: Carnegie Endowment for International Peace, 1979), p. 161.

19. Ibid., p. 162.

advocate of regional stability and the peaceful settlement of disputes. During his campaign for the presidency, Jimmy Carter said that the United States "cannot be both the world's leading champion of peace and the world's leading supplier of weapons of war."[20] Arms sales could actually diminish U.S. influence with some countries unless they are adequately restrained.

Diplomatic Influence. One of the most often cited benefits of arms sales is the diplomatic influence that supplier nations can acquire with recipients. Critics contend that just as arms sales are not always synonymous with U.S. security, they cannot always be equated with the power to influence nations.

The United States was perhaps in a better position to influence arms recipients when most weapons were given to friendly nations as grant aid, before the 1970s. Sales since then have become the primary method by which arms transfers occur. Recipients not only have become more diverse in the extent of their sympathy with American interests, but also have often considered their debts to the United States paid in full when they pay cash for arms.[21]

Perhaps the best example of the use of arms sales to acquire American influence is the negotiations to resolve the Arab-Israeli conflict. The United States has sold arms to Israel and Egypt to induce political compromise and territorial concessions from both parties. The Ford and Carter administrations generously provided arms on easy credit terms at various times following the 1973 war to keep the negotiating process alive. In selling arms to the Middle East, however, the United States must always walk a fine line to avoid making either party to the dispute insecure. Most important, Washington must recognize that nations will ultimately pursue their own interests regardless of how intimate their arms relationships may be with other countries.

Critics cite numerous examples where arms suppliers have been unable to influence recipients. Perhaps the most significant setback occurred in the early 1960s when China turned against the Soviet Union. Other prominent examples of setbacks to the Soviets include Egypt and Somalia.

20. "The Views of Two Presidents," in Kincade and Porro, *Negotiating Security*, p. 261.

21. For a discussion of the issue of influence and arms transfers, see William H. Lewis, "Political Influence: The Diminished Capacity," in Stephanie G. Neuman and Robert E. Harkavy, eds., *Arms Transfers in the Modern World* (New York: Praeger Publishers, 1979), chap. 11.

The Soviet Union and Czechoslovakia began an arms sales relationship with Egypt in 1955 that lasted for two decades. Egypt became dependent on Soviet arms and was Moscow's largest recipient in the third world after North Vietnam. Soviet heavy-handedness in managing its arms relationship with Cairo, however, eventually led President Sadat to expel all Soviet advisers from Egypt in 1972 and later to abrogate the Treaty of Friendship and Cooperation with Moscow. The Soviets have had difficulties with other arms recipients in the Middle East (Syria and Iraq), in Africa (Congo, Ghana, Guinea, Somalia, Sudan), and in Latin America (Peru).

Somalia merits closer examination. Moscow's arms relationship with Somalia began in the early 1960s and included the sale of naval vessels and MiG-21 fighters. Somalia in return permitted the Soviets to establish a base at the port city of Berbera, on the Gulf of Aden. When the 1976 coup overthrew the pro-Western government of Emperor Haile Selassie in Ethiopia, Moscow saw an opportunity to establish relations with the new revolutionary regime. The Soviet arms relationship with Somalia was not sufficient to dissuade that country from invading Ethiopia's Ogaden region in 1977, however, and in the ensuing turmoil the Soviets sided with Ethiopia and were summarily expelled from Somalia. The Soviet navy lost its base at Berbera, and Somalia turned to the United States and conservative Arab nations for arms and support.[22]

The record of American arms sales relationships, which is perhaps better than that of the Soviets, is still unsettling in the eyes of the critics. A report by the Senate Foreign Relations Committee in 1980 noted that "the history of [U.S.] arms sales is marked with both foreign policy successes and failures."[23] America's generosity toward South Vietnam was not enough to prevent Saigon from vetoing successive U.S. peace proposals. Nor did the virtually open-ended pipeline of America's most modern weapons keep the shah of Iran from advocating ever higher oil prices at OPEC meetings. According to one observer, "It was perfectly obvious" that the shah "needed higher revenues from oil exports to pay for the expensive arms purchased from the West in the first place."[24]

22. Soviet arms transfer policy is examined in Center for Defense Information, "Soviet Weapons Exports: Russian Roulette in the Third World," *The Defense Monitor*, January 1979; and in Pierre, *The Global Politics of Arms Sales*, pp. 73-83.

23. U.S. Congress, Senate, Committee on Foreign Relations, *U.S. Conventional Arms Transfer Policy*, Report to the Senate, 96th Congress, 2nd session, June 1980, p. 6.

24. Pierre, *The Global Politics of Arms Sales*, p. 151.

Some of America's closest friends and allies have eluded Washington's influence. Not only did the close U.S. arms relationship with the Greek military regime fail to avert actions that precipitated the Cyprus crisis of 1974, but similar U.S. ties to Turkey did not prevent that country from using American arms to invade Cyprus. Saudi Arabia and Jordan continue to resist American efforts to engage them in the Camp David peace process despite the sale of F-15s and AWACS aircraft to Saudi Arabia and tanks and anti-aircraft missiles to Jordan. Even Israel, our closest ally in the Middle East, has successfully resisted U.S. attempts on numerous occasions to extract diplomatic leverage from arms sales. In 1975, President Ford threatened a suspension of American military and economic aid to get Israel to agree to Egyptian terms for a second Israeli withdrawal from the Sinai. The Israeli government hardened its position and rejected the terms, causing the negotiations with Egypt to collapse.[25] The Reagan administration had to take punitive steps after Israel used American combat planes against Lebanon and Iraq in 1981. The administration suspended aircraft deliveries and withdrew economic support for joint military projects. These setbacks demonstrate to those who oppose an unconstrained arms sales policy that there is limited diplomatic leverage provided by arms sales. Whatever influence the arms supplier may acquire over a recipient, it is likely to be short-lived and confined to issues that are not important to the recipient.

Economic Interests. Arms sales proponents point to economic benefits as a justification for not significantly curtailing arms sales. They usually cite improvements in the U.S. balance of payments, employment, industrial base, and weapons costs as arguments for selling arms overseas. They also argue that if the United States does not sell arms, then another country will do so and will reap the economic rewards. Critics say these arguments overstate the economic benefits of arms sales.

U.S. balance of payments. Following the 1973–1974 oil price increases, the Nixon administration appointed an interagency task force to stimulate exports of arms and other goods.[26] The objective was to help cover the costs of energy imports, but critics say the effort was shortsighted. Arms sales to other countries cover only a small fraction of U.S. oil import bills each year: they accounted for

---

25. On the U.S.-Israeli arms relationship, see Thomas R. Wheelock, "Arms for Israel: The Limits of Leverage," *International Security,* vol. 3, no. 2 (Fall 1978).
26. Pierre, *The Global Politics of Arms Sales,* p. 24.

only about 4–5 percent of total American exports in 1980. Arms sales make a smaller contribution to the exports of Britain and France.[27] Critics also note that rising arms sales to oil-exporting nations may stimulate even higher oil prices to cover the cost of arms. If the United States curtailed its arms sales to oil-exporting countries in the Middle East, according to a 1977 Treasury Department study, up to 30 percent of the funds not spent on American weapons would still end up in the United States in the form of long-term investments.[28]

It is also argued that the U.S. balance-of-payments situation receives only short-term benefits from arms sales. Most third-world countries need nonmilitary imports from the United States over the long run to build their economies and infrastructure. Greater purchases of equipment and services needed for development could partially offset lost arms sales revenue. Justifying arms sales by citing improvements in the balance of payments could constitute an open-ended rationale that can apply to any and all arms exports.

Employment. Critics cite several studies indicating that the contribution of arms sales to employment in the United States is relatively minor. A 1976 study by the Congressional Budget Office (CBO) showed that a ban on arms exports would raise the unemployment rate in 1981 by 0.3 percent above then current projections. According to CBO, each $1 billion in arms exports accounts for approximately 42,000 jobs. A study by the Carter administration estimated that 38,000 jobs were owed to each $1 billion in arms sales overseas.[29] Another study, by the Department of Labor in 1977, concluded that 277,000 jobs in the United States—0.3 percent of total national employment—were the result of arms exports.[30] Most proponents of arms sales restraint do not argue for a complete end to weapons exports but only for a significant curtailment; thus they believe displaced workers could be relocated and retrained for new jobs in fields such as mass transit and energy development.

Industrial base. Representatives of American defense industries contend that weapons exports are necessary to keep the arms industry viable financially and competitive internationally. Profits from foreign

27. Ibid., pp. 25-26.

28. Cited in Clark, "Needed: A Policy of Restraint," p. 9.

29. Congressional Budget Office, *The Effect of Foreign Military Sales on the U.S. Economy* (Washington, D.C.: Congressional Budget Office, Staff Working Paper, July 23, 1976), pp. 21, 25; and Anne Hessing Cahn, "The Economics of Arms Transfers," in Neuman and Harkavy, *Arms Transfers in the Modern World*, p. 179.

30. Cited in Pierre, *The Global Politics of Arms Sales*, p. 26.

military sales, they argue, are often used to keep their industry competitive by independent research and development efforts and to build more efficient production lines. Statistics show, however, that few of the top American arms manufacturers are significantly dependent on overseas sales. Only one of the top ten contractors with the Pentagon in 1977, for example, was heavily dependent on arms exports. On average, the remaining nine contractors relied on arms exports for about 12 percent of their sales.[31]

Weapons costs. Proponents of arms sales also contend that weapons exports can lead to economies of scale that result in lower unit costs for arms bought by the Pentagon. By lengthening production runs of weapons and equipment and by spreading research and development costs over a larger number of units, efficiencies are realized, and the cost of each item to U.S. forces can be reduced. U.S. military services, recognizing these potential benefits, have at times promoted sales overseas. According to one former State Department official, the air force wanted to sell the AWACS aircraft to NATO allies and Iran to lower its unit cost and to make its procurement for American forces more affordable.[32]

Critics of arms sales cite several government studies to show that the unit cost savings realized by arms sales are not large. A Congressional Budget Office (CBO) study in 1976 concluded that substantial savings may be realized for certain high-technology weapons systems, but "large savings do not seem generally characteristic of foreign military sales."[33] Another 1976 CBO study estimated that only $560 million was saved on foreign military sales of $8 billion a year (based on the then current mix of weapons, services, and construction), a savings equal to less than 1 percent of annual Pentagon budgets at the time of the study. Those cases where substantial unit cost savings from arms exports are realized are high-technology aircraft and missiles. For most categories of items sold abroad (ships, artillery, ammunition, and services), the cost savings are negligible. According to a 1977 Pentagon study, "there is only a loose relationship between production readiness and cost economies on the one hand, and the total dollar volume of transfers on the other."[34]

31. Clark, "Needed: A Policy of Restraint," p. 11; and Pierre, *The Global Politics of Arms Sales*, p. 71.

32. See Whittle, "Reagan Policy Renews Arms Sales Debate," p. 724.

33. Quoted in Clark, "Needed: A Policy of Restraint," p. 11.

34. Congressional Budget Office, *Budgetary Cost Savings to the Department of Defense Resulting from Foreign Military Sales* (Washington, D.C.: Congressional Budget Office, Staff Working Paper, May 24, 1976), pp. ix, 13-15. The Pentagon study is quoted in Pierre, *The Global Politics of Arms Sales*, p. 26. See also

It is also argued that arms sales provide an opportunity to recoup research and development expenditures for new weapons. Critics contend that the value of this recoupment to the United States is often exaggerated. CBO, for example, found that of the $560 million in savings noted above, only about $160 million was attributed to recoupment of research and development costs. As one former senator familiar with the issue of research and development remarked, "Selling arms just to recoup a small portion of these research and development costs would be letting the tail wag the dog."[35]

Proponents of arms sales point out that Britain and France, the major European arms exporters, depend on arms sales more than the United States does to sustain their arms industry and to lower unit costs of weapons needed by their own forces. According to this argument, British and French weapons manufacturers could be expected to rush in to fill even more orders for arms if the United States significantly curtailed its arms exports to the third world.

Those who favor arms sales restraint claim that there are policies the United States could adopt that would alleviate the need for France and Britain to sell arms to less-developed countries. It has long been recognized that NATO's military capabilities have been plagued by a multiplicity of aircraft, missiles, communications systems, and other equipment that the Warsaw Pact has been able to avoid through standardization. A similar effort on the part of the Western allies would reduce the need for separate logistics systems, which are costly and which degrade the combat effectiveness of NATO.

One way to address NATO's goal of standardization would be for the United States and its European allies to embark on a genuine two-way street, whereby each country would specialize in producing those types of weapons and equipment for which it has a natural advantage. Thus longer production runs and economies of scale could be realized for the sophisticated arms needed by Western military forces. Each country could be guaranteed a fair share of the NATO market and would not have to rely on third-world sales for the health of its arms industry. NATO's standardization goals could be met, and a sound basis for multilateral restraint on arms sales to the third world would be created among the major Western arms exporters.[36]

Cahn, "The Economics of Arms Transfers," pp. 180-81. Pierre (p. 105) cites a report of Parliament's Public Accounts Committee as having reached conclusions similar to those of the CBO report with regard to unit cost savings from British arms sales.

35. Clark, "Needed: A Policy of Restraint," p. 11.
36. Pierre, *The Global Politics of Arms Sales*, p. 300.

Last, there is the argument that if the United States does not sell a particular weapon to a prospective buyer, another nation will. According to one observer, "within governments this preemptive rationale is probably the most widely used justification for arms sales."[37] It is true that in certain instances other countries have rushed in to make sales that the United States preferred not to make. The Soviet Union and France, for example, sold advanced jet fighters to Latin American countries after the United States refused to do so. Some developing countries have even begun their own arms industries to reduce their dependence on overseas suppliers.

Critics of arms sales contend that these examples demonstrate the necessity for multilateral restraints on weapons exports by the major suppliers. They also argue that the historical record is not as clear-cut as proponents of arms sales maintain. A study by the Senate Foreign Relations Committee in 1979 found that in five out of twelve cases where President Carter refused to approve a sale, the European allies sold comparable weapons. In most of the other cases the prospective buyers had nowhere else to go for the same type of weapon.[38] The Congressional Research Service has listed the following turndowns by the Carter administration as successes, in that the sales requests were not filled by other countries: F-5Es for Guatemala, A-7s for Pakistan, F-4s for Taiwan, F-4Gs for Iran, and F-16s for Greece and Turkey.[39]

There are several reasons why countries that are denied a particular American weapons system do not all rush to other suppliers. If the potential buyer has equipped most of its forces with American arms, turning to another supplier could require costly retraining of personnel to operate and maintain the new system. Moreover, other major suppliers are often seen as less reliable than the United States when it comes to training and providing spare parts. Another problem the potential buyer may face is systems incompatibility. Mixing arms from several countries can result in noncomplementary systems that could degrade the military effectiveness of the weapons on hand. Last, the potential buyer may invite strained relations with the United States should it turn to another country for arms.[40] Of course, these problems would have to be dealt with only if there was another country that could supply a comparable weapon and was willing to do so. If these conditions could not be met, the buyer might be per-

37. Ibid., p. 43.

38. Cited in Whittle, "Reagan Policy Renews Arms Sales Debate," p. 723.

39. Congressional Research Service, *Changing Perspectives on U.S. Arms Transfer Policy*, p. 30.

40. Ibid., p. 54.

suaded to settle for a weapon of lesser capability from the United States.

In short, the critics of arms sales believe the economic arguments in favor of selling arms overseas are exaggerated and shortsighted. They also argue that the only proper justification for arms sales is the contribution they can make to the security of the United States and its allies and close friends.

Arms Sales and Conflict

Supporters of arms sales restraint have long argued that weapons exports to unstable regions of the world can have the unintended effect of exacerbating existing tensions and feeding regional arms races. A vicious circle of competitive arms buildups and heightened tensions can result, increasing not only the prospects of war but also the destruction that would ensue. Given the global character of U.S.-Soviet rivalry, the outbreak of armed conflict anywhere in the world poses the risk of superpower involvement and confrontation.

Few regions of the world can claim an absence of tensions—particularly in the third world. Between 1955 and the beginning of 1979, all but six of the more than 120 armed conflicts in the world involved less-developed countries.[41] There are many reasons for these conflicts, and in some cases arms transfers have been seen as a contributing factor. Territorial disputes dating back to colonial times or earlier, ethnic rivalries, ideological competition, and the search for scarce natural resources have all been responsible for regional tensions. Arms shipments to a country can lead to offsetting arms acquisitions by surrounding states, an exacerbation of tensions, and an increase in the opportunities for armed conflict. Such regional arms races are evident in the Middle East, South Asia, Latin America, the Persian Gulf, and East Africa. When one country in a region builds up its forces to match the combined forces of several neighbors, each neighboring country may feel even more threatened. The result can be a spiraling arms race. Examples of this phenomenon include Iran's rivalry with Saudi Arabia and Iraq, Iraq's concerns about Iran and Syria, and Peru's competition with Ecuador and Chile. Although supplier nations may consider their arms sales to a particular country necessary to restore a regional balance of power, other countries in the region may view these sales in a different manner.

Critics cite several examples where American arms sales have played a role in regional arms races. The cross-cutting rivalries among

41. Pierre, *The Global Politics of Arms Sales*, p. 132.

Middle East and Persian Gulf states explain much of the arms buildup in those regions during the last decade. Iran's fears of Iraq were responsible for many of the sophisticated American arms that the shah bought in the 1970s. Meanwhile, Israel's efforts to rebuild its military forces with American arms following the 1973 war encouraged Syria to acquire large quantities of Soviet weapons. Iraq's concerns went beyond its rivalry with Iran to include the regime in Syria. Saudi Arabia, fearing the imperial designs of the shah and the radical regime in Iraq, acquired the latest in American weaponry. Iran, in turn, responded to the buildups in Iraq and Saudi Arabia, and the cycle continued.[42] Another Persian Gulf state may be drawn into this arms race. Oman, fearful of the F-14 fighters the United States sold to the shah that are now in the hands of Islamic fundamentalists, is considering the acquisition of its own advanced combat aircraft, possibly the F-16. The United States could find itself hard pressed to refuse such a request at the risk of losing its access to Oman's military facilities for the Rapid Deployment Force.[43]

Another potentially explosive situation confronts the United States in South Asia. The perennial arms race between India and Pakistan may be about to spiral upward once again, according to critics. When India and Pakistan went to war in 1965 using American and British arms, Washington and London imposed an arms embargo against both combatants. The embargo was not lifted until 1975, but in the meantime India and Pakistan shopped elsewhere for weapons and developed their own arms industry. The Carter administration rejected a Pakistani request for A-7 aircraft in part out of concern that the sale would be viewed as a threat by India. When Carter offered instead the shorter-range F-5E, Pakistan turned to France and bought the Mirage III. The Reagan administration now intends to sell Pakistan the F-16. Critics say President Reagan may believe this sale is necessary because of the presence on Pakistan's border of Soviet military forces in Afghanistan, but the Indian government may view the situation in a different way. Some believe that India's recent purchase of forty Mirage 2000 fighters is partly a response to the F-16 sale to Pakistan.[44]

Latin America has also seen a competitive arms buildup. Peru and Chile have been locked in an Andean arms race—the legacy of a war fought a century ago in which Peru lost its southern terri-

---

42. Clark, "Needed: A Policy of Restraint," p. 6.

43. David B. Ottoway, "Oman Expects U.S. Help for Use of Its Bases," *Washington Post*, April 7, 1982.

44. See Felix Kessler, "France Remains a Major Arms Dealer," *Wall Street Journal*, May 4, 1982; and Pierre, *The Global Politics of Arms Sales*, pp. 221-25.

tories—for years. Ecuador has also been drawn into this arms race out of fear that Peruvian arms could be used to seize its oil fields. The United States has tried to dampen this arms race by denying Peru's request for F-5 aircraft and by vetoing a proposed sale of Israeli Kfir fighters (with American-made engines) to Ecuador, but other arms suppliers have rushed in to fill the vacuum. Ecuador bought the Mirage F-1 from France, and Peru acquired in desperation Soviet SU-22 fighter-bombers, tanks, and other weapons. Although Peru has become one of the ten largest recipients of Soviet arms, Moscow's influence with the military regime in Lima is minimal. The lesson to be drawn from this account, according to those who favor arms sales restraints, is not that the United States should be more forthcoming in supplying arms to participants in the Andean arms race. It is, rather, that Latin America is perhaps the region that most lends itself to multilateral restraints by the major arms suppliers.

President Carter's policy of arms sales restraint was predicated on the belief that arms sales could spark the outbreak of war. Several historical examples support this view. The competitive arms buildup by Germany and Austria on the one hand, and by Britain and France on the other, before August 1914 so heightened tensions in Europe that the assassination of an archduke at Sarajevo was enough to spark the outbreak of World War I. Soviet arms shipments in 1950 gave North Korea a military advantage against its southern neighbor. Critics see the Reagan administration, however, as drawing a different lesson from history. Instead of seeing the competition for arms sales as a cause of tension and contributor to regional instability, the administration has apparently taken the position that instability can be remedied by arms sales. Not all officials in the Reagan administration subscribe to this belief. Testifying before the Senate Foreign Relations Committee in April 1982, the assistant secretary of state for Near East and South Asian affairs said that "over any long period of time, clearly the accumulation of large numbers of weapons by potential adversaries has the logic of the outbreak of war."[45]

The lack of significant restraints on arms sales has also been seen as contributing to the destructiveness of wars. The shipment of vast quantities of sophisticated weapons to the third world has made conflict more destructive and violent. The 1973 Middle East war saw the largest tank battle in history. Precision-guided munitions for anti-tank and air-to-ground combat have greatly increased the quantities of arms destroyed, and the superpowers could be drawn in to resupply

45. Quoted in "Administration Denies Overemphasis on Military Assistance to Middle East," *Washington Post*, April 16, 1982.

their clients as a result. The Soviet Union's threat in 1973 to send its own troops to save Egyptian forces from being overwhelmed by the Israelis resulted in a tense confrontation with the United States, as Washington raised the level of its nuclear alert to deter Soviet intervention.[46]

The United States has exercised some restraint in selling particularly destructive arms. Washington has, for example, refused to sell Israel Pershing I surface-to-surface missiles and concussion bombs. With a range of up to 450 miles, the Pershing missile would represent a significant offensive threat to Arab cities and noncombatants. The threat to noncombatants was also part of the reason for refusing to sell concussion bombs. Proponents of arms sales restraint argue that controlling the export of long-range, high-yield, and indiscriminate weapons should be in the interests of all arms suppliers. Such restraint will help to limit not only the violence and destructiveness of wars but also the risk that the superpowers will be drawn into the conflict.

In summary, critics do not see arms sales as a remedy for regional instability and international tensions. Unless weapons exports are significantly controlled, they could become the spark that ignites conflict and superpower confrontation.

Arms Sales and Recipients

Arms sales are more than just business deals between countries. They often symbolize a deeper political commitment on the part of the United States to the security and stability of a recipient nation, because arms sales are a transfer of military power from one country to another. Unless one assumes that sales are made solely for commercial profit, which is not the case, one is drawn to the logical conclusion that selling weapons to other countries entails (whether intentionally or not) commitments to those countries.

Such commitments, of course, have been the intended consequence of many arms sales relationships the United States has consummated in the postwar period. Arms sales to Cairo since the 1973 war constitute deliberate decisions on the part of successive American presidents to commit the United States to the security of Egypt. Similarly, the extensive arms sales to Saudi Arabia and Iran (before 1979) could, according to one observer, turn "into the functional equivalent of a treaty."[47] Before the United States enters into

46. Henry Kissinger, *Years of Upheaval* (Boston: Little, Brown and Company, 1982), pp. 583–88.
47. Gelb, "Arms Sales," p. 16.

any new arms relationship abroad and whenever it is asked to sell additional weapons to past recipients, a careful reassessment of the domestic and foreign policies of those countries should be made to determine whether American political and security interests would be served by the sale.

Some critics question whether the United States should associate with repressive regimes by selling arms to them. Unfortunately citizens of many third-world countries continue to endure violations of fundamental human rights at the hands of their own governments. Thus a decision to sell arms to any of these countries may reflect a conclusion that the benefits of the sale for the security of the United States and its vital interests will outweigh the negative consequences for U.S. international prestige and self-image of association with a repressive regime. Arms sales to South Korea and the Philippines are perhaps the clearest cases where U.S. security interests are seen as outweighing human rights. Critics argue that when such sales are contemplated, special attention should be given to whether American weapons and related equipment could be used against internal dissidents to prop up unpopular regimes.

Congress has adopted several pieces of legislation over the years in response to a perceived cavalier attitude by the executive branch toward human rights violations by regimes that either receive U.S. security assistance or buy American weapons. Congress adopted the Kennedy amendment to the Foreign Assistance Act of 1974, prohibiting arms sales and security assistance to the military junta in Chile that overthrew the Allende government the previous year. When Congress passed the International Security Assistance and Arms Export Control Act in 1976, it included a provision prohibiting arms transfers except in extraordinary cases to any country "which engages in a consistent pattern of gross violations of internationally recognized human rights."[48] The same law requires the president to report to Congress each year on the human rights policies of countries receiving U.S. security assistance. When the Carter administration decided to reduce arms aid to Argentina, Uruguay, and Ethiopia because of their human rights records, both Latin American countries rejected further assistance from the United States, and Ethiopia expelled American personnel. Brazil was so incensed by allegations of human rights violations that it rejected U.S. military credits and canceled a military assistance treaty with Washington. The Reagan administration last year requested that the congressional ban on arms sales to Argentina, which was enacted in 1978, be withdrawn. The

48. Quoted in Pierre, *The Global Politics of Arms Sales,* p. 32.

administration also supported repeal of the ban on sales to Chile. A mandatory embargo on arms transfers to South Africa was voted by the UN Security Council in 1977 in response to South Africa's apartheid policies and repression of black dissidents. Critics contend, however, that arms sales to repressive regimes continue to be the norm rather than the exception.

Apart from human rights considerations, another factor that should be taken into account before deciding to sell arms to another country is its foreign policy objectives. How likely is it that the arms could be used for aggressive purposes? Does the prospective recipient harbor any irredentist claims against neighboring territory? Somalia's initial request for American arms after its expulsion of the Soviets in 1977 was rejected by the Carter administration on the grounds that the weapons could be used in the war with Ethiopia over the Ogaden region or against other neighboring states whose borders with Somalia are in dispute. The United States eventually agreed to supply Somalia with arms in return for access to the port of Berbera following the Soviet invasion of Afghanistan in late 1979. Somalia also promised that it would not use American arms in the Ogaden. The recent military seizure of the Falkland Islands by Argentina illustrates how arms sold overseas can be employed for purposes other than those intended. Britain's attempt to reclaim the islands by force could be met by Argentina's use of American A-4 fighter-bombers flying off an aircraft carrier sold to Buenos Aires years ago by Britain.

Advocates of additional restraint on arms sales also contend that large weapons purchases by many third-world countries could have the unintended effect of weakening ruling regimes by feeding internal unrest. Some arms purchases can have adverse economic, social, and political consequences for recipient countries. The Arms Export Control Act of 1976 recognizes these possibilities and requires that any less-developed country that diverts U.S. development assistance or "its own resources to unnecessary military expenditures, to a degree which materially interferes with its development" be found ineligible for future arms sales.[49]

It is true that most third-world countries do not spend much money on arms, but critics contend that far too little is spent on health, education, and other social needs. Some regimes may actually see it as in their interest not to encourage rising expectations among their people for fear of losing their grip on power, especially if they are unable or unwilling to satisfy popular demands for a better qual-

---

49. Quoted in Ball and Leitenberg, "The Foreign Arms Sales Policy of the Carter Administration," p. 540.

ity of life. Although there is no guarantee that all money diverted from arms purchases would be used to help lift the masses from poverty, it is likely that some of it would be so used. Scarce foreign exchange that might have paid for weapons could be used instead for more productive imports. More than one-third of the ninety-four less-developed countries that imported arms in 1978 were among the poorest in the world, with average per capita incomes of less than $500 a year.[50]

Critics argue, however, that the United States should not be concerned only about the possible deleterious effect of arms sales on the stability of the regimes in the poorest countries. Even as prosperous and seemingly stable a country as Iran in the late 1970s was not immune to these problems. The massive flow of American arms to Iran was intended to make that country the guardian of Western interests in the oil-rich Persian Gulf. The shah was assigned this enormous responsibility in part because American policy makers regarded his regime as highly stable. U.S. arms sales policy responded to the shah's own assessment of his country's military needs; American defense officials were instructed not to question the shah's requests for weapons. It appears that little consideration was given in Washington to what use might be made of Iran's arsenal should the monarchy fall from power. In the words of one expert on American arms sales policy, "The United States, in failing to examine the possible long-term consequences of its arms sales to Iran, exhibited a degree of irresponsibility or shortsightedness seldom matched in the postwar period."[51]

Some civilian officials in the Pentagon raised serious and fundamental questions about the premises of American arms sales policy toward Iran even before the dramatic rise in oil prices began filling the shah's treasury with petrodollars. Many of these concerns were prophetic: the shah might not have enough money both to fulfill his grandiose plans for the military and to meet the many pressing social needs of his people; domestic unrest was probable and could eventually topple the shah; the projected influx of American weapons and technical advisers might associate the United States too closely with the shah's repressive secret police; advanced American weapons technology could fall into the wrong hands if the shah fell from power; an unrestrained appetite for arms and other modernization programs could force the shah to boost the price of oil even higher; and neigh-

50. Pierre, *The Global Politics of Arms Sales*, p. 36.
51. Ibid., p. 150.

boring states were unlikely to permit Iran to achieve a clear military superiority in the Persian Gulf.[52]

Of course, American arms sales policy toward Iran does not by itself explain the revolution in 1979 and the subsequent anarchy. Critics argue, however, that the money spent on arms reflected an ordering of priorities that ultimately weakened the political, economic, and social fabric of the country. Up to 25 percent of Iran's national budget was devoted to defense; yet over half of the population remained illiterate.[53] Diverting money to pay the bills for weapons left construction projects half built and resulted in housing shortages and high unemployment. When the end came in 1979, the shah was not the only victim; the close association of the United States with the shah's policies prompted mobs in the streets of Tehran to seize the American embassy and hold U.S. diplomats hostage for over a year. U.S. arms sales policy toward Iran had helped to undermine American strategic interests in the vital Persian Gulf region.

Summary

The case for significantly curtailing U.S. arms sales rests on five basic arguments.

First, arms sales are not always in the national security interests of the United States. Critics contend that the national security argument is applied too freely and that it is often made without adequate consideration of how arms sales can harm U.S. interests. The preceding analysis has identified six ways in which arms sales can harm U.S. security:

• U.S. weapons technology could fall into the hands of adversaries and compromise weapons currently deployed with U.S. forces.
• Arms sold to another country could someday be used against the United States and its allies or could be employed for purposes inconsistent with U.S. interests.
• Arms sales could result in a situation where U.S. policy options are circumscribed, especially if a large number of U.S. military personnel and dependents are stationed in recipient countries or if the United States has acquired base rights in exchange for arms sales.

52. Robert J. Pranger and Dale R. Tahtinen, "American Policy Options in Iran and the Persian Gulf," *AEI Foreign Policy and Defense Review*, vol. 1, no. 2 (1979), p. 4.
53. Pierre, *The Global Politics of Arms Sales*, pp. 151 and 152. See also Moran, "Iranian Defense Expenditures and the Social Crisis."

• Arms sales can deplete existing stocks of weapons and equipment for U.S. forces or delay acquisitions of needed arms by U.S. military services, thereby reducing the readiness of U.S. forces.

• Arms sales could be counterproductive for another important U.S. policy goal: preventing the spread of nuclear weapons to other countries.

• Arms sales, unless substantially curtailed, could harm the international prestige and influence that the United States enjoys as an advocate of regional stability and the peaceful settlement of disputes.

Second, arms sales do not always provide the United States with diplomatic leverage over recipients. Critics argue that the recent history of U.S. arms sales demonstrates that recipients often ignore the wishes of the United States on issues that are important to those countries. Although Soviet setbacks in China, Egypt, and Somalia were perhaps more serious than those the United States has endured in the postwar period, Washington has had its share of difficulties with countries that buy American arms. NATO allies like Greece and Turkey, a close friend like Israel, and moderate Arab regimes that have resisted U.S. efforts to elicit their support for the Camp David peace process are often cited by critics to demonstrate the tenuous nature of the diplomatic influence the United States may acquire from arms sales.

Third, the economic benefits often claimed by proponents of arms sales are viewed by critics as overstated and often not worth the risks to U.S. security that arms sales entail. In particular, five points are made by the critics:

• Earnings from exports of weapons cover only a small fraction of U.S. oil import bills, and arms sales constitute only 4–5 percent of total U.S. exports, thereby contributing relatively little to the balance of payments of the United States.

• The employment benefits from arms sales are relatively minor; a significant curtailment of sales, as opposed to a total ban, would not create serious unemployment problems.

• Few top U.S. defense contractors depend on overseas sales for their economic survival.

• Most of the military items and services sold by the United States to other countries do not result in significant unit cost savings and recoupment of research and development costs for Pentagon purchases.

• There are good economic and military reasons why countries denied particular American weapons do not always buy comparable items, if available, from other supplier nations.

Fourth, arms sales can exacerbate existing tensions among neighboring countries and destabilize regional balances, thereby increasing the risk of war. Critics also contend that sales of sophisticated weapons to the third world can make wars more destructive and, if the belligerents are close friends of the United States and the Soviet Union, increase the chance of direct superpower confrontation.

Fifth, arms sales can adversely affect the internal stability of countries friendly to the United States. Critics also contend that U.S. arms sales to governments that violate human rights or spend excessively on arms, at the expense of economic and social development needs, can be perceived as symbolizing U.S. approval of those policies. A similar image may be signified by arms sales to countries that harbor aggressive aims against neighboring states.

Those who favor significantly curtailing U.S. arms sales to other countries believe that the risks in selling arms often outweigh the potential gains. The United States has vast economic and technical resources, as well as diplomatic skills, that often could be used more effectively to address the problems of less-developed countries. In short, arms sales should not be the policy of first resort.

4

The Case against Significantly Curtailing U.S. Arms Sales

This chapter presents the major argument for a less restrictive U.S. arms sales policy. It does not, however, support the removal of all constraints. Arms sales have always been limited. To argue for an open-ended, easy-access sales policy would be irrational and counterproductive in the long term. Likewise, proponents of arms sales are quick to point out that policies of unilateral restraint have proved to be flawed both in theory and in practical application. There is a middle ground.

The first priority of arms sales is to support U.S. national security goals. Each case must be evaluated on its own merits in light of many political and economic considerations. Often the decision to sell or not sell is based solely on current politics. This chapter, though not exhaustive, enumerates the relevant factors in support of a liberal sales policy.

Arms Sales and U.S. Security

The most important responsibility of a nation-state is to provide for the security of its people. As one means of accomplishing this goal, the United States, since World War II, has entered into a number of collective security arrangements with other nations. Through these arrangements, it has contributed to regional and global stability by providing a counter to Soviet aggression worldwide. Security assistance, and in particular arms sales, are an increasingly important dimension of U.S. policy, which seeks to ensure the security of friends and allies and thereby enhance its own. A stable, secure environment is of first priority and is essential to economic and social development at home and abroad.

Through security assistance measures, such as arms sales, the United States enables allies to undertake regional responsibilities that it would otherwise have to assume. The sale of arms to an ally is an alternative to deploying U.S. troops in the region. Proponents of arms sales cite several examples. Greece and Turkey perform duties critical to U.S. security interests by protecting the southern flank of NATO. Turkey occupies a strategic position controlling access to the Mediterranean from the Black Sea and faces the Soviet Union over the longest land border of any NATO country. With modern arms these countries can effectively counter Soviet moves to the south without the presence of U.S. troops.

A similar case can be made for Pakistan, given its strategic location and the proximate Soviet threat in Afghanistan. A strong, confident Pakistan capable of withstanding Soviet intimidation is essential to protect U.S. and free-world interests in the area.[1] Consequently, the United States is exploring options for modernizing Pakistani forces to deter Soviet aggression in that area.

Arms sales are also recognition that nations have their own legitimate security needs that require an adequate defense against regional adversaries. Security assistance "furnishes tangible evidence of U.S. support for their independence and territorial integrity, thus deterring possible aggression."[2] Although the United States has become increasingly aware of its inability to police the world alone, it continues to have a major interest in the survival of other nations. Maintaining their strength serves U.S. military interests by promoting regional stability and reducing the potential for direct U.S. involvement. These nations should be independently capable of deterring attacks from their neighbors. The assistance provided Thailand, for example, helped bolster Thai resolve in the face of Soviet-supported Vietnamese forces positioned along its eastern border.[3]

Arms sales to Taiwan are another example where the United States promoted self-sufficiency and regional stability. Self-sufficiency, however, is not a justification for unrestrained arms sales. According to one observer, "the role of arms sales in supporting American security must be highly contingent, because interests outside Europe are diverse, conditional and inconsistent." Unfortunately advocates of restraint "often do not take seriously the recipient's military

1. Jane A. Coon, deputy assistant secretary of state for Near Eastern and South Asian affairs, "Aid to Pakistan," statement before subcommittees of the House Foreign Affairs Committee, April 27, 1981. *Department of State Bulletin*, June 1981, p. 53.

2. James L. Buckley, under secretary of state for security assistance, science, and technology, "FY 1982 Security Assistance Requests," statement before the Subcommittee on International Security and Science Affairs of the House Foreign Affairs Committee, March 19, 1981. *Department of State Bulletin*, May 1981, p. 63.

3. Ibid.

requirements, and see proliferation of weaponry as a counterproductive indulgence that may precipitate the United States into self-destructive involvements in conflict."[4]

The Nixon Doctrine established arms sales and the training of indigenous military forces as a substitute for U.S. presence. Supplying arms to friendly forces was economically less burdensome and politically less controversial than stationing American combat troops in other countries. Arming friends and relying upon their troops could produce larger armies at lower cost. South Korea, for example, can maintain twenty troops for the cost of one U.S. soldier; Turkey can maintain twelve.[5]

Under the Reagan administration, arms sales are again seen as an "integral component of our global defense posture."[6] Sales to allies and friendly third-world nations are seen as complementing U.S. military forces. Consequently, the United States is not only rebuilding its own military strength but also giving attention to the security needs of its friends and allies "whose strength and support are major pillars of our own security."[7] This is not to suggest that all arms sales can be justified by using the specter of containment; arms can support purposes other than superpower competition.

As the major force for Arab moderation in the Middle East, Egypt plays a pivotal role in support of U.S. interests. Egypt has its own legitimate security needs as well. It must provide security for its ally Sudan, for the Nile River as an economic lifeline, for Egypt's coastlines, and particularly for the Suez Canal. There are also external threats from Libya and other sources.[8] Arms sales will allow Egypt to modernize its forces, increase its confidence, and match Israel's strength. Much of the equipment being sold is replacing obsolete and unserviceable weapons obtained from the Soviet Union many years ago. By aiding Egypt's military modernization, the United States contributes to regional stability and encourages continuation of the Camp David peace process.

Opponents of arms sales argue that high arms levels are destabilizing. As President Carter put it, "The virtually unrestrained spread of conventional weaponry threatens stability in every

---

4. Richard K. Betts, "The Tragicomedy of Arms Trade Control," *International Security*, vol. 5, no. 1 (Summer 1980), p. 82.

5. Cited in David J. Louscher, "The Rise of Military Sales as a U.S. Foreign Assistance Instrument," *Orbis*, vol. 20, no. 4 (Winter 1977), p. 957.

6. Buckley, "FY 1982 Security Assistance Requests," p. 63.

7. Ibid.

8. Ibid., p. 64.

region of the world."[9] Proponents point out that this assessment is only partially correct because the existence of arms within a region does not by itself create instability. Instability results from unequal strength between adversaries. Maintenance of regional arms balances and diplomatic efforts to reduce tensions and resolve differences peaceably are the key to regional stability. High levels of arms can be stabilizing as long as a real or perceived balance is maintained. The Middle East and Persian Gulf were not "made more volatile by the [arms] transfers; rather, the transfers were prompted by the volatility."[10] Large arms sales to Israel at concessional terms reflect the longstanding commitment of the United States to the security of Israel and the desire for stability in the region. Israel has been able to maintain a qualitative edge in arms to balance the large numbers of its Arab adversaries.

Regional imbalance leading to conflict occurred in the 1930s in Europe. European nations allowed their military capabilities to degrade while Germany was clandestinely rearming. Even after German aggression was apparent, attitudes of appeasement prevailed. Without an effective counterforce, Germany, free to attack its neighbors, did so with little risk. Another example was the perceived exclusion of South Korea from the U.S. security perimeter in the Far East. This is often cited as a contributing cause of North Korean aggression in 1950.

Access to military operating bases overseas is another benefit of arms sales often cited by proponents. Facilities on a permanent basis are needed to support forward-deployed U.S. forces. This adds credibility to security alliances and maintains a U.S. presence in various regions. Besides serving the traditional functions of overseas bases—staging areas, replenishment depots, and repair facilities—they are increasingly important in supporting intelligence collection and communications.

Facilities in Europe are available under provisions of the NATO agreement, but they may not always be available to support non-NATO operations, as was the case during the U.S. resupply of Israel in the 1973 Middle East war. At that time, most NATO allies did not permit staging from European bases, overflight, or refueling during airlift operations. Fortunately, Portugal permitted the United States to use the Azores as an aircraft refueling stop on the way to Israel. Loss of intelligence facilities in Iran has made the ones in Turkey all the

9. "President Carter Announces Policy on Transfers of Conventional Arms," *Department of State Bulletin*, June 13, 1977, p. 625.

10. Betts, "The Tragicomedy of Arms Trade Control," p. 87.

more necessary. Arms sales to Spain have been tied to continued access by U.S. forces to bases in the area, which is of great importance to maintaining the U.S. defense posture in Europe. In the Philippines, arms assistance is regarded as a quid pro quo for the use of Clark Air Base, Subic Naval Base, and related U.S. facilities. These bases are critical to America's remaining an Asian and Pacific power and to the projection of U.S. power into the Indian Ocean.[11]

In Southwest Asia, the United States is seeking military access to strategically located facilities. In exchange for use of ports and airfields in Oman, the United States will upgrade these facilities for its own purposes and for Oman's permanent use with a $1–1.5 billion military construction program. Oman is also seeking an additional $200 to $250 million in arms from the United States, including advanced fighter aircraft.[12] Oman's position overlooking the Strait of Hormuz at the mouth of the Persian Gulf makes it a key factor in America's Persian Gulf posture. The United States is also seeking access to facilities in Kenya and Somalia. The sale of F-5E fighters to Kenya has allowed U.S. forces to use the port of Mombasa and, possibly, staging facilities for patrol aircraft.[13] Arms sales to Somalia have improved the chances that American military forces will be able to use port facilities in that country to enhance access to the Arabian Sea and Indian Ocean and have improved the ability of the United States to counter growing Soviet naval strength in the area.

Arms sales do not always result in access to operating bases. Questions of sovereignty, resentment of U.S. support to adversaries (as in the Middle East), and the absence of effective leverage are other factors that can affect whether the United States acquires overseas bases. In cases where such bases are neither required nor offered, it may suffice to have access to port and interim staging facilities or even overflight rights.

In addition, the United States desires cooperative military arrangements with countries that can enhance the projection of its power and support joint military operations during crises. Providing arms and

11. "Congressional Presentation: Security Assistance Programs, FY 1982," in U.S. Congress, House of Representatives, Committee on Appropriations, Subcommittee on Foreign Operations and Related Agencies, *Foreign Assistance and Related Programs Appropriations for 1982*, 97th Congress, 1st session, 1981, part 6, p. 757.

12. David B. Ottoway, "Oman Expects U.S. Help for Use of Its Bases," *Washington Post*, April 7, 1982.

13. Cited in Robert E. Harkavy, "The New Geopolitics: Arms Transfers and the Major Powers' Competition for Overseas Bases," in Stephanie G. Neuman and Robert E. Harkavy, eds., *Arms Transfers in the Modern World* (New York: Praeger Publishers, 1979), p. 143.

support ensures that the logistics pipeline would already be in place, facilitating rapid response by U.S. military forces into an area. Thus regional security can be enhanced by mutually beneficial defense relationships that provide common equipment to U.S. allies.

Critics of arms sales to third-world nations have argued that those nations often buy arms beyond their means, spending money that should be used for economic development. Proponents contend that this argument ignores the fact that a government's most important task is providing for the security of its people. Proponents observe that without security, economic development is not possible. Moreover, the evidence shows that these countries have not been spending very much on arms. Military expenditures of the developing world (as a share of GNP) actually decreased from 5.8 percent in 1970 to 5.5 percent in 1979. Military expenditures as a percentage of central government expenditures declined from 33.3 percent to 22.9 percent over the same period, providing additional insight into their impact on development.[14] Arms purchases by non-OPEC developing nations (as a share of GNP) have remained steady at 0.6 percent and are thus no more of a burden today than they were a decade ago.[15]

The U.S. role in this activity has not appreciably changed. The volume of transfers by the United States has remained fairly stable over the last decade, except for the Middle East. Transfers have averaged $6 billion per year (in constant 1978 dollars), remaining within a range of $5–7 billion.[16] The United States has attempted to evaluate the security needs of third-world countries and to provide arms accordingly. Of course, dollar value is only one measure of the volume of arms transfers. One should consider the number and types of items transferred to form a clearer picture of the nature and substance of U.S. arms sales.[17]

Arms spending levels in general have not jeopardized development programs. Arms sales agreements often foster military and civilian construction programs that provide infrastructure such as roads, housing, and electrical generating facilities. Such projects contribute substantially to the economic and social development of the recipient country. In Saudi Arabia, for example, the United States is building roads and air bases. Once completed, the roads will support the civilian community. Military construction of this type has in-

14. U.S. Arms Control and Disarmament Agency, *World Military Expenditures and Arms Transfers 1970-1979* (Washington, D.C.: ACDA, March 1982), p. 43.

15. Ibid. (derived from tables I and II).

16. Ibid., p. 123.

17. For example, see ibid., table IV.

creased significantly during the last decade.[18] In fact, were military construction, training, and other technical services counted in the arms transfer aggregates reported by the Arms Control and Disarmament Agency (ACDA), the total value of U.S. military-related exports would be two-thirds greater.[19]

Assistance in the form of training contributes to the overall educational level of recipient countries because basic skills must be mastered to understand technical manuals and to repair and operate weapons systems. Many technical skills are readily transferable to the private sector.

Limiting sales to other countries on the basis of need (as the U.S. defines it) can be counterproductive and unnecessarily paternalistic. These nations are sovereign and should be able to assess their own requirements. U.S. judgments of the threat and the development needs of the country in question may not always be sound because our perspective is different. American arms sales policy must serve the security interests of the United States as the first priority, but then the security and economic needs of the recipient as *it* perceives them should prevail.

Arms Sales and Foreign Policy

Proponents argue that arms sales are a foreign policy tool, and under some circumstances they can be the most effective instrument available to policy makers. Sales are an added element that can satisfy U.S. foreign policy objectives. These objectives may be longstanding or recently derived from a change in regional alignments or internal political regimes. Arms sales may provide political influence, either potential or actual, or they may produce direct leverage over a recipient's behavior in ongoing events.

Political influences may result from access to the decision-making elites within the recipient country. The continuing dialogue with the military and political leadership on issues of mutual interest, such as arms sales, can often be directed toward cooperative efforts in other policy areas. In this regard, purely military rationales for sales may not be as important as establishing or maintaining rapport (this has

18. Department of Defense Security Assistance Agency, *Foreign Military Sales, Foreign Military Construction Sales and Military Assistance Facts* (as of September 1981) (Washington, D.C.: Data Management Division, Comptroller, DSAA, n.d.), pp. 13-14. (DSAA distinguishes between military construction and other defense-related items.)

19. William H. Lewis, "Arms Transfers and the Third World," in ACDA, *World Military Expenditures and Arms Transfers 1970-1979*, p. 29.

been the case in Latin America). U.S. arms support has provided an opportunity to influence government policies on human rights.

Sometimes the United States can derive influence from actions that are symbolic, such as a demonstration of friendship toward a nation that is pro–United States or independent in its political orientation. Influence could result from an expression of ideological support for a regime that is favorable to the United States but facing domestic instability. Special relationships that can evolve not only are mutually beneficial politically, but also can preempt the competition's attempts to gain influence. The appearance of closeness between the United States and the recipient may send appropriate signals to third parties, such as the Soviet Union.

Influence tends to be subtle and difficult to measure. Critics of constraints observe that a decision to sell arms may produce only marginal benefits to the United States, but a decision not to sell can have enormous negative consequences. There are a number of examples of such negative fallout. Congress banned sales to Turkey after it invaded Cyprus using American arms. The United States not only lost what influence it had there, but also was restricted in the use of intelligence collection facilities located in the country. Peru turned to the Soviet Union for arms after the United States refused to sell the F-5 fighter. The United States argued that Peru had no need for such an aircraft. The Soviets took advantage of the situation and supplied a wide variety of arms on generous terms. In addition to the SU-22 Fitter aircraft, they provided tanks, helicopters, and artillery. Jordan has also turned to the Soviets, ordering mobile anti-aircraft missile systems after the United States refused to sell mobile Hawk missiles. The American missiles purchased by Jordan in the mid-1970s were set in concrete at U.S. insistence.[20]

Arms sales can provide leverage to achieve specific goals. They can bring pressure on the recipient to pursue certain national policies or to alter its behavior. They can be used manipulatively to impose a resolution of conflict. Sometimes greater leverage results from the threat of withholding arms than from continuing to supply them. This is especially true where an agreement to provide arms had been previously established. It has been suggested, for example, that the United States used its control over Israeli military supplies and spares in the 1973 Middle East war to pressure Israel to cease military action after cutting off the Egyptian Third Army.

The United States has used arms sales to encourage both Israel and Egypt to modify their positions and agree to a peace

20. "Jordanian Officials Turn Down F-5G Proposal," *Aviation Week & Space Technology*, April 19, 1982, p. 16.

settlement. In addition to maintaining Israeli strength, President Carter agreed to provide arms to Egypt. The sale of arms to Egypt encouraged a troubled Sadat to continue to work toward the Camp David accords. Israel has been made to feel both militarily secure and rewarded for withdrawing from the Sinai. The United States has guaranteed the replacement of military equipment while maintaining Israel's technological edge. It has also guaranteed the replacement of the air base facilities that were given up in the Sinai. A disproportionately large share of security assistance funding has been earmarked for Israel and Egypt as a positive consequence of their agreements at Camp David.

Another form of leverage often cited by proponents of arms sales is found in the Symington provision of the 1976 Arms Export Control Act. This provision calls for the United States to withhold military assistance from a state that receives nuclear technology without appropriate international safeguards. By linking U.S. assistance to acceptance of restrictions on the use of nuclear technology, the provision is meant to encourage agreement to International Atomic Energy Agency (IAEA) inspections designed to prevent proliferation of nuclear weapons.

Conventional arms sales have provided the leverage to dissuade South Korea, Iran, and perhaps Pakistan from developing nuclear weapons. The United States threatened to cut off sales to South Korea if it bought a nuclear fuel reprocessing plant. Iran was simply to retain its open-ended commitment of sales from us.[21] Pakistan's continued reluctance to submit to IAEA inspections has prevented the United States from selling that nation arms. It appears, however, that recent events in Southwest Asia may demonstrate that restrictions of this nature require exceptions.

Access to conventional weapons reduces the likelihood that a recipient would resort to nuclear weapons. With nuclear power technology available from many developed countries, an insecure would-be nuclear power can acquire the technology transferable to nuclear weapon development. Worldwide proliferation of nuclear weapons is a continuing and serious concern. Some of the developing countries have been encouraged to invest in nuclear-powered electric generation facilities, but to preclude weapon development, the fuel enrichment/reprocessing technology has not been transferred. This practice, as well as the requirement for inspection, is resented as an infringement of sovereignty. Reducing the incentive for acquiring nuclear weapons

21. Leslie H. Gelb, "Arms Sales," *Foreign Policy*, no. 25 (Winter 1976-1977), p. 12.

by providing sophisticated conventional arms is seen by proponents as being more effective than rigid enforcement of safeguards.

The United States can offer, at reasonable prices, a wide range of sophisticated, maintainable weapons that would not only enhance the military capability of recipients but also provide flexibility not offered by nuclear weapons. Conventional weapons are needed to deter conventional conflict. Making these weapons available does not guarantee against the recipient's developing nuclear capabilities. To deny conventional systems necessary to maintain regional balances and national security, however, could create the wrong incentive. Deprived of U.S. equipment, the insecure nation might take the necessary steps to produce nuclear weapons.[22]

Economic Benefits of Arms Sales

Arms sales earn foreign exchange and improve the U.S. balance of payments. Proponents note that in the 1960s the United States sold arms to European allies to offset the costs of American troops committed to NATO. In the 1970s, the United States vigorously pursued arms sales to Persian Gulf countries to recoup dollars spent on oil. Today, the world arms market is even more lucrative, as significant foreign exchange earnings accrue to the United States.

Arms sales made up 3.1 percent of total U.S. exports in 1979 (0.2 percent of a $2.4 trillion GNP). Though often dismissed as having little relative value with respect to total economic activity, arms transfers in absolute terms ($5.6 billion in 1979) are significant.[23] As indicated earlier, these figures actually understate the true value of military-related exports because they do not include military construction, training, technical services, and certain items, such as medical equipment and foodstuffs, that have alternative civilian uses.

Arms sales can be used to ensure access to critical raw materials, such as Middle East oil. A guns-for-oil barter arrangement is fostered, creating a mutual dependence between the United States and the arms recipients. One would hope that Saudi Arabia and other countries in the region would be reluctant to interrupt the sale of oil to the United States given their reliance on American arms, military and civil construction, spare parts, technical services, and training. The relationship explains in part why almost one-half of our sales go to

22. See Richard Burt, "Nuclear Proliferation and the Spread of New Conventional Weapons Technology," in Neuman and Harkavy, *Arms Transfers in the Modern World*, pp. 89-108.

23. U.S. Arms Control and Disarmament Agency, *World Military Expenditures and Arms Transfers 1970-1979*, p. 123.

the Middle East. This is in contrast to the situation in 1973, when we had little arms leverage to exercise. During the oil embargo, the shah of Iran supplied both the United States and Israel with oil (to the displeasure of his Arab OPEC partners) in part because of his special arms relationship with the United States.

A number of studies have shown that arms sales increase employment. The Congressional Budget Office (CBO), for example, analyzed the macroeconomic effects of sales, using 1976 FMS of $8.2 billion as the base line. (FMS as identified at that time constituted over 90 percent of U.S. arms sales.) Assuming a complete ban on sales as of 1977, by 1981 there would have been 350,000 fewer jobs in private industry than if FMS had continued at the constant 1976 rate.[24] Put another way, roughly 42,000 jobs are provided from $1 billion in arms sales. Employment effects go beyond those directly involved in the defense industry (for example, the prime contractors, subcontractors, and vendors). Many more jobs are created among the suppliers' suppliers; that is, the effects reach the secondary and tertiary levels. The impact should not be minimized. A study by the Bureau of Labor Statistics in 1977 estimated that foreign military sales in 1975 provided 277,000 jobs.[25] Industry officials estimate that for every $1 billion in arms sales, more than 30,000 jobs are created directly and 60,000 more are created in related activities.[26]

Another benefit of arms sales often cited by proponents results from cost savings from economies in expanded production. These savings are passed on to buyers in the form of a lower unit cost of each item produced. These lower unit costs may permit the United States to buy needed weapons in numbers that were previously unaffordable.

Research and development (R&D) expenses are an easily identifiable savings from foreign sales. They are typically incurred early in the systems acquisition process and would be borne totally by the United States in the absence of sales abroad. The U.S. government can recoup a portion of these expenses by attaching a prorated surcharge to the price of those weapons sold overseas. Although other savings are more difficult to measure, they nonetheless contribute to lowering systems' unit cost.

24. Congressional Budget Office, *The Effect of Foreign Military Sales on the U.S. Economy* (Washington, D.C.: CBO, Staff Working Paper, July 23, 1976), p. 1.

25. Cited in Andrew J. Pierre, *The Global Politics of Arms Sales* (Princeton, N.J.: Princeton University Press, 1982), p. 26.

26. "Arms Sales Policy," in *U.S. Defense Policy: Weapons, Strategy and Commitments* (Washington, D.C.: Congressional Quarterly, 1980), p. 94.

Arms sales generate overhead savings. That is, certain fixed costs, which do not vary with the volume of sales, are passed on to the buyer. Such costs are often associated with design engineering staffs and facilities and would be spread over more units. The assumption in the analysis is that in the absence of foreign sales, the weapons production base would not change significantly.

Savings from learning curve effects result from longer production runs for a particular weapons system. That is, the average cost of a system decreases as the number of units produced increases. The cause is primarily the increased efficiency of the work force and improved management techniques gained from experience. Savings from economies of scale result from expanding the *rate* of production by fully using existing capacity. Both types of production savings—neither of which appears in a cost assessment directly—can lead to significant reduction in unit costs.

If foreign sales allow a production line to remain open for subsequent U.S. production, thereby eliminating shutdown and start-up fees, savings may be generated, and skilled employees may be retained in the industry. These effects are also difficult to measure because they are predicated on production plans that may not be executed.

Finally, foreign sales may generate savings by absorbing a portion of the cost of expanding or accelerating a particular production run that would otherwise have been required to satisfy U.S. inventory requirements. Implicitly, a greater than equal share of the nonrecurring cost of new tooling is passed on to the foreign buyer.[27]

CBO studied these cost savings phenomena. On the basis of an $8 billion 1976 FMS program of thirty-five weapons systems with no change to the production base, it estimated that $560 million in savings were generated.[28] The study noted that not all sales generate savings (for example, training and repair services, which constitute a large share of the dollar value). Ships are unique: they require virtually no R&D (excluding weapons systems) and have no learning curve effects. Aerospace systems (aircraft and missiles), along with vehicles and communications gear, do generate significant savings. The savings from sales of systems that generate savings averaged $0.14 on the dollar, of which R&D accounted for $0.04.[29] These figures translate into many hundreds of millions of dollars in today's vibrant market.

---

27. Congressional Budget Office, *Budgetary Cost Savings to the Department of Defense Resulting from Foreign Military Sales* (Washington, D.C.: CBO, Staff Working Paper, May 24, 1976), pp. 3-5.

28. Ibid., p. ix.

29. Ibid., p. 17.

On a more practical note, recoupments resulting from sharing R&D costs and those attributable to nonrecurring production costs of tooling required to accommodate the foreign arms purchase can be identified. Recoupment from the sale of 213 F-18s to Canada and Australia is almost $1 million per aircraft, primarily for R&D. (The overall savings to that program as a result of foreign sales is $1.3 billion.) The projected recoupment based on a hypothetical program for the modified Harrier (AV-8B), a joint U.K. and U.S. effort not yet into foreign sales, is $0.9 million per aircraft, of which $0.7 million would be attributable to R&D.[30] Similar recoupment can be expected from the $1.3 billion in sales of 350 F-16s to seven countries. Case by case, the figures are impressive because they have a large impact on the economic viability of the acquisition program.

The aerospace industry is of particular interest, as aircraft and missiles account for over 50 percent of the value of U.S. FMS deliveries.[31] It has the greatest potential to generate savings. R&D costs are recouped routinely, even from systems that have been in production for some time. Learning curve effects are well known, particularly for aircraft, and to the extent that both aircraft and missile production lines operate at full capacity because of foreign sales, overhead savings are significant.[32]

The value of military aircraft exports in 1981 was $1.5 billion, a 58 percent increase over 1980, which had recorded a 13 percent increase over 1979. For 1982, exports of 600 aircraft valued at $1.9 billion are forecast. The long-term prospects are for even greater sales. Large increases in missile exports are expected through the decade as well.[33] The potential for new employment and improved foreign exchange earnings in this sector are substantial.

Proponents also believe that arms sales are an alternative, at least in the short term, to increasingly prolific indigenous arms industries in third-world countries. Although there are few such countries capable of producing sophisticated weapons (Brazil, Israel, and India are the principal ones), many nations in the developing world are trying to build some form of arms industry. They are motivated

30. Office of the assistant secretary of defense (comptroller), Selected Acquisition Reports, December 31, 1981.

31. Department of Defense Security Assistance Agency, Foreign Military Sales, Foreign Military Construction Sales and Military Assistance Facts (as of September 1981), p. 75.

32. Congressional Budget Office, Budgetary Cost Savings Resulting from Foreign Military Sales, p. 13.

33. U.S. Industrial Outlook 1982 (Washington, D.C.: U.S. Department of Commerce, January 1982), pp. 254-63.

in part by a desire to reduce their susceptibility to the political and economic influence of the major arms suppliers, or at least to minimize their dependence on the industrialized world by substituting locally produced spare parts, if not entire weapons systems. Today, there are fourteen developing countries capable of producing military equipment other than small arms.[34]

The most significant activity of indigenous arms industries, from a U.S. perspective, is the production of combat-capable jet aircraft and missiles, the savings-generating industries. Five third-world countries are producing jet aircraft of indigenous origin or under license (Brazil, South Africa, Taiwan, Israel, and India). Israel has also produced two types of missiles, one surface-to-surface, one air-to-air. Other nations are still in the R&D phase. Many countries produce less-sophisticated military aircraft, and a handful have developed the capability to manufacture tanks and/or armored vehicles. The greatest proliferation has been in small arms and ammunition production, most of it under European license.[35]

The capacity for greater self-reliance in arms would appear to be growing. There is, however, a catch: "Instead of creating independence, indigenous production usually creates a new set of dependencies. Most often the machinery, the patents, and the high technology components all have to be updated."[36] This requires returning to the original suppliers for the new technology. The problem is particularly acute in aircraft and tank production, because third-world countries are unable to provide adequate engines to power these weapons and must use those available from the major suppliers. Electronics and avionics production is equally difficult.

Indigenous arms producers may eventually master the required technology, but their dependence on major suppliers will be difficult to break. Weapons technology is advancing so quickly that by the time a nation acquires proficiency with a class of weapons, it is obsolete, and the fledgling producer must again turn to the industrialized world for the next generation.

Another aspect of dependence involves the selection of suppliers. With advanced weapons systems, the most efficient way to procure and operate them is to rely on a single source of supply. To seek

34. Cited in Lewis, "Arms Transfers and the Third World," p. 28.

35. Michael Moodie, *Sovereignty, Security, and Arms*, Washington Papers, vol. 7, no. 67 (Beverly Hills and London: Sage Publications, 1979), pp. 14-22.

36. Anne Hessing Cahn and Joseph J. Kruzel, "Arms Trade in the 1980s," in Anne Hessing Cahn, J. Kruzel, P. Dawkins, and J. Huntzinger, *Controlling Future Arms Trade* (New York: McGraw-Hill, 1977), p. 78.

multiple sources, as Iran did, is expensive. The services of skilled technicians and engineers are not cheap, and elaborate supply and support networks are required. The cost of acquiring the most up-to-date systems may be to subject the recipient to the dictates of the supplier.

Changing suppliers is costly in the short term. Retraining is required, and support systems, already in place, must be altered. New and old weapons systems are frequently incompatible. Egypt is changing suppliers and completely rearming at a cost of $27–32 billion over the next eight years.[37] Egypt initially turned to Eastern Europe, India, and North Korea for spare parts for its Soviet-supplied equipment, and it is now seeking engines from the West to retrofit its aircraft. The market potential is quite promising, as Egypt seeks to diversify its supply sources.

Standardization of equipment among friends and allies, a particularly timely issue for NATO countries, can be a benefit of arms sales. From the European perspective standardization has generally meant the purchase of U.S. military goods. Despite efforts to reverse the trend, the U.S. share of sales has increased from a ratio of 3.6 in U.S. sales to 1 in European sales in 1976 to a 9.4 to 1 ratio in 1980.[38] The essentially one-way flow of arms from the United States has meant stifling competition for emerging European defense industries and trade deficits. Europeans have felt obliged to pursue their own political and economic self-interest and arm themselves domestically, with little attention to commonality of equipment. Unlike the United States, Europe cannot sustain its defense industries without foreign markets. The Europeans have insisted that the United States be more forthright in its market dealings and allow greater competition and freer transfer of technology if improvements in standardization are to be made. A number of cooperative efforts are now under way, including reciprocal procurement arrangements, the families-of-weapons concept for allocating development responsibilities, and, most important, coproduction of systems well along in development.

Coproduction under U.S. license offers the Europeans an opportunity to acquire advanced technology and to participate in the production of sophisticated equipment for all NATO partners. Systems currently in coproduction are F-16 aircraft of U.S. origin

37. Clarence A. Robinson, Jr., "Cairo Turns to West for Weapons," *Aviation Week & Space Technology*, December 14, 1981, p. 42.

38. "Senators Propose Agency to Select NATO's Arms," *Aviation Week & Space Technology*, May 10, 1982, p. 21.

and produced by Belgium, Denmark, the Netherlands, and Norway; AIM-9L Sidewinder air-to-air missiles developed by the United States and produced by a West German–led consortium; Infrared Seeker for Missiles (MOD FLIR) produced by the United States and West Germany; the Armor Machine Gun developed by Belgium and to be produced in the United States; and the AV-8B, a U.S. version of the British Harrier vertical and short takeoff and landing (V/STOL) aircraft, to be jointly produced by the United States and Great Britain.[39] Significant opportunities exist for other collaborative efforts to share technology, to broaden the production base, to increase equipment interoperability, and ultimately to enhance standardization. Removal of U.S. restrictions on the sale of coproduced items in third-world markets, an outlet so critical to the viability of the European defense industries, would further these efforts.

Arms Sales Restrictions and Loss of Markets

Perhaps the most practical consideration of all, to borrow a cliché, is "if we don't sell, others will." Refusal on the part of the United States to sell arms simply leaves the market to other countries. The proponents believe that availability of other suppliers, some of which are willing to sell arms and follow-on services at financial discounts and with few political restrictions, is the heart of the issue. Potential recipients are less willing to accept the dictates of the United States, and they increasingly seek to diversify their sources of supply. Critics of the Carter administration's restrictive and unilateral arms sales policy point to the results as evidence for this argument.[40]

The value of U.S. arms transfer agreements to the third world during the Carter years, which is the clearest reflection of the policy's impact, was essentially constant in nominal terms and thus declined in real terms. During the same period, the Soviet Union nearly doubled the value of the agreements it had the previous four years. In 1979, for the first time, the estimated value of Soviet arms deliveries exceeded that of U.S. deliveries. Likewise, France tripled its agreements, and Great Britain, West Germany, and Italy each doubled theirs. The United States relinquished its worldwide lead in sales of four of the standard twelve weapons categories, and its dominance

39. Caspar Weinberger, *Annual Report to Congress, Fiscal Year 1983* (Washington, D.C.: Department of Defense, February 8, 1982), pp. III-116 to III-120.
40. See, for example, Stephen P. Gibert, "Arsenal Diplomacy: Problems and Prospects," *International Security Review*, vol. 5, no. 3 (Fall 1980); and Betts, "The Tragicomedy of Arms Trade Control."

as an arms supplier slipped in varying degrees in all the regional markets.[41]

When the Carter administration turned down the sale of F-5Es and vetoed Israeli export of Kfir aircraft with U.S. engines to Ecuador, the French provided Mirage F-1s. India purchased British Jaguar aircraft when the United States vetoed Swedish export of the Viggen fighter with engines built under U.S. license. Argentina purchased French helicopters and German submarines and bought Mirage fighters from Israel after it was prohibited from buying weapons from the United States.[42] The record shows that the Carter program of quantitative and qualitative controls on sales did not achieve the goal of reducing worldwide arms transfers. The U.S. attempt to go it alone lost business for the American arms industry and "may have undermined some established supplier-client relationships with specific countries in the Third World."[43] The Soviet Union and France increased their market shares at our expense, and most suppliers were more than willing to satisfy the market demand.

The competition continues to be keen. The Soviets routinely overproduce for export purposes. Their low prices and liberal credit arrangements for preferred customers tend to be politically motivated. They have accepted barter goods in exchange for new and used weapons, and they are now the principal supplier of arms to third-world nations. Western European governments actively encourage overseas sales with foreign exchange assistance and help in promoting exports. France and Britain are neck-and-neck for markets in Africa, the Middle East, and Latin America, markets that were once dominated by the United States.[44] In retrospect, it appears that where there is a potential sale that does not threaten U.S. security and where there are other available suppliers, it serves no useful purpose for the United States to deny the sale.

Summary

The case against significantly curtailing arms sales rests on several arguments. A realistic, well-developed policy for the sale of U.S.

41. Congressional Research Service, *Changing Perspectives on U.S. Arms Transfer Policy*, Report to the Subcommittee on International Security and Scientific Affairs of the Committee on Foreign Affairs, U.S. House of Representatives, September 25, 1981, pp. 12-26.

42. Ibid., p. 30.

43. Ibid, p. 28.

44. See Pierre, *The Global Politics of Arms Sales*, pp. 73-82; Lewis, "Arms Transfers and the Third World;" and "Arms Sales Policy."

arms to other nations can make important contributions toward fulfilling U.S. national security and foreign policy goals, and can improve our economic posture. A unilaterally restrictive policy, on the other hand, has not been effective in reducing the international trade in arms. Such a policy only jeopardizes U.S. security when others, particularly the Soviet Union, show no real interest in limiting transfers. Proponents of arms sales make the following arguments:

- Arms sales are advantageous to the United States because they promote global stability as a counter to Soviet aggression. Sales to friends and allies complement U.S. force structure.
- Equipping other nations with American arms strengthens them so they can fulfill regional and unilateral security needs, thus reducing the potential for direct U.S. military involvement.
- U.S. arms sales can restore regional military balances, creating stability.
- Arms sales can result in cooperative arrangements for operating bases for U.S. forward-deployed forces. By providing equipment compatible with U.S. systems, the United States can gain logistics bases for regional deployment of its forces in times of crisis.
- Contrary to the view that arms sales impede economic development, sales help nations to establish and maintain the security and infrastructure essential for economic and social progress. Paternalistic views, which dictate arms needs to third world nations, are detrimental to our relations with them and to their security.
- By selling necessary arms, the United States is often able to influence nations to support its foreign policy. Sales provide access to political elites and thus the potential to influence them. Not selling arms often can have far-reaching negative consequences.
- Sales can be used as leverage in convincing recipients to modify their behavior or pursue certain policies compatible with U.S. interests. Sales may be used to dissuade a nation from developing nuclear weapons.
- Sales improve U.S. trade balances and may provide access to raw materials.
- The industrial base is strengthened and employment opportunities are created by arms sales.
- Savings from expanded production are generated. Research and development costs are prorated over a larger number of units. Larger production runs realize learning curve effects, economies of scale, and continuity of operation, which result in implicit savings that reduce unit costs.

• Sales can discourage third world countries from developing indigenous arms industries.

• Purchases of advanced systems lead to dependency on the United States for technical support and spare parts, which can be used as a vehicle for political influence.

• Standardization of equipment and doctrine, particularly in NATO, and reduced European reliance on third-world markets to maintain viable arms industries are byproducts of reciprocal sales and coproduction arrangements among NATO allies.

• Since the United States is not the sole source of sophisticated military equipment, unilateral arms sales restraint will not reduce the international trade in arms. Such a policy will only leave the market to competitors, primarily the Soviet Union, France, and Great Britain, and unfairly penalize U.S. defense industry.

Arms sales, guided by an enlightened process of review, have served important foreign policy and security objectives. As a policy tool, they are not immune to error or risk. U.S. policy should be based on principle yet also be pragmatic. Policy must address, in practical terms, the legitimate security needs of the United States and reflect economic reality. A policy of overbearing restraint—unilaterally imposed—is unworkable and ultimately undermines the security of the American people.

Bibliography

Baker, Steven J. "Arms Transfers and Nuclear Proliferation." In *Negotiating Security: An Arms Control Reader,* edited by William H. Kincade and Jeffrey D. Porro. Washington, D.C.: Carnegie Endowment for International Peace, 1979.

Ball, Nicole, and Leitenberg, Milton. "The Foreign Arms Sales Policy of the Carter Administration." *Alternatives: A Journal of World Policy* 4 (March 1979): 527–56.

————. "The Foreign Arms Sales Policy of the Carter Administration." *Bulletin of the Atomic Scientists* 35 (February 1979): 31–36.

Barnett, A. Doak. *The FX Decision: "Another Crucial Moment" in U.S.-China-Taiwan Relations.* Washington, D.C.: Brookings Institution, 1981.

Barton, John H. "The Developing Nations and Arms Control." *Studies in Comparative International Development* 10 (Spring 1975).

Bennet, Douglas J., Jr. "Congress in Foreign Policy: Who Needs It?" *Foreign Affairs* 57 (Fall 1978): 40–50.

Benson, Lucy Wilson. "Turning the Supertanker: Arms Transfer Restraint." *International Security* 3 (Spring 1979): 3–17.

Berry, Clifton, Jr., and Schemmer, Benjamin F. "How Europe Sells." *Armed Forces Journal International* 114 (August 1977): 15, 18.

Betts, Richard K. "The Tragicomedy of Arms Trade Control." *International Security* 5 (Summer 1980): 80–110.

Blechman, Barry M.; Nolan, James E.; and Platt, Alan. "Pushing Arms." *Foreign Policy,* no. 46 (Spring 1982): 138–54.

Buckley, James L. "Conventional Arms Transfer Policy." *Department of State Bulletin,* September 1981, 61–64.

————. "U.S. Assistance to Pakistan." *Department of State Bulletin,* August 1981, 83.

Burt, Richard R. *Developments in Arms Transfers: Implications for Supplier Control and Recipient Autonomy.* Santa Monica, Calif.: Rand Corporation, P-599a, September 1977.

————. "Nuclear Proliferation and the Spread of New Conventional Weapons Technology." In *Arms Transfers in the Modern World,* edited by Stephanie G. Neuman and Robert E. Harkavy. New York: Praeger Publishers, 1979.

Cahn, Anne Hessing. "The Economics of Arms Transfers." In *Arms Transfers in the Modern World*, edited by Stephanie G. Neuman and Robert E. Harkavy. New York: Praeger Publishers, 1979.

―――. "Have Arms, Will Sell." In *Negotiating Security: An Arms Control Reader*, edited by William H. Kincade and Jeffrey D. Porro. Washington, D.C.: Carnegie Endowment for International Peace, 1979.

Cahn, Anne Hessing; Kruzel, J.; Dawkins, P.; and Huntzinger, J. *Controlling Future Arms Trade*. New York: McGraw-Hill, Council on Foreign Relations, 1977.

Callaghan, Thomas A., Jr. *U.S./European Economic Cooperation in Military and Civil Technology*. Washington, D.C.: Center for Strategic and International Studies, September 1975.

Carter, Jimmy. "President Carter Announces Policy on Transfers of Conventional Arms." *Department of State Bulletin*, June 13, 1977, 625–26.

Center for Defense Information. "Soviet Weapons Exports: Russian Roulette in the Third World." *The Defense Monitor* 8 (January 1979).

―――. "U.S. Weapons Exports Headed for Record Level." *The Defense Monitor* 11 (March 1982).

Chubin, Shahram. "Iran's Security in the 1980s." *International Security* 2 (Winter 1978): 51–80.

Clark, Dick. "Needed: A Policy of Restraint for United States Arms Transfers." *AEI Defense Review* 2 (1978): 2–15.

Comptroller General of the United States. *Foreign Military Sales—A Growing Concern*. Report to the Congress. Washington, D.C.: General Accounting Office, ID-76-51, June 1, 1976.

―――. *Foreign Military Sales—A Potential Drain on the U.S. Defense Posture*. Report to the Congress. Washington, D.C.: General Accounting Office, LCD-77-440, September 2, 1977.

Congressional Budget Office. *Budgetary Cost Savings to the Department of Defense Resulting from Foreign Military Sales*. Staff Working Paper. Washington, D.C.: May 24, 1976.

―――. *The Effect of Foreign Military Sales on the U.S. Economy*. Staff Working Paper. Washington, D.C.: July 23, 1976.

―――. *Foreign Military Sales and U.S. Weapons Costs*. Staff Working Paper. Washington, D.C.: May 5, 1976.

Congressional Quarterly. *U.S. Defense Policy: Weapons, Strategy and Commitments*. 2d ed. Washington, D.C.: Congressional Quarterly, 1980.

"Conventional Arms Sales in the Carter Administration: An Interview with Leslie Gelb." *Arms Control Today* 10 (September 1980).

"Conventional Arms Transfer Policy." Reagan Administration Policy Statement. *Department of State Bulletin*, September 1981, 61–62.

Cottrell, A.; Hanks, R.; and Moodie, M. *Arms Transfers and U.S. Foreign and Military Policy.* Washington, D.C.: Center for Strategic and International Studies, Significant Issues Series, vol. 1, no. 7, 1980.

Cullin, William H. *How to Conduct Foreign Military Sales.* Washington, D.C.: American Defense Preparedness Association, 1977.

Daly, John Charles (moderator). *Arms Sales: A Useful Foreign Policy Tool?* Washington, D.C.: American Enterprise Institute, AEI Forums series, 1982.

Debating the Direction of U.S. Foreign Policy: 1979–1980 High School Debate Analysis. Washington, D.C.: American Enterprise Institute, 1979.

Department of Defense Security Assistance Agency. *Foreign Military Sales, Foreign Military Construction Sales and Military Assistance Facts* (as of September 1981). Washington, D.C.: Data Management Division, Comptroller, DSAA, n.d.

Dorfer, Ingemar. "Arms Deals: When, Why, and How?" In *Arms Transfers in the Modern World*, edited by Stephanie G. Neuman and Robert E. Harkavy. New York: Praeger Publishers, 1979.

Evron, Yair. "The Role of Arms Control in the Middle East." *Adelphi Papers*, No. 138. London: International Institute for Strategic Studies, Autumn, 1977.

Farley, Philip J.; Kaplan, Stephen S.; and Lewis, William H. *Arms Across the Sea.* Washington, D.C.: Brookings Institution, 1978.

Frank, Lewis A. *The Arms Trade in International Relations.* New York: Praeger Publishers, 1969.

Franko, Lawrence G. "Restraining Arms Exports to the Third World: Will Europe Agree?" *Survival* 21 (January/February 1979): 14–25.

Freedman, Lawrence. "Britain and the Arms Trade." *International Affairs* 54 (July 1978).

Gail, Bridget. "The Fine Old Game of Killing: Comparing U.S. and Soviet Arms Sales." *Armed Forces Journal International* 116 (September 1978): 16–20.

———. "The Fine Old Game of Killing: Part Two." *Armed Forces Journal International* 116 (November 1978): 37.

Gelb, Leslie H. "Arms Sales." *Foreign Policy*, no. 25 (Winter 1976–1977): 3–23.

Gervasi, Tom. *Arsenal of Democracy: American Arms Available for Export.* New York: Grove Press, 1978.

Gibert, Stephen P. "Arsenal Diplomacy: Problems and Prospects." *International Security Review* 5 (Fall 1980): 375–406.

———. "Implications of the Nixon Doctrine for Military Aid Policy." *Orbis* 16 (Fall 1972): 660–81.

———. "Soviet-American Military Aid Competition in the Third World." *Orbis* 13 (Winter 1970): 117–37.

Gibert, Stephen P., and Joshua, Wynfred. *Arms for the Third World: Soviet Military Aid Diplomacy.* Baltimore: Johns Hopkins University Press, 1969.

Glassman, John D. *Arms for the Arabs. The Soviet Union and War in the Middle East.* Baltimore: Johns Hopkins University Press, 1975.

Gray, Colin S. "Traffic Control for the Arms Trade?" *Foreign Policy,* no. 6 (Spring 1972): 153–69.

Greenwood, David. "The Defense Policy of the United Kingdom." In *The Defense Policies of Nations: A Comparative Study,* edited by Douglas J. Murray and Paul R. Viotti. Baltimore: Johns Hopkins University Press, 1982.

Hahn, Walter F., and Cottrell, Alvin J. *Soviet Shadow over Africa.* Miami, Fla.: Center for Advanced International Studies, University of Miami, 1976.

Hamilton, Lee H., and Van Dusen, Michael H. "Making the Separation of Powers Work." *Foreign Affairs* 57 (Fall 1978): 17–39.

Hammond, Paul Y., Louscher, David J., and Salomon, Michael D. "Controlling U.S. Arms Transfers: The Emerging System." *Orbis* 23 (Summer 1979): 317–52.

Harkavy, Robert E. *The Arms Trade and International Systems.* Cambridge, Mass.: Ballinger, 1975.

Holland, Max. "The Myth of Arms Restraint." *International Policy Report* 5 (May 1979).

Howe, Russell Warren. *Weapons: The International Game of Arms, Money and Diplomacy.* Garden City, N.Y.: Doubleday & Co., 1980.

Husbands, Jo L. "How the United States Makes Foreign Military Sales." In *Arms Transfers in the Modern World,* edited by Stephanie G. Neuman and Robert E. Harkavy. New York: Praeger Publishers, 1979.

Kemp, Geoffrey. "Dilemmas of the Arms Traffic." *Foreign Affairs* 48 (January 1970): 274–84.

Klare, Michael T. "The Political Economy of Arms Sales." *Bulletin of the Atomic Scientists* 32 (November 1976): 11–18.

Leitenberg, Milton, and Sheffer, Gabriel, eds. *Great Power Intervention in the Middle East.* New York: Pergamon Press, 1979.

Lewis, William H. "Political Influence: The Diminished Capacity."

In *Arms Transfers in the Modern World*, edited by Stephanie G. Neuman and Robert E. Harkavy. New York: Praeger Publishers, 1979.

Louscher, David J. "The Rise of Military Sales as a U.S. Foreign Assistance Instrument." *Orbis* 20 (Winter 1977): 933–62.

Louscher, David J., and Salomon, Michael D. "New Directions and New Problems for Arms Transfer Policy." *Naval War College Review* 35 (January–February 1982): 40–47.

Luck, Edward C. "Does the U.S. Have a Conventional Arms Sales Policy?" In *Negotiating Security: An Arms Control Reader*, edited by William H. Kincade and Jeffrey D. Porro. Washington, D.C.: Carnegie Endowment for International Peace, 1979.

Mann, Paul. "Defense, State Ask Eased Arms Sales." *Aviation Week & Space Technology*, April 12, 1982, pp. 20–21.

The Military Balance 1981–1982. London: International Institute for Strategic Studies, 1981.

Moodie, Michael. *Sovereignty, Security, and Arms.* Washington Papers, series no. 67. Beverly Hills and London: Sage Publications, 1979.

Neuman, Stephanie. "Security, Military Expenditures, and Socioeconomic Development: Reflections on Iran." *Orbis* 22 (1978): 569–94.

Pierre, Andrew J. "Arms Sales: The New Diplomacy." *Foreign Affairs* 60 (Winter 1981/1982): 266–86.

———. "Beyond the 'Plane Package': Arms and Politics in the Middle East." *International Security* 3 (Winter 1978/1979): 178–92.

———. *The Global Politics of Arms Sales.* Princeton, N.J.: Princeton University Press, 1982.

Pierre, Andrew J., ed. *Arms Transfers and American Foreign Policy.* New York: New York University Press, 1979.

Pranger, Robert J., and Tahtinen, Dale R. "American Policy Options in Iran and the Persian Gulf." *AEI Foreign Policy and Defense Review* 1 (1979).

———. *Implications of the 1976 Arab-Israeli Military Status.* Washington, D.C.: American Enterprise Institute, 1976.

———. *Nuclear Threat in the Middle East.* Washington, D.C.: American Enterprise Institute, 1975.

———. *Toward a Realistic Military Assistance Program.* Washington, D.C.: American Enterprise Institute, 1974.

Pryor, Leslie M. "Arms and the Shah." *Foreign Policy* 31 (Summer 1978): 56–71.

Ra'anan, Uri; Pfaltzgraff, Robert L., Jr.; and Kemp, Geoffrey, eds. *Arms Transfers to the Third World.* Boulder, Colo.: Westview Press, 1978.

Redick, John R. "Prospects for Arms Control in Latin America." In *Negotiating Security: An Arms Control Reader*, edited by William H. Kincade and Jeffrey D. Porro. Washington, D.C.: Carnegie Endowment for International Peace, 1979.

Rogers, Gen. F. Michael, USAF. "The Impact of Foreign Military Sales on the National Industrial Base." *Strategic Review* 5 (Spring 1977): 15–21.

Ross, Andrew L. *Arms Production in Developing Countries: The Continuing Proliferation of Conventional Weapons.* Santa Monica, Calif.: Rand Corporation, 1981.

Rubin, Barry. *Paved with Good Intentions: The American Experience and Iran.* New York: Penguin Books, 1981.

Sabrosky, Alan Ned. "The Defense Policy of France." In *The Defense Policies of Nations: A Comparative Study*, edited by Douglas J. Murray and Paul R. Viotti. Baltimore: Johns Hopkins University Press, 1982.

Salomon, Michael D., and Louscher, David J. "Conventional Arms Sales in the Carter Administration: Dilemmas of Restraint." *Arms Control Today* 10 (September 1980).

Salomon, Michael D.; Louscher, David J.; and Hammond, Paul Y. "Lessons of the Carter Approach to Restraining Arms Transfers." *Survival* 23 (September/October 1981): 200–208.

Sampson, Anthony. *The Arms Bazaar: From Lebanon to Lockheed.* New York: Viking Press, 1977.

Samuelson, Lewis J. "FY1982 Security Assistance Legislation." *DISAM Newsletter.* Spring 1982.

Schriever, Bernard A. "Jimmy Carter's Arms Transfer Policy: It Won't Work." *AEI Defense Review* 2 (1978): 16–28.

Tahtinen, Dale R. *Arms in the Persian Gulf.* Washington, D.C.: American Enterprise Institute, 1974.

———. *National Security Challenges to Saudi Arabia.* Washington, D.C.: American Enterprise Institute, 1978.

Tahtinen, Dale R., with the assistance of John Lenczowski. *Arms in the Indian Ocean: Interests and Challenges.* Washington, D.C.: American Enterprise Institute, 1977.

Tower, John G. "Congress versus the President: The Formulation and Implementation of American Foreign Policy." *Foreign Affairs* 60 (Winter 1981/1982): 229–46.

United Nations Association of the United States of America, National Policy Panel on Conventional Arms Control. *Controlling the Conventional Arms Race.* New York, November 1976.

U.S. Arms Control and Disarmament Agency. *World Military Expenditures and Arms Transfers 1970–1979.* Washington, D.C., March 1982.

U.S. Congress, House of Representatives, Subcommittee on International Security and Scientific Affairs, Committee on Foreign Affairs. *Changing Perspectives on U.S. Arms Transfer Policy.* Report prepared by the Congressional Research Service, Library of Congress. 97th Congress, 2d session, September 25, 1981.

U.S. Congress, Senate, Committee on Foreign Relations. *U.S. Conventional Arms Transfer Policy.* Report to the Senate. 96th Congress, 2d session, June 1980.

U.S. General Accounting Office. *Arms Sales Ceiling Based on Inconsistent and Erroneous Data.* Washington, D.C., FGMSD-78-30, April 12, 1978.

Warner, Edward L. III. "The Defense Policy of the Soviet Union." In *The Defense Policies of Nations: A Comparative Study,* edited by Douglas J. Murray and Paul R. Viotti. Baltimore: Johns Hopkins University Press, 1982.

Weiss, Seymour. *President Carter's Arms Transfer Policy: A Critical Assessment.* Washington, D.C.: Advanced International Studies Institute, University of Miami, 1978.

Wheelock, Thomas R. "Arms for Israel: The Limits of Leverage." *International Security* 3 (Fall 1978): 123–37.

Whittle, Richard. "Controls on Arms Sales Lifted After Failure of Carter Policy to Reduce Flow of Weapons." *Congressional Quarterly Weekly Report* 40 (April 10, 1982): 797–802.

―――. "Reagan Policy Renews Arms Sales Debate." *Congressional Quarterly Weekly Report* 40 (April 3, 1982): 719–24.

Selected AEI Publications

AEI Associates Program

Concerned
Intervention

❧

When Your Loved One
Won't Quit Alcohol or Drugs

JOHN & PAT O'NEILL

NEW HARBINGER PUBLICATIONS, INC.

Copyright 1993 by John and Pat O'Neill
New Harbinger Publications, Inc.
5674 Shattuck Avenue
Oakland, CA 94609

Cover design by SHELBY DESIGNS AND ILLUSTRATES
Illustrations by Mike Krone

Library of congress catalog number: 92-061813
ISBN 1-879237-36-9 Paperback
ISBN 1-879237-37-7 Hardcover

An earlier version of this book was published under the title *Help to Get Help*, by Creative Assistance Press, Austin, Texas. Copyright 1989, distributed by Texas Monthly Press, Inc.

First printing October 1992 5,000 copies

To our adult children, Catherine, Julie, John Jr., and Dan, with love and gratitude for all they have taught us.

And to the late Donald E. Hunter, who, as an Air Force chaplain, first helped our family to get help.

Contents

Our Own Experience • The Dilemma • Common
Sense to the Rescue—Sort of • First Families—No
Exception • Even the Warriors Fell • Facts We Do
Know • Other Factors

Part Four: Finding the Resources

About the Authors

John and Pat O'Neill are human relations training consultants based in Austin, Texas. They have worked with over 200 companies and agencies and have presented seminars and workshops to over 80,000 people.

The O'Neills are Licensed Chemical Dependency Counselors and National Certified Addiction Counselors who have worked as a husband-wife counseling team since 1973. They trained at the Johnson Institute in Minneapolis and have since studied and worked with many of the top names in the field. They were among those who pioneered the concepts of concerned person intervention and family treatment.

Over the past fifteen years John and Pat have served as consultants to many Fortune 500 companies, the U.S. Armed Forces, numerous other government agencies, as well as national treatment organizations. They have developed ongoing community information presentations, designed and managed employee assistance programs, and helped organize alcohol and drug abuse education programs at all educational levels.

Though possessing considerable clinical experience, the O'Neills see their mission as advocates for families suffering from alcoholism and related diseases. Their special focus is educating the public about effective intervention methods and quality treatment and advocating for addictive disease research. John and Pat are frequent media guests and popular presenters at regional and national gatherings.

Their book, *Concerned Intervention*, is a guide to family recovery from chemical dependency and co-dependency. The book is based on lessons learned from their experience with hundreds of families seeking intervention, counseling, and treatment. Special emphasis is placed on ways to identity healthy, properly trained professional counselors, affordable patient-centered treatment, and compatible self-help groups.

Acknowledgments

Concerned Intervention summarizes two decades of learning from thousands of people who have touched our personal and professional lives. We thank each of them for their love, support, encouragement. and most of all for the pushes, shoves, and nudges that kept us on the path.

We are also grateful for the legacy of the pioneering professionals who discovered these practical and direct routes to wellness. Until their efforts, the road to recovery was a faint and winding trail through a wilderness of public apathy and professional indifference. But today, thanks to them, the roadway is clearly illuminated by the glow of community awareness and the light of new medical and mental health interest.

Gratitude and respect to mentors and professional peers, too numerous to possibly mention, who, in spite of the frustrations and pain, continue in their commitment to help families overcome this disease.

Thanks to our families of origin, who may not always have understood our mission but have respected and supported our work.

Introduction

Through the years we have worked with hundreds of suffering families and friends of alcoholic or otherwise chemically dependent persons. We have presented educational programs to thousands more, many of whom have shared their stories with us. Two facts have become increasingly clear. First, there is a well-defined and proven sequence of specific choices and actions that mark the road most individuals and families follow on the way to intervention and recovery. And second, if caution is not used, there is potential for many expensive, time-consuming—even deadly—detours and cul-de-sacs on the route. So this book is about staying on a proven path and avoiding the hazards along the way.

Families and friends of chemically dependent persons need practical answers to these questions: What has happened? Why my family, friend, or co-worker? What can I do about it? To whom should I turn? Whom can I trust? Where will I find the courage and support to take action? Why is quality help for alcohol and other drug problems often illusive? How can I avoid misguided excursions in the quest for recovery? Our folklore about these matters is full of harmful myths. But, worse yet, until recently there was hardly any validated information in school curriculums at any level—especially in the universities. For most people, no matter how otherwise well-educated and informed they might be, these questions require updated answers. There are now many excellent books available on the separate subjects of alcoholism and drug abuse, family systems, intervention, and treatment. But there was not a complete, easy-to-apply, self-contained basic training manual for the personal war on drugs that begins when someone important to you becomes harmfully dependent on mood-altering chemicals and you are hurting. We wrote *Concerned Intervention* to meet that need by pointing out a clear, straight, proven path to intervention, treatment, and recovery.

Concerned Intervention is about tragedy, turmoil, and trouble. Yet it is a hopeful book full of facts that lead to understanding and positive change, with suggestions that the reader can use—right now—to reach out for effective, affordable, approachable help. Our intended reader is the family member, friend, co-worker, or employer who is trying to deal with someone else's drinking or drugging problem. But we believe that executives and managers at all levels, schoolteachers, counselors and administrators, and judges and law enforcement officials will also find the information helpful in their work. Certainly, if we had our way, every physician, clergy person, marriage counselor, psychologist, and social worker would hand a copy of the book to almost all their clients. For the evidence is growing by the day that most, yes most, of the people seen by such helping professionals are experiencing illnesses, dysfunctions, and relationship breakdowns because of an underlying alcohol or drug problem—either in themselves or someone they love.

This is not a theoretical work. We are not scholars. We are experienced-in-the-trenches alcohol and drug abuse counselors.

Concerned Intervention is based on our firsthand experience and the legacy of the pioneering professionals who discovered these practical and direct routes to wellness. Until their efforts, the road to recovery was a faint and winding trail through a wilderness of public apathy and professional indifference. But today, thanks to them, the roadway is clearly illuminated by the glow of community awareness and the light of new medical and mental health interest. We believe that our extensive personal and professional experience in the application of these principles can also make a contribution, especially because of our somewhat unique role as a counseling couple.

The book is divided into four parts: "Getting Started," "Taking Action," "Understanding the Problem," and "Finding the Resources." The four parts track with the questions uppermost in the minds of most readers: Should I act? What should I do? Why should I do it? Where can I get the help I need? The chapters in each part are essentially self-contained. In fact, each could be a separate booklet on its particular subject. This compartmentalization required some repetition among chapters. But this resulted in a more reader-friendly, functional, and easy-to-use book. By referring to the chapter descriptions in the Table of Contents or to the Index, readers will be able to quickly locate the information they need.

Finally, *Concerned Intervention* is a book about pain—why it happens and how to make it go away. It is said that there are no guarantees in life. Maybe so. But we know this. When suffering people have come to accept the ideas synthesized here and followed the courses of action suggested, lives change for the better, people get well, families mend, and the pain goes away.

Perhaps earlier sincere but unsuccessful efforts to find help have you feeling confused, frustrated, and disillusioned. Maybe you've chosen or been sent into blind canyons, unmarked detours, and deadends in the search for a straight path to recovery. Unquestionably, many genuinely concerned people, truly wanting to take right action and willing to accept professional guidance, often pay a shocking price in time, money, and emotional pain for help that doesn't help. In some cases the "professional" assistance has even caused real harm.

Still, in spite of the many valid reasons for fear, doubt, and hesitation, there is even more basis for hope. For it has been our special privilege to view the renewed personhood, restored health, and revived love that blooms in the happier place that lies beyond this stormy disease. The thousands of families who have found or rediscovered such wellness testify to the possibilities of recovery for you and your family. Their proven success, collective strength, and genuine willingness to help you along the way are powerful and realistic reasons for hope and confidence. It is a happy truth that today thousands are winning the family battle against alcohol and drugs. Their victories show that, armed with basic information, equipped with proven guidelines, connected to the right help resources, and encouraged by the support of those who have gone before, you and your loved ones don't have to hurt anymore.

Maybe you're thinking, "This sounds too easy. They don't understand. Our situation is a lot more complicated than all this sounds." Be warned that perhaps the greatest barrier to recovery is clinging to the idea that your situation is so different that what worked for others will not work for you. To view a chemically dependent person or your particular situation as unique is to sentence him or her and you to continued suffering. It is only by accepting the idea that you are dealing with a universal illness—one that responds to proven interventions and treatments—that recovery can begin. And such is truly the case.

As the title implies, this is a help book. So use it in any way that will help. There are four parts. "Getting Started" does just that; it gives reasons why you need to get moving and how to avoid harmful directions. "Taking Action" suggests specific, proven intervention and treatment steps and offers guidelines on how to recognize quality help. "Understanding the Problem" provides an optimistic update on today's national effort to understand, prevent, and remedy alcoholism and other drug dependencies. "Finding the Resources" deals with where to turn and how to pay the costs involved, and lists specific help resources nationwide as well as recommended reading.

The four parts encompass thirteen chapters. In addition, each major paragraph has a headline summarizing its content, so you can jump from topic to topic if need be. In a crisis scan the Index at the end of the book to locate immediate, helpful information. By all these means, *Concerned Intervention* is designed to be very reader-friendly and immediately useful. So skip around all you want. We think the organization is logical and the book is best read from front to back. But this disease is not always logical. Accordingly, read what seems important at the moment and come back for the rest later. In other words, do whatever it takes to find the help you need. The idea is to provide *Concerned Intervention*.

Concerned Intervention

Part One

Getting Started

1

Straight Answers to Key Questions

Nothing in life can prepare us for the storms that a chemical obsession unleashes within a family or group of friends. The auto accidents, arrests, breakups, batterings, and bankruptcies; the ruined plans and shattered dreams; the heartache and bewilderment—these things really do happen. Even if conditions are not that bad, as alcohol or other drugs gain more and more control, the emotional connections within the family begin to disintegrate. And that's disaster enough. There is great and growing pain when once-loving relationships turn into tortured contests for survival. We know this to be true from personal experience and many years of interacting professionally with families and other groups of concerned persons being torn apart by alcohol and drug problems. Still, if someone you care about has a problem with alcohol or other drugs, there is hope. There is help. It does work. Here is how to find it.

If you are trying to live or work with someone who has a serious alcohol or other drug problem, such optimism may ring hollow. Yes! You are right. There are no quick, magic solutions. But if you will trust the real-life experiences of people just like yourself, be willing to open-mindedly consider some useful facts, and risk a few new and different choices, there is a way out.

Let's get started!

The Usual Starting Point

This book is primarily for those trying to deal with somebody else's alcohol or drug problem. In our experience most want answers to these three key questions before they feel right about taking action:

1. Is alcohol (or some other drug) truly the primary problem?

2. How do I justify confronting someone else if I drink or drug myself?

3. Is it really possible to help when he or she won't admit there is a problem?

Is Alcohol (or Another Drug) Really the Problem?

How can you tell, with certainty, if someone you care about has become dependent on alcohol or other drugs? What's the difference between acceptable use of mood-altering chemicals, abuse of these substances, and the pathology called chemical dependency? How do you know that the person is not just being bad, stupid, or crazy—or all three? These questions are frequently asked by family members and other concerned persons who are living or working with a person who is experiencing life problems as a result of drinking or drugging.

Suspect the Obvious

Very few people live part of their life as good, intelligent, sane people and then start acting bad, stupid, and/or crazy unless alcohol and drugs are the culprit. So when we see behavior changes in those we love, we should first suspect and investigate the obvious. Certainly there are emotional and psychiatric illnesses. And occasionally people will turn morally sour. But such dysfunctions are relatively rare. Alcohol and drug-related problems, on the other hand, are encountered in one of every three American families. If someone you care about is acting in ways that concern you and there is reason to believe he or she drinks or drugs, look at that issue first. You will probably save a lot of time, heartache, and money by doing so. Even if there are underlying physical and emotional problems, those conditions cannot be dealt with until the alcohol or drug use is first addressed. Chemical dependencies are always primary.

How Can I Tell?

Clearly, there is a difference between a groom toasting his bride with a single glass of fine champagne and the skid row drunk trying to get his shaking hands on a pint of cheap muscatel. Or between the postsurgical patient taking pain killers for a few days and the chronic heroin addict willing to rob or even kill for a fix. But just where along the line between these extremes are the points that distinguish between acceptable use, harmful abuse, and pathological "ism"?

Use/Abuse/Dependency

The following definitions may be useful:

Use
Legal mood-altering chemicals consumed by choice, in safe amounts, at appropriate times and places, in ways not harmful to self or others.

Abuse
Mood-altering chemicals *still being used by choice*, but in unsafe amounts, or at inappropriate times and places, or in ways harmful to self or others.

Dependency
Powerlessness over mood-altering chemicals characterized by episodes of loss of control and/or the apparent inability to modify drinking and drugging even after experiencing negative consequences. Sometimes but not always accompanied by physical addiction to the chemical. Dependency may or may not be preceded in life by a history of abuse.

Are They Really Hooked?

How can you tell if someone has crossed the line and become dependent? First of all, the fact that you're reading this information makes it a very real possibility. Being concerned enough to want to read this book is a strong indication of how many clues you're picking up. But if there is doubt in your mind, here is a simple quiz. Answer the questions on the basis of your observations of the person about whom you are concerned.

1. Does he/she do things under the influence of alcohol and/or other drugs that violate his/her own rules for behavior?

2. Does he/she break promises to himself/herself about the use of alcohol and/or other drugs?

3. Is he/she paying an emotional price (shame, guilt, fear, remorse, self-directed anger, etc.) for using alcohol and/or other drugs?

4. Does he/she seem to have a different version of his/her own drinking/drugging behavior than witnesses?

5. In your opinion, would he/she become defensive, rationalize, or even lie if you asked him/her these questions?

(From here on, for convenience, we will most often use masculine pronouns. But everything said applies to both sexes. Chemical dependencies are definitely equal opportunity diseases.)

If you think that the person about whom you are concerned would have failed this quiz, there are two possible explanations. Either he is deliberately choosing to abuse chemicals in the face of adverse consequences—a highly unlikely case—or he has become dependent on chemicals and is sick and in need of help. If his sickness is causing you pain, you may find it helpful to learn more about the nature of this illness so you can take positive steps to intervene.

Chapters 9 through 11 contain more detailed information about alcoholism and other drug dependencies. But, assuming a crisis led you to this book, there may not be time or the inclination to read all that information now. For the time being, we suggest the following attitude toward someone who appears hooked on alcohol or another drug: they are sick. They have a pathology in every sense of the word. The mainstream scientific consensus is that alcoholism and other chemical dependencies are physiological diseases with a powerful genetic component. This is a most unique pathology, however, because it surrounds itself with an array of emotional and behavioral symptoms that make it difficult to diagnose, hard to intervene upon, and demanding of highly specialized long-term treatment and aftercare. Such a view is, beyond all else, extremely practical because those who approach this malady with that picture in mind are usually successful in bringing about change in the situation. Those who choose to moralize, analyze, or chastise tend to stay stuck in their pain. So, if you want to stop hurting, approach this disease like any other disease. Such an attitude will get results.

How Can I Confront When I Use Alcohol/Drugs Myself?

Maybe you can't! If chemicals are causing a serious problem in your life, then you yourself are probably chemically dependent. In such a case the only way you could help someone else is to say, "I'm going for help. Why don't you come along?" But, assuming your own use is under control, you can certainly be a help to others. To be effective, however, you will need to take these steps:

1. First, deal with the ways the other person's drinking/drugging has affected you.

2. Stop doing things that enable that person to escape the consequences of drinking/drugging.

3. Learn how to confront the behavior without attacking the person.

4. Become familiar with help options that can be accepted without loss of dignity.

Making those changes in your relationship with the chemically dependent person will place you in a posture of love and concern. And love and concern gives you a right to try to help. Thus, if the person says something like "Where do you get off talking to me about alcohol? You drink as much as I do!" the simple response is "Because I care about you and am concerned."

Caution: Personal Experience Need Not Apply

There is another caution regarding our own use of alcohol/drugs. Most of us form strong opinions on the subject from our own experiences. Many readers will have, at some time or other, abused alcohol or other mood-alterers and thus, in certain respects, believe they "understand" the problem. But there is a trap to the idea of using your own drinking or drugging experience in dealing with someone else's. If you are like the vast majority of temporary alcohol and drug abusers, you were probably able to learn from the negative physical, behavioral, and emotional consequences and modify your use with willpower and reason. Since you were able to change your drinking and/or drug use as the result of such "Wow! I'll never do that again" experiences, it's easy to conclude that everyone else ought to be able to do likewise, especially when the victim is someone you love and respect. But that's the trap. Not everyone else can.

Your personal experiences notwithstanding, there is blended into our drug-using/abusing culture a significant and tragic minority of people who permanently lose control over alcohol and other drugs. These people become pathologically dependent not because they are evil, ignorant, or insane but because of a complex and far-reaching disease process. It is complex because it affects every area of the victim's life and far-reaching because it causes pain in the lives of family members, friends, and even co-workers. So any approach to a loved one about an alcohol and/or other drug problem should be tempered by awareness that our own experience with chemicals may not apply and our own pain may even distort reality and block appropriate action. And of course, as mentioned before, there is always the possibility that we are chemically dependent ourselves and are in as much denial as the person about whom we are concerned.

How Can I Help If He Won't Admit There Is a Problem?

Few people are able to break out of a chemical dependency without help. Most who do recover follow a strikingly similar path. First, some significant event or person(s) intervenes and helps them to see the reality of their condition. This new awareness generates a willingness to accept outside help. Then the outside help is successful in getting them to accept their powerlessness, inspiring them to clear away the wreckage of the past and develop new and positive programs for alcohol- and drug-free living.

There are many respected contemporary theories about alcoholism and other chemical dependencies, just as there are a number of plausible models through which to view the family impact of these addictions. Some of these concepts make more sense than others. But, as yet, there is insufficient evidence to prove any of them conclusively. What is important and beyond theoretical controversy is the readily observable truth that some victims of alcohol and drug dependencies die and others get well. Those who recover are the fortunate few who had loved ones caring enough or hurting enough to reach out for help. Recovery is almost always the result of "outside interference." The momentous tragedy of this disease is that it first destroys love, and the resulting unloved victim—helpless from within and abandoned from without—dies. Yes, it is possible to intervene, but your assistance is crucial.

Does the Help Really Work?

Until the 1970s, the only readily available sources of assistance were self-help programs such as Alcoholics Anonymous, based on the renowned Twelve Steps. Such programs were literally lifesavers for those willing to admit there was a problem and be open to help. But the unwilling were sentenced to more suffering and, all too often, death.

Over the last twenty years or so, there has been widespread introduction of excellent health-care-based intervention and treatment models that seem better able to reach the unwilling. These programs accelerate recovery, enhance the benefit of twelve-step programs, and also deal more effectively with the physical and emotional aspects of the disease. At the same time, a much clearer understanding of the family impact of chemical dependency has emerged, accompanied by specific therapies to deal with these issues. Alongside these positive developments in treatment has been the outgrowth of innovative and potent intervention methods that facilitate the chemically dependent person's entry into treatment. So, in spite of yet unanswered questions about specific causes and the lack of a single magic remedy, the prognosis for early intervention and lasting recovery is excellent. In fact, it has become a truism that of all the nation's major health problems, chemical dependency is the most treatable. Again, *there is hope because there is help and it does work.* And you can play a vital role.

Chemical Dependency—C.D.

By now you have perhaps recognized the awkwardness of trying to continually refer to "alcoholism and other chemical dependencies" or "alcoholic or otherwise chemically dependent person." Yet today's drug dependency problem has expanded far beyond just alcohol. To simplify this poly-drug situation, the term *chemical dependency* has been coined.

Nowadays, when someone has become harmfully hooked on a mood-altering chemical, including alcohol, the professionals in the field refer to such persons as chemically dependent and call the disease chemical dependency. This is a very useful term that the press and the public would do well to more fully adopt. In fact, the longer the term is used, the more sense it makes.

In the past, the primary drugs of choice—alcohol, marijuana, and heroin—were actually grown as crops and processed almost like food products. Consequently, many people had trouble thinking of addicts to these earthborn substances as chemically dependent. Then along came real "drugs" such as tranquilizers, amphetamines, and laboratory derivatives of cocaine—closer to our general notion of chemicals. In fact, many of today's chemicals of abuse are just that: chemicals. They are not being harvested from the earth but rather are being synthesized in laboratories, legal and illegal. (It is not the least bit unfair to describe distilleries and breweries as laboratories for turning food products into mood-altering drugs.) Thus, the term *chemical dependency*, if anything, has grown more accurate, descriptive, and acceptable as an all-purpose term to describe a pathological dependency on any mood-altering substance. It seems wise to have a standard, agreed-upon name for a disease that has reached epidemic levels in our proliferating drug culture. To encourage greater acceptance and wider use of this term, as well as to keep this book more concise and readable, the victim of chemical dependency will hereafter be referred to as the C.D. person. Similarly, we will refer to the disease as C.D.

Focus

The C.D. experts advise those trying to deal with someone else's drinking or drugging to focus on practical steps and measures in the here and now rather than wasting energy on why it all happened in the there and then. Understanding alone doesn't arrest alcohol and/or other drug problems; choosing to act and getting the help to do so, however, does. So this is a "what works here and now" book. Our aim is to break down this seemingly overwhelming problem into a series of smaller, less intimidating challenges and then provide the pertinent information, clear guidelines, and practical skills to meet them.

A Starting Point

For starters, we suggest the following logic: If someone you love is putting mood-altering chemicals into his body and if doing that is messing up his life and if he either can't or won't change, then he is unquestionably harmfully dependent. If what you're doing to help the situation isn't working and if doing nothing only seems to make things worse, try something else! And if you're going to change strategies, follow the paths that have led to solutions for the most people. Just take it a step at a time and draw courage from the success stories of those who not only made it through this challenge but report being better human beings for having made the journey.

A Touchstone of Power

Consider also that deep emotions are touched when alcohol or other drugs run wild in a family. It may seem at the moment that those negative energies will destroy your loved ones. But there are positive forces at work as well. There is love, concern, and courage still buried within suffering families and friends as well as much dedication among professionals who work in the field. All the emotional energy, professional skill, and moral support you need is out there waiting for you to connect. Thus, we are confident that, if you're willing to reach for help, wellness for you and yours is close at hand.

2

To Families and Friends

"Let It Begin With Me"

As the song suggests, change around us begins with change within us. It is difficult and painfully frustrating to try to help a C.D. person until we first understand and begin repairing the damage the disease has done to us. One of the first things we tell our clients is "You need to put yourself back at the top of your own priority list." There is no way you can help someone else until you first take care of your needs, your pain, your self. So an important part of getting started is gaining an understanding of just why *their* disease is making *you* sick.

The One You Love Is on Booze or Drugs

Your love is rejected. Your help is refused. Your threats are ignored. You do what needs to be done to keep the family together, but much energy is spent hiding feelings and dealing with pain. Trying to uphold the family image by pretending, fixing, and controlling people and situations becomes physically, emotionally, and mentally exhausting. You don't understand what has happened to your once loving family or even where to find a glimmer of hope.

We have worked with lots of people just like you who felt trapped in an intolerable, painful situation and didn't know where to turn. Frequently seeking out traditional helpers such as clergy, physicians, and psychologists, who lacked the specialized skills to really be of value, family members were left with hope dashed, fears reinforced, power untapped, and questions unanswered. Why? How do families work? What happens when this unique disease takes charge? How can you begin to change your situation? What kind of help truly helps?

More Than Dick and Jane Families

Depending upon the situation, you may be wondering whether you are indeed a member of a family. Rest assured, you are. Families are simply groups of individuals tied together with an emotional bond. Families today are more than the traditional "Dick and Jane" family consisting of Mom, Dad, and kids. They appear in many other diverse forms as well. There are extended families composed of stepparents, stepchildren, adopted children, and sometimes other relatives. There are borrowed families, groups of people with whom you can be close and get needs met when your own family is not available. And there are institutional families: those at work, at school, in the military, or even in a treatment facility.

In all these kinds of families an emotional bonding takes place. When that family unit is healthy, the bonding is positive and healthy. But when a disease such as chemical dependency enters the picture, the picture changes. The bonding becomes negative, feelings become buried alive. People feel trapped, unable to see a way out or make healthy choices until and unless they receive better information and guidance, strong emotional support, and sometimes even loving confrontation. Family members become survivors. Moms, dads, sisters, brothers, daughters, sons-in-laws, co-workers, employers, friends—all begin to learn what it takes to survive in a relationship with someone who is chemically dependent. So when we speak of C.D. families, we are referring to any system suffering from the painful effects of chemical dependency.

Co-Dependency—Another Name for Survival

Living in a C.D. family has been likened to being held hostage. When you feel trapped, survival becomes the focus of your life. Unable to be objective or rational, those living with a C.D. person have to develop techniques, behaviors, responses, and defenses in order to survive. There is little doubt that people living in these situations develop their own pathology. What to call this pathology, however, has been the subject of considerable dialogue over the years. The terms *co-alcoholic*, *para-alcoholic*, and *co-dependent* have at one time or another been used to describe someone who has become full of emotional pain and taken on an array of defensive behaviors. Currently, *co-dependency* and *co-dependent* are the most widely used terms to describe this disease and its victims. In our experience, all who have been emotionally bonded with a chemically dependent person suffer some degree of co-dependency. When you have lived, loved, reacted to, and learned how to survive with someone else's chemical dependency, it is impossible to escape co-dependency. You can't be rich enough, smart enough, protected enough, or powerful enough to escape the trauma or avoid the consequences. We are only human, and our humanity is what makes us all vulnerable.

How Does It Happen?

Life in a C.D. family breaks the rules for healthy living. Time after time, promises are broken. People say things they don't mean and don't say what they really mean. The environment becomes a "crazy" place where reality is harder and harder to figure out. Reading minds becomes a necessary skill. You can't trust the people in your system, and you begin to forget what it was like to trust your own reality. Family members desperately want to believe that all will be well, but are disappointed over and over again. Yet they continue to hope, try to give the C.D. person the benefit of the doubt, and, wanting so badly to trust someone, pretend he is as trustworthy as he once was.

The disappointments multiply, the fears and hopes become intermingled, and the pain gets deeper. Consider, for example, the young girl whose dad promises to show up at her school play. She secretly and silently hopes he will be there. Rationally and objectively it is doubtful that he will appear, but C.D. family members are neither rational nor objective about those they love. On the one hand, she wants him there to share her happiness; on the other, she worries that he will show up drunk and humiliate and embarrass her in front of friends. She fears having to make excuses if he never arrives or alibis for his condition if he shows up drunk—all the while wishing that this time will be different.

Family members desperately want to trust: the next party will be fun, Friday's paycheck will go toward bills, tonight's meal will be peaceful, the chores will be done, future promises will be kept, and on and on and on. Trust is so important to family members that they believe in the unbelievable—that the situation will change or simply go away. And through tears, shed and unshed, people who care or once cared about a C.D. person are revolving around him and his drinking/drugging behavior regardless of the fearful consequences to themselves.

Silent Fears

To live in a C.D. family is to live with unspoken fear. Will he be home for dinner? And in what condition? Will there be peace or battles? Will you be able to study for an important test or be dodging an abusive parent? Will your C.D. co-worker do his share of the job or will you have to cover for him? Agonizing concerns such as these put the family focus on the C.D. person and downgrade the needs and wants of others.

Coping with unpredictable and aberrant behavior demands so much time, energy, and concern that the co-dependent persons have little left for themselves. Being the constant target of blame chips and chips away at self-esteem and sense of worth. So you try harder, believing the "craziness" is your fault. No longer do family members expect honest answers, promises kept, time for themselves, respect, cooperation, love. *Yet the real craziness is that the non-C.D. family members are now feeling worthless and accepting responsibility for the chaos caused by someone else's totally unacceptable drinking and drugging behavior. Beyond all else, co-dependency is a disease of misplaced responsibility. Its victims stop managing their own lives in an attempt to control another's.* As a result, all those involved cease being what they were meant to be and become pathological actors in a drama of human destruction. Their internal dialogue says, "Tell me what you want me to be today so that you don't have to drink and drug, and I'll be it. How do you want me to look? What do you want me to say and how do you want me to say it? How do you want me to love you? Who can I have as friends? What can I do to make it easier for you so that you won't have to drink or drug?

The struggling players try to manipulate the C.D. person's drinking or drugging by being, saying, doing, not doing, looking, loving—in short, behaving—as they think the C.D. person wants, believing that controlling the environment will bring the miracle of change. And with that change will come attention, love, and respect. This obsessive notion that you can change another person's drinking or drugging by controlling and manipulating is what co-dependency is all about. Life is driven by the compulsion to meet the needs of the C.D. person so that he will stop drinking, love you, respond to you, care for you, and *be a part of your family.* How sad and how untrue. Real change begins only when someone in the family has the courage to acknowledge this powerlessness and reach out for positive help.

What's Real?

Family members find it increasingly difficult to talk to others about what's really happening. And efforts to speak with the C.D. person meet with wrath, denial, hostility, and conflicting versions of reality:

> "You're making too much of this!"
> "Stop nagging!"
> "You're just imagining things."
> "It wasn't that bad."

Spouses of alcoholics experience this kind of rebuff so often they think they are losing their minds; they react by screaming and sobbing, even hiding from the C.D. in fear—yet pretending to the rest of the world that everything is O.K. You must be "crazy"! The C.D. person powerfully projects his painful emotions on those closest, seeing his anger, fear, loneliness, and disgust in others. His inadequacy becomes their inadequacy. The house isn't clean enough, the kids aren't quiet enough, the boss isn't fair enough, the weather isn't sunny enough, etc. So you try harder and harder: scrub floors until they shine, hush kids until they whisper, cover up for him at work, and pray for the weather to change. You try everything; yet things get worse as chemical dependency and co-dependency progress.

Your home becomes a house of fear. There may be screaming, name-calling, and even violence, creating recurring terror. You become afraid to risk the wrath of the C.D. person, becoming secretive and not daring to talk about what is really going on. Please note that not all C.D. persons act out with violence, abuse, D.W.I.'s, or job losses. Some just withdraw and gradually abrogate responsibilities as spouses, parents, citizens, and employees. This isolation can be as painful as the fear. But no matter how the C.D. person acts out his illness and reacts to the family—quietly withdrawn or loudly abusive—family members pay the highest emotional cost.

Who Buried My Feelings?

Chemical dependency and co-dependency are diseases of feelings buried alive. When it's not O.K. to feel, feelings get stuffed. Once-positive feelings for the C D. person are often erased or at least superimposed by many negative feelings. You might attempt telling the C.D. about your sadness or anger—how unloved you feel. But someone in pain has little empathy for the pain of others, and the feelings are thrown back in your face. So you stuff your real feelings and start to pretend.

Because there is so much pretense, feelings get all mixed up. Burying negative feelings also puts a lid on positive feelings—the joy, happiness, and love that give meaning to our lives. Unfeeling family members become robot-like creatures, responding from habit, prior conditioning, and stress rather than through thoughtful consideration of reality.

When behavior is automatic and feelings are denied, the body may react in physical illness—recurring migraine headaches, back problems, gastrointestinal problems, and other conditions that won't go away in spite of many trips to the doctor. Seldom will the physician ask about family life or possible alcohol or other drug problems. So...another illness and another, as nothing in your life changes. It's as though your body is crying out, "Pay some attention to the hurt, the anger, the hopelessness I feel!"

"I Am Not Angry!!!"

It's perfectly natural to become very angry when you are being used, abused, and discounted. But showing that anger can have serious, even dangerous consequences for you. Open, honest anger is nearly impossible. Sometimes anger is stored up, exploding in self-defeating ways. A friend became so frustrated with her unresponsive alcoholic husband that she found herself stopping in disbelief just a breath away from shooting him with his own hunting bow and arrow. Most retaliation is less violent and comes in the form of passive-aggressive behaviors such as being late, spending money, not doing things the C.D. person likes to do, or turning the children against him. Co-dependency forms behaviors that violate your own values and deepen the guilt. You buy booze for him with food money, prostitute yourself by having sex with a smelly drunk, lie to cover up and maintain a false family image.

To overcome the guilt, you buy what the kids want instead of what you need, struggling to give them the attention the C.D. person doesn't.

Isn't Mom Wonderful!

Control the kids, run the household, get a job if necessary, and still find time to be "Volunteer of the Year." Has this happened to you? Do you feel worth the time and energy you give others? Do you spend any money on yourself or, at the opposite extreme, try to spend as much as the C.D. person squanders on alcohol? Do you order what you want in a restaurant or what is cheap? How long has it been since you made a choice for yourself? Do you feel deserving of *anything*?

Children of Silence

The children can't talk about what's really happening, either. When they try to talk to Mom and Dad, they often find themselves targets of angry frustration. If the parent is a C.D., he will either pay no attention, strike out, or switch behaviors. Or, one youngster complained, "He is either buying me a football or kicking me around the house. I don't know what to expect." The other parent, preoccupied with the desperation of the moment, can't hear what the children are saying or respond to their needs. The non-C.D. parent may even insist that everything is alright when the children see that it isn't. Under these stresses, children lose trust in their parents, become fearful, and feel guilty and unwanted. Children sense being torn apart when parents try to get them to take sides. They may hesitate to talk to their sisters or brothers, thinking the other kids don't know what's going on. Older siblings may in fact tell the younger ones that nothing is wrong in order to spare them pain. When no one talks about what's real, the youngest children fear they are hearing things and seeing things that may not even be happening. The kids also begin to believe they are the "crazy" ones. Such troubled youngsters are usually too embarrassed to turn to a school counselor, clergy person, relative, or friend for help. Instead they pretend—fantasizing about a loving, kind, caring, sane family. We have encountered adult children of alcoholics who suffered emotional and physical abuse and even incest and yet insisted that they came from a "normal" family. Children have a tremendous sense of loyalty to family, no matter what the cost. What a high price to pay. Kids who can't trust their parents lose trust in themselves and the security of their world. Without help, these children grow into adults unable to trust anyone.

Older Than Their Years

Children living in C.D. families take on responsibilities far too difficult for their years. Dedicated to family survival, they will do whatever is needed to keep the dysfunctional unit together. If children think the family needs someone to be perfect and take charge, they will. If they think it is necessary to take some focus off the chemically dependent person, they may act out and even get in trouble. If humor is needed, they will provide fun and games to the point of being obnoxious. Children will try to be perfect, serious, intellectual, or rebellious and troublesome, or even funny and cute—whatever works for right now. It is an exhausting job that makes young people quickly feel tired and scared, but they never stop trying. They fight paralyzing feelings of loneliness and guilt. There is no one to turn to, so the tears aren't shed and the screams aren't uttered.

Children get lost playing parts in the drama of the chemically dependent family. They lose touch with who is inside the pain, not allowing anyone—including themselves—to see, know, or love the person residing within the wall of defenses. It sometimes becomes necessary to withdraw or even become invisible to help the family. So some kids get harder and harder to find, suffocated beneath the weight of survival.

Where does childhood go for these children? It doesn't even exist. Adults who grew up in chemically dependent homes are typically intellectually overdeveloped and emotionally underdeveloped, often displaying compulsive behaviors like drinking, drugging, overeating, undereating, overworking, gambling, smoking, and indulging in promiscuous sex. They feel overtired, overworked, and overburdened and need help to deal with and grow out of their co-dependency. Without help, they will carry that pathology with them for as long as they live. Not only is their childhood taken away by this disease but, without help, healthy adulthood is impossible. It is critical to educate and intervene in the lives of young family members to stop this cruel cycle.

What's Family to a Child?

Kids in C.D. families believe that what is going on is "normal" unless someone tells them otherwise. We met an eleven-year-old whose dad would get drunk, get an ax, hold the child's head on a chopping block, and pretend he was going to cut off the boy's head. The youngster got so used to living this way that he thought being awakened in the middle of the night by a raging, drunken father and thrown against the wall was "normal." It is so important to reach these children and give them some idea of what a real family can be. Children living in a C.D. home also believe that the problems are their fault. Even the youngest must be told that they didn't cause chemical dependency and the living problems associated with this disease. A three-year-old girl once told us, "It's my fault that Daddy gets drunk." Then she would go stand in the corner and bite her arm until it bled. Even at this early age she was blaming herself.

Children must be told that they are not responsible. It is also important to break the no-talk rules in the family. When no one talks about what is real, people, particularly children, may not be able to distinguish reality. How does a child feel when he hears at school that love and moms and dads and pets and play are what families are all about and then goes home and sees drunkenness, physical fighting, and vomiting? And he listens to the screaming and the glass shattering in the night, trying to hide the fear by burying his face under the pillow and wondering what is real. What is family? What was family to the dark-eyed four-year-old girl at the Battered Women's Center who had lived through so much terror she couldn't talk to us, didn't react, didn't do anything—except sit and stare. What was family to the nine-year-old boy who thought he was the only one in his whole school living in a family like his? He felt so different and so scared. Relief shined in his eyes when he was told that many of his classmates lived in families just like his. He couldn't wait to join a group where he could talk to kids his own age who wouldn't think he was "crazy." Families?

Beware of Powerlessness

Family members try to stay in charge to survive. They pretend everything is going to be alright, developing a sense of powerlessness and resistance to change. The intolerable known becomes more acceptable than the frightening unknown. Family members seem to be saying to themselves, "Here at least I know my role, what I have to do to survive. Out there—who knows?" The fears seem insurmountable: where to go, what to do, who can help, where the money will come from. With trust gone, no one to talk to, and feelings buried, the idea of change—taking action and letting go of the chemically dependent person—is terrifying. They cling to the false security of the familiar. That is one of the reasons why adult children of alcoholics very often marry alcoholics—to repeat the role they have rehearsed. Often professionals hear co-dependent people describe their situation as intolerable. They can't continue and must do something. Yet after planning a course of action, they won't act, blocked by a wall of powerlessness. It is not easy to take back power and begin change. Staying stuck is much easier. It takes courage, trust, and action to recover, but the rewards are worth the risk.

A First Step

Recovery can begin by learning how to stop enabling. Those surrounding a chemically dependent person tend to do all the wrong things for all the right reasons: make excuses, pretend it's not so bad, lie, give the C.D. money, buy booze and drugs, bail the C.D. out of jail, and other rescue and cover-up operations. After a while, enabling becomes a difficult pattern to stop. Calling the boss and making excuses for the alcoholic gets easier. You believe that if you just get your child out of jail one more time, he will have learned his lesson and not drive drunk again. You learn just where to look for your husband's car after a night of drinking.

Enabling means accepting responsibility for the actions of the C.D., hoping that by doing all these helpful things you can stop him from drinking and drugging. But in fact, *by enabling, you are perpetuating the disease*. As long as the chemically dependent person pays little price for the drinking and drugging behavior, he has no reason to quit. Letting go of the reins is difficult. But when tempted to enable, remember you are literally loving him to death. By protecting the C.D. from the consequences of his unacceptable behavior, you deny him the opportunity to touch the true severity of the situation.

It is painful to let your husband lose his job, watch your child in jail, and listen to the abuse when you don't do what the C.D. person wants. It hurts to be reprimanded by well-meaning but ill-informed relatives and friends who think you should just care for him, love him, and pray for him until he recovers. Stop the enabling! Allow him the privilege of his pain! To do so, you will need the support of those who understand what you're going through, what works, and what doesn't work. Enabling is difficult if not impossible to stop without help. Feeling responsible and guilty will too easily lead back to enabling behaviors because they make you feel a little better about yourself, at least for a while.

Who Hits Bottom?

They speak of alcoholics "bottoming out." But what about family members hitting bottom? We usually think of family members as one day having enough and filing for divorce or insisting their C.D. adolescent accept treatment or disavowing their alcoholic parents or some other dramatic positive step. But this is not how co-dependent persons usually bottom out. Rather, it is more common to see them try to escape their pain through negative, self-defeating actions, which only aggravate their situation. For example, a wife may say, "I can't beat him, so I'll join him," and starts drinking abusively until she has her own drinking crisis. Or the child who simply cannot take any more turns to negative alternatives: drugs, dropping out, suicide. Tragically the family member may suffer as much trying to escape from the pain of co-dependency as the C.D.

experiences in the grips of chemical dependency. Who hits bottom? Everyone touched by this disease.

What Price Secrecy?

It's not easy to step outside of yourself and reach for help when your self-worth is constantly being bruised and battered. This blame-try-fail, blame-try-fail cycle wears away at self-esteem. Family members no longer feel confident enough to share the situation with others. They hide the pain—the physical illness, spiritual despair, terrible nightmares, shattered dreams, obsessions, compulsions, depressions, troubled relationships, failing grades, awful fears, isolation, the silent array of costly secrets. Ending this agony demands breaking this conspiracy of silence. And you'll need outside help to do it. A safe phone call is usually the easiest place to start.

Getting Started

Look in the yellow pages of your telephone directory under Alcoholism. Find Al-anon, Alateen, or Adult Children of Alcoholics support groups. If these groups are not listed, call Alcoholics Anonymous and ask about meetings for the families and friends of C.D. people. Request a call from Al-anon or Alateen.

If you are a teenager, talk to your school counselor, nurse, or teacher about support groups within the school system. In such groups and in Alateen you will meet young people your age living in similar situations.

Meetings for the adult children of alcoholics have sprung up all over the nation. The groups are called ACOA or ACA Al-anon groups. Another organization, Co-dependency Anonymous, is found in some communities. These various support groups can save your life. They are not meant to be therapy groups, but they do provide a source of experience, strength, and hope.

It is important to find a place where you can express your true feelings and where it's safe to talk about them. Listen closely. The people who are sharing may express a feeling that you yourself have been afraid to voice. Hold on to them for support until able to express your own. Newcomers are welcome and very special. Check it out. Discover you're not alone! Seek out a more experienced member, someone you can trust who will keep you in touch with reality and help you escape the vicious cycle. This person, called a sponsor, will be someone to talk with, contact in crisis, and assist you in launching your recovery. Find someone who really cares about you. When your family is no longer there for you emotionally, it is crucial to find a substitute place where it's safe to talk and feel.

Just How Serious Is This?

Co-dependency, without help, is a lifelong permanent condition affecting the victim in all subsequent relationships. Untreated co-dependents pass on delusion, repression, and compulsion to their own children. Recovery requires therapy or treatment. You cannot simply learn or think your way out of co-dependency because it is burned into your heart and soul.

An eighteen-year-old high school senior, tears running down his cheeks, approached us after a presentation. He told us that he never knew that the behavior of his alcoholic parents could have a lifelong affect on him. Now he understood why he was like he was and wanted help to change. He was weary from his struggle to survive the chaos of an alcoholic home.

A Special Word to Parents

Parents of chemically dependent offspring also take on enabling roles and survival behaviors. So most of what has been said concerning spouses and children in co-dependency applies to parents as well. However, the major trap for most parents is that they give up their authority. They allow the troubled child to take charge of the family, control its emotional life, and drive its behavior.

Parents must regain their rightful power. Mothers and fathers of children with alcohol or drug problems should first learn the laws of their state concerning compulsory treatment. It may be that they can require their son or daughter to enter an appropriate recovery program. Above all, parents need to set limits and stick to them. This may even require involving law enforcement officials. More than one C.D. adolescent has gone from a judge's chambers to a treatment center. To demonstrate such tough love, parents will need the help of a support group, such as Toughlove Parents or Al-anon. Co-dependency is multigenerational and moves in all directions. You can get it from your kids.

A Road Now Well-Traveled

Fortunately, excellent individual co-dependency treatment and family-based chemical dependency treatment are now available. Support groups as well as co-dependency-focused therapy groups are available in nearly every community. Keep in mind there is no blame in either chemical dependency or co-dependency. These are diseases that nobody asked for and everyone got. But it is no longer necessary to just survive. The right kind of help can free your real feelings from the depths of your pain and restore your authentic self. Family members who have cried and screamed their way through layers of hurt and pain come out the other side knowing that, deep down, they are real. Real, feeling human being.

3

Hazards on the
Way to Help

Caution: The Usual Help...May Not!

Finding the excellent care now available for chemical dependency and co-dependency poses special challenges. The inclination is for suffering families to turn to the mainstream helping professions: physicians, psychologists, clergy persons, marriage counselors, social workers. After all, that is where our experience teaches us to go for "professional help." Yet, for alcohol and other drug-related problems, such resources must be carefully screened.

As late as the early 1980s, very few schools of medicine, ministry, psychology, or social work offered in-depth courses in alcoholism or other chemical dependencies. The general theme in the health care professions reflected society's view that alcohol and drug abuse were behavioral or criminal justice problems. Consequently, most physicians, clergy, psychologists, and social workers were not trained to deal with these issues as primary illnesses. C.D. was seen as secondary to some underlying moral, behavioral, or psychological problem.

How Bad Is It?

He'd recently been fired from a bank presidency. His once significant net worth was in virtual collapse. Now he was sitting across from us weeping. "Why didn't anybody tell me these things before?" he asked through the tears. Let's call him John. John had told us a story we'd heard many times before. Job stress drove him to his doctor, who prescribed a tranquilizer and continued to do so for years. Several physicians, jobs, and cross-country "geographical cure" moves later, his life was in shambles—all because of the pills. He was experiencing panic attacks, chronic anxiety, bouts of paranoia, every area of his life was falling apart. Another psychiatrist prescribed a different tranquilizer. Then a psychologist referred him to a third doctor, whose solution was more pills. None of the physicians, psychiatrists, or psychologists involved in his case for over ten years ever questioned his use of or need for tranquilizers. In a real sense, they were his pushers.

The banker entered C.D. treatment and—glory be!—a miracle. His stress, panic attacks, anxiety, paranoia, and eventually his professional and financial problems faded from his now sober and productive life. The banker's wife and teenage children, who had been severely affected by this chaos, also underwent treatment. They are a normal happy family again.

Beware the Professional Enabler

It is fair to say that many helping professionals have entered the business of treating chemically dependent and co-dependent people without the proper education and training. In the 1970s and 80s, many physicians, counselors and therapists of other disciplines opened treatment centers and clinics or offered therapy groups in response to increased public awareness and demand for treatment. Most of these health professionals made the effort to gain the pre-requisite skills needed to offer excellent programs. But a few were simply incompetent and/or dollar-driven, with their facilities staffed with profit rather than professional competency in mind. One could witness the inappropriate prescribing of tranquilizers to already chemically dependent persons, the charging of high fees for ineffective talk therapy, ACOA groups conducted by counselors who should have been in one…and the list could go on.

In recent years the system has purged itself of much of this abuse. But the unwary can still blunder into what is called profes-sional enabling. So a warning is in order. There are at least seven ways untrained, unhealthy, or ill-intended helping professionals can enable a C.D. person to continue in self-destructive ways.

1. Not recognizing and diagnosing the primary problem as chemical dependency or co-dependency.

2. Not confronting the patient about drinking/drugging.

3. Prescribing or dispensing mood-altering chemicals.

4. Failing to refer patients to specialized treatment and, in-stead, employing inappropriate forms of psychotherapy.

5. Rescuing, judging, problem-solving, or avoiding the real issues, thus provoking even deeper feelings of powerless-ness, inadequacy, guilt, and isolation in the chemically dependent person and/or family.

6. Suggesting ineffective courses of action based on lack of information or misinformation.

7. Being actively chemically dependent themselves.

Where to Turn

Until recently there were few formal courses in alcohol or other drug dependencies. It is only in the last five years or so that degree programs have emerged. Consequently, most of the professionals competent in the C.D. field achieved their knowledge and skill through continuing education programs and specialized internships rather than in their initial professional education and training. Consequently, top-notch C.D. specialists are quite knowledgeable, intensely dedicated, and very capable, but not always easy to find. They are now beginning to surface in mainstream health care. One reason is that, until the mid 1970s, there was little insurance coverage for treatment of alcoholism and other chemical dependencies. Consequently, with little economic incentive, few conventional hospitals or psychiatric facilities were interested in providing care to "drunks, dope fiends, or their crazy friends and relatives," especially since these patients denied they had a problem, resented attempts to be helped, were often belligerent, and sometimes even smelled bad. To fill these voids, a network of paraprofessional counselors and freestanding nonhospital treatment facilities evolved during the fifties, sixties, and seventies. However, a combination of government funding, expanded insurance coverage, and growing public enlightenment led to new involvement on the part of the orthodox helping professions and institutions.

The paraprofessionals and free-standing programs deserve credit for developing the early treatment models. But it must be acknowledged that the conventional helping professionals and health care institutions have the credentialing networks and financial wherewithal needed to mass-produce this help for the many millions in need.

The best of both worlds was emerging in the eighties and nineties. The proven programs and skills developed by the dedicated pioneers were adopted by the national health care organizations that, with their business acumen and financial strength, could deliver them on a large scale. At present, however, the intervention and treatment of alcohol and other drug dependencies is still in a state of transition. The concept of "managed care," which one critic described as "neither," has emerged. Originally, a positive step to curtail rising health care costs, managed care has evolved into an antagonistic dialogue between insurance providers and care givers.

This growing negative component in our national health care system is much too complex to deal with here. Until this jockeying for position settles down, finding affordable, effective help for your situation may require some effort in order to avoid help that doesn't help. (See Chapters 12 and 13 for help in finding quality resources.)

So for Now, Be Careful

Our clients have revealed how a naive walk through the Yellow Pages looking for help wound up costing time, money, and emotional pain with no results. There are many variations, but the essence of the tale usually goes as follows. It seems they had first sought help where conditioned to seek it: psychiatrists, clergy persons, physicians, marriage counselors, psychologists, school counselors, and social workers. Yet often the information received was outdated or inaccurate and the advice inappropriate. Worst of all, expensive, unnecessary, and even harmful medication or therapy was often prescribed. The message is this: if care is not taken, you may encounter professionals who can delay, block, and even do harm to recovery while charging a lot of money. These perhaps well-intended "professional enablers" in one way or another permit suffering families to continue on destructive courses of action. Consider the following real-life examples.

Case Study—"The Woman Who Had Everything"

Not only did Ruth have everything, but it seemed she was taking everything there was for it. Ruth first got into "help" when she showed up in the hospital emergency room with an apparent allergic reaction. The emergency staff failed to note that Ruth's eyes were bloodshot, speech slurred, gait very unsteady, and breath nearly flammable. The doctor prescribed a shot and referred her to an allergist. He suggested an isolation diet, which she carefully followed. But she continued drinking her bourbon because the doctor never mentioned that.

A few days later another reaction sent her back to the emergency room. Her puzzled allergist ran a comprehensive series of skin and blood tests, and prescribed twice-weekly desensitization shots and powerful antihistamines. Still no questions about her alcohol use. Ruth paid little attention to the warnings about mixing the pills with alcohol because she "didn't drink that much." She found herself awakening drowsy from the pills and discovered that a Bloody Mary got her moving.

Later, while seeing her doctor for a sore throat, she reported extreme nervousness. He prescribed "a tranquilizer to tide her over the rough spots." Still no discussion of alcohol use except a reminder not to drink while taking the tranquilizer. Ruth interpreted this as meaning "Don't wash it down with a beer." By this time her alcoholism had progressed to the point where her blood pressure was elevated and required drugs to control. Her doctor also detected mild diabetes and added medication for that condition as well. He did caution her to restrict her drinking, but there was no real discussion of alcohol as a possible factor in her growing array of physical problems.

As Ruth's alcoholism progressed, she developed gastrointestinal problems that led to many examinations, x-rays, and medications but no clear diagnosis. Finally, her various physicians began refusing to renew her tranquilizer prescription. One eventually referred her to a psychiatrist. After reviewing her medical epoch, he prescribed antidepressant drugs. By now Ruth was suffering from allergies, sleep disorders, nervousness, headaches, gastointestinal distress, diabetes, high blood pressure, and depression—for all of which she was taking some kind of medication. And like most chemically dependent people, she was further assaulting her body and central nervous system with huge doses of nicotine and caffeine.

Ruth's family attended a community information program we presented. Coming up to us afterwards, her husband described all the maladies from which she was suffering and exclaimed, "We hate to say anything about her drinking because she's so sick all the time. Her bourbon is all she has to look forward to." After education, training, and counseling they successfully intervened and entered family treatment. The medical director, a specialist in C.D., weaned her from all medications within a week. Miraculously, her allergies, high blood pressure, nervousness, sleep problems, gastrointestinal distress, depression, and diabetes disappeared as she recovered from her primary disease—alcoholism.

Is this an isolated or far-fetched example? Ask the medical director of any good C.D. treatment center. He or she could keep you up nights relating countless similar medical melodramas. The reality is that most physicians and psychiatrists are neither trained to recognize or motivated to confront anything but very late, near-fatal symptoms of alcoholism: cirrhosis, acute pancreatitus, delirium tremens, and specific kinds of skin disease and muscle weakness. Short of that, they will, as in Ruth's case, usually just diagnose and treat symptoms. Like many of us, physicians are reluctant to question patients about alcohol use either because they consider it a personal matter, because there is an implied stigma, or because it brings into question their own alcohol or drug use.

Lesson: Alcoholism, when present in an ill person, is almost always the primary chronic disease. Except for emergency treatment of acute injuries, internal bleeding, or overdoses, it is futile to treat C.D. persons for other diseases until they first undergo treatment of their primary illness.

Case Study—"The Battered Christian"

Sarah approached us cautiously after one of our information programs. Her bruised arms and face bore witness to recent violence. After some evasion and many furtive glances, Sarah admitted that her alcoholic spouse beat her severely on frequent occasions. Her reason for not leaving or at least seeking help was her minister's counsel that her husband was just a sinful man who needed to repent. He insisted it was her Christian duty to remain with him and that all she could do to help was pray. The preacher suggested that Jesus would want her to turn the other cheek.

In all our programs we urge people living in physical abuse situations to seek help through local shelters for battered women, law enforcement agencies, or appropriate social service organizations. The first priority should be their own life and limb. And they certainly can't earn a living, care for children, or help the chemically dependent person if paralyzed with fear, physically incapacitated, or dead.

After some urging, the terrified woman sought safety and counseling at the Battered Women's Center. We also referred her to a minister of her faith who had more current and enlightened education about chemical dependency and family violence. With his support, her husband was confronted about the abuse and offered treatment for his alcoholism and associated violent behavior. Grudgingly he agreed, only because she refused to come home if he did not.

This points out an exciting reality of modern C.D. treatment today: quality treatment is effective even when the C.D. person enters a program under coercion and filled with anger. And so it was in this case. During his treatment for alcoholism, the husband learned that his abusive behavior was related not only to his alcohol use, but also to his upbringing in a family where his own father had been an abusive alcoholic. He learned how someone raised in this kind of emotionally deprived family develops a disturbed emotional life and an array of self-defeating survival behaviors. Consequently. the husband had to deal with the emotional and behavioral impacts of not only his own alcoholism but also his family's.

After a period of sobriety, the husband joined an ACOA therapy group. Here he was able to purge his repressed childhood anger and to deal with frustration without resorting to physical violence. The family is now living and growing together in peace.

Lesson: Clergy are not necessarily trained C.D. counselors. If there is a need for pastoral counseling, contact the local council of churches or the seminary that educates the ministers of your church. They can probably steer you to someone qualified.

Case Study—"The Medicated Family"

Kathy, the oldest daughter, spoke to us after a program we presented at her college. Through slowed and halting speech, Kathy told us she was having trouble with her schoolwork and was under the care of a physician who had prescribed antidepressants. She sensed that somehow her problems were related to her father's alcoholism. After some encouragement, Kathy brought her mother to our next information session. The mother confirmed her husband's alcohol problem and added that he also took sleeping pills and tranquilizers. Prescribed by the same doctor who was treating the daughter, this mixture was supposed "to help him deal with his job stress and cut down on his drinking." Further discussion uncovered that Mom was using large amounts of tranquilizers daily prescribed by—you guessed it—the same doctor "to help her cope during this trying time." And Debbie, another daughter, was taking medication for her hyperactivity, also dispensed by the family doctor. To round out the chemical scene, their teenage son, we learned, was a heavy marijuana smoker. So here was an entire family under the influence of some kind of mood-altering chemical. And all this drug use, except the son's, was courtesy of the well-intended family physician.

After much counseling, a successful intervention on Dad's alcoholism led to treatment. During Family Week at the treatment center, the chemical use by the rest of the family was revealed. After outpatient treatment for all of them and a considerable period of aftercare, the entire family was chemical-free. A sober Dad, equipped with a clear head and putting in a full day's work, found that most of his "job stress" had been generated by alcoholism. Mom accepted her powerlessness over tranquilizers just as her husband had alcohol. She learned how to deal with her feelings openly and honestly, to assert her needs before she became angry and frustrated, and to feel good about herself. She joined a self-help group with a program for living that led to new, positive, and supportive friends. Down the drain went her remaining tranquilizers. Kathy, whose courage in reaching out for help no doubt saved the family, was taken off medication by the knowledgeable physician at the treatment center who suspected that her depression was not primary, but the result of living in an alcoholic family.

Frequently the depression seen in chemically dependent family members is simply anger turned inward because it's not safe to express it openly. In this case, after Kathy was able to process her anger in the safety of family treatment, her depression and the need for medication disappeared. Likewise, Debbie's hyperactivity quickly faded once peace returned to the family. And so too her need for medication. Junior's marijuana abuse was confronted in family treatment and, after learning that his grandfather and great grandfather had both been alcoholic, he wisely chose to abstain.

Unsnarling drug-controlled families like this isn't easy. A family, presenting a complex array of problems such as depression, job stress, marriage conflicts, hyperactivity, and teenage rebellion, usually requires specialists to diagnose this underlying primary disease.

Lesson: If you suspect alcohol or drugs are a problem in a family member, find out whether your doctor has special training in C.D. If not, get the name of one who does from a local treatment center.

Case Study—"Super Drunk"

Like most C.D. people, Walter's disease began to disrupt all areas of his life—professional, family, health, spiritual, and financial. And like many other C.D. victims, he tried to fix each of these in turn with counseling, enlightenment, self-improvement programs, and greater effort. In his own words, "First my wife and I went to marriage counseling because she thought that one of the reasons for my drinking and pot-smoking was communication problems. In counseling I learned to express my needs more honestly, give feedback, listen actively, and empathize with Shirley's feelings.

At the counselor's suggestion, Shirley attended assertiveness training and I went to a stress management course. After that, whenever Shirley would very assertively confront my drinking, I would listen attentively with glass in hand, accurately feed back what she had said, empathize with her concern, and acknowledge that she deserved a sober mate. Then, I'd take another drink to calm my nerves. Later, I got into yoga, and if things got too hot and heavy, I'd ask for some space and go meditate." Walter went to night school for two different work-related graduate degrees. And, as part of this "higher" education, mastered the use of uppers and downers to orchestrate his study habits. He also got into cocaine as a "recreational drug" by way of a relationship with a female fellow student who "understood him" better than his wife. She understood him well enough to bring on a divorce, which left him so broke that she quickly stopped understanding him. All this time he was on a fast track at the company after a series of rapid and important promotions. Then came the crash. Walter made the papers with a D.W.I. So, when Walter began to make mistakes at work, the company was already primed to intervene and insist he accept help.

Underneath all his apparent success, Walter's drinking and drugging had created three very dysfunctional families; he was beginning to show signs of liver disease; and, while under the influence of drugs, he had made some very questionable business deals. All of this, plus fear of losing his job, made Walter despondent. As he said, "The headline was about to read 'Young Businessman's Success Story Ends in Shocking Suicide.'"

Walter's story is not uncommon. Many C.D. people cover up their disease with overachievement on and off the job. Walter tried to overcome his loss of control over alcohol by demonstrating that he was too smart and capable to get hooked on alcohol and drugs. He tried to conquer the unacceptable conduct, emotional pain, and defensive behavior by proving over and over that he was sane, intelligent, successful, and physically fit. This piecemeal approach to conquering C.D. is like attending to pest control when the house is on fire.

Lesson: Just as C.D. is the primary disease and must be treated first, so too it is the primary life problem and must be dealt with before attempting to overcome whatever other problems it may have caused.

Far Too Many

Helping professionals can be constrained by the threat of stigmatizing their patients, limited by poor training, and confused by the myths that still surround C.D. These deficiencies can affect the way they interact with chemically dependent people and their families. And many of these professionals may themselves be suffering from co-dependency. Whatever the reason, their ineptness can actually worsen the condition. These are not isolated cases. This "harmful help" is still evident in many communities. Even in today's more enlightened times, many practicing physicians, psychiatrists, psychologists, clergy, and social workers have received little current education in the intervention and treatment of C.D. There are notable exceptions, but it is true that most of the schools they attended devoted only a few hours of curriculum to what many feel is the nation's number one health problem. University schools of psychology and social work are still teaching future therapists that alcoholism and other chemical dependencies are symptoms of underlying psychological or emotional disorders. And at the many workshops we've conducted for the clergy of numerous denominations, priests and ministers report little or no training in what, after a few years in a position, they consider to be the major problem in their congregations.

Shining Examples

On the other hand, we fondly remember a clergyman very dear to us who encountered a family he couldn't help because he knew so little about alcoholism. Recognizing this need in his ministry, he went back to school for a year to study C.D. We also know a young psychiatrist who admitted his ignorance about chemical problems and, with an open mind, set about becoming a nationally respected medical expert on chemical dependency.

We are aware of many respected professionals who give of their time and talents to those unable to pay. There are such quiet heroes in the professional ranks. We've also encountered physicians who gave up time from their practices to present their medical opinions in family intervention sessions. Their presence had a powerful impact on the outcome. Finally, we especially applaud those courageous physicians, clergy, and other helping professionals who have publicly announced their own recovery from chemical dependency. In some cases these disclosures jeopardized their positions but seemed worth the price in order to help end the suffering of others.

C.D. Is a Speciality

There are many such horror stories in our experience, but perhaps this is enough evidence to make the point: proceed with hope but be careful. Clearly the intervention and treatment of chemical dependency and co-dependency requires special education, training, and skills as well as a high level of personal growth on the part of the professionals involved. It is, therefore, important to seek out healthy, properly trained, and effective help resources. As with any other disease, look for the highly regarded specialist with a record of success. Qualified physicians can be identified by their certification from the American Society of Addiction Medicine.

Addictionology is now an identified medical speciality with 3,500 members nationally. Check with your county medical society for the names of local physicians who have this special training and background. The National Association of Alcoholism and Drug Abuse Counselors has 15,000 members. This organization has set rigid and high standards for certification in this challenging health specialty. Thus, there is a high-quality, affordable, effective care available for the intervention and treatment of chemical dependency and co-dependency. These professional resources are set firmly atop a national network of specialty help programs such as A.A., Al-anon, Alateen, Adult Children of Alcoholics, Narcotics Anonymous, Tough Love Parents, Cocaine Anonymous, and many others.

Follow the proven paths. Join an appropriate support group. This network of new friends and acquaintances can help in recommending and checking out potential therapists, intervention counselors, and treatment programs. And remember, the resources you choose should work for you. Tell them the truth and cooperate with them. But if things don't change, move on—examine other options. Find a person or program that works.

Part Two

Taking Action

4

Six Critical Actions

What Does It Take?

There are direct, dollar-wise paths to reversing the course of C.D. and its family impact. Quality, affordable help is out there for the asking. Still, the situation can seem overwhelming—a bit like opening your child's new bicycle box on Christmas Eve, seeing all those loose parts and complicated directions, and realizing the project should have been started a long time ago. Yet carefully following the tested directions can produce a gift that brings years of joy. That's also what it takes for family recovery. Following tested directions works. Just face each piece of the task one at a time and heed proven guidelines; the end product will be the gift of lifetime wellness for you and your loved ones.

The way is now quite clearly defined by those who have gone before you. Helpful choices and positive actions—based on accurate information, professional guidance, and clearly defined goals—can reverse the damage that has been done and lead to full recovery.

There Is a High Road

The ideal scenario is timely intervention followed by quality treatment leading to lifetime recovery. Not just for the C.D. person but for all those impacted by the disease. Such a level of restoration may seem an abstract idea or an imagined wonderland. Yet if you take the right actions, you will eventually cross the magic line beyond which you are no longer a suffering person seeking wellness but a well person growing toward your highest potential. You'll wake up one day and recognize that your personal world has become a far more open, honest, congruent place. A more positive environment, where healthy loved ones relate as equals and from which the unhealthy have been denied citizenship. An atmosphere in which honest feelings are now respected and individuality is possible. As distant and elusive as all that may sound, such a level of wellness is entirely possible within the present state of the intervention and treatment art. Getting there is a matter of wanting it bad enough to do what it takes. Recovery requires willingness, risk, effort, and, most of all, new and better choices leading to critical actions.

Recovery Planning

Like any complex human endeavor, recovery from this family illness will demand time, money, energy, and motivation. So it is wise to plan carefully. With a bit of forethought you'll get there faster, spend less money, and achieve higher levels of wellness for you and your family. Recovery is simply undoing what C.D. did. It is a move-by-move strategy to deal one by one with the components of the disease. This takes a willingness to be open to new ideas and normally requires the help of trained professionals.

In this chapter, the focus will be on the Six Critical Actions we usually observe in those who have successfully reversed the damage done to them and their families by alcohol or other drugs. These choices are a logical sequence to recovery, attacking the disease in much the same sequence as it unfolded.

Six Critical Actions

The following is a checklist of the sequential components of recovery:

1. Seek accurate, current information.

2. Arrange a professional assessment.

3. Join a support group.

4. Learn intervention skills.

5. Pursue the goal of family-based treatment.

6. Follow through after treatment.

The following is a description of each Critical Action and suggestions on how to carry it out. These actions can be postponed or dragged out for years, or they can all be commenced in the course of a single day. But sooner or later most people find them critical to the pursuit of quality recovery.

1. Seek Accurate, Current Information

A nonthreatening and easy-to-take first move is to seek out books, articles, films, and community education programs that provide up-to-date information about how alcohol and other drugs affect individuals and families. The first stop on the road to recovery ought to be the library or book store. Book therapy can be invaluable because it is helpful, inexpensive, and nonthreatening. And books only charge for the first visit.

There is a short list of recommended reading in the back of this book. Our clients have consistently found these titles helpful. All of the authors listed have achieved national recognition for breakthroughs in understanding and treating chemical dependency and co-dependency.

As you examine potential reading material, keep in mind that these diseases primarily reside at the feeling level. Be suspect of heady intellectual books. Leave these scholarly works with the psycho-babble titles to the expert in search of greater expertise. In-depth information can come later. For now, intervention and initial recovery requires but few facts and much action. The hurt cannot be understood or intellectualized away. It must be owned, experienced, and converted to positive energies. These are not diseases that require a lot of clinical language to explain. The word *power-lessness* has more clarity than *compulsivity*, and *unloved* is easier to understand than *emotional deprivation*. Certainly, the specificity of clinical verbiage has a place in the training of professionals, but in early recovery it's best to keep it simple. The goal is not to get smarter but to feel better and live life more fully.

Community Information Programs

Reading will probably increase your desire to know more about how alcohol and drugs affect families. Workshops, seminars, and other community information programs have advantages over simply reading about these problems. Such gatherings remove some of the sense of isolation, allow you to ask questions, and assist in identifying help resources.

Hospitals and other treatment facilities recognize the community relations value derived from sponsoring free community information lectures or seminars about alcohol, drugs, and family intervention. Consequently, professionally conducted introductory presentations are likely to be available at little or no cost. Call the local Council on Alcoholism for the schedule. The council, which is listed in the Yellow Pages under "Alcoholism Information" (the term "drug abuse" may also be in the title), is a United Way agency found in nearly every major community. If receiving mail from the council will not cause problems for you, it's a helpful idea to get your name on the mailing list for its very informative newsletters.

Do They Know What They're Talking About?

Once the various information programs available in your town are identified, there are ways to check out their quality. Call the sponsoring agency and ask: Who presents the program? What is it about? How long has the program been offered? How large is the usual attendance? Is it open to the general public? There are no right or wrong answers to these questions. Any program presented by a reputable treatment organization will likely be helpful. What is important, however, is how your questions are answered. If the community information program is professionally done, well organized, and successful in attracting large and diverse audiences, it will be a source of pride to the organization. Listen for professionalism as your questions are answered. Be wary if the call is passed to several persons or no one seems to know about the program. Or if responsibility for the program is rotated through several staff members or the schedule of presentation dates and times is not readily available. All these are signs that the program doesn't have much priority in the organization and is probably not of high quality.

2. Arrange a Professional Assessment

Once you have a clearer understanding of what is happening, it is time to meet with a professional alcohol and drug abuse counselor to discuss your situation and sort things out. He or she can help develop an overall intervention and treatment plan for your family. But finding the right person for the job is not easy. Here are some precepts to keep in mind when selecting a counselor or other helping professional:

- Alcohol and drug abuse counselors, psychologists, and other professional helpers are fundamentally service providers—they work for you. They should honor their appointment times, answer your questions satisfactorily, empathize with your feelings, and provide real help for your problems. On the other hand, counselors have a right to respect, to full and truthful information, to cooperation with recommended treatment, to on-time arrivals for appointments, and to timely payment for services rendered.

- It's O.K. to fire incompetent help. If the professional person to whom you have turned for assistance doesn't respond to your needs—terminate. But keep in mind that, although your feelings deserve empathy and questions should be answered satisfactorily, you may not always like the professional who is trying to help you. Often the counselor may have to get tough, be confrontive, suggest scary risks, or even terminate the therapy in your own best interests. But through all of that, you as a client should feel important, respected, and—most of all—that you're being helped. If nothing is changing, you have a perfect right to seek out someone else.

- Check out the professional with the community. Helping professionals quickly get a reputation—good or bad. Ask around at self-help meetings. Talk to friends you trust. Ask other professionals. Nurses are a valuable source of information about physicians. Clergy can often recommend ethical therapists. The local Council on Alcoholism can suggest alcohol and drug abuse counselors, intervention consultants, and treatment programs. A bit of effort will find competent people with the right skills and solid professional reputations.

3. Join a Support Group

Getting involved in Al-anon, Alateen, Adult Children of Alcoholics, Tough Love Parents, or a similar group is vital. You just can't do all this alone. If you could, you would have done so a long time ago. Now that you are making these better choices, you'll need a positive program for living in this negative situation and a source of emotional support for taking the remaining actions.

Self-help programs, especially those based on the famous Twelve Steps of A.A., can be of most value if viewed as one part of the total framework of recovery. First of all, self-help programs, as important as they are to recovery, do not fully meet the needs of everyone. A.A., for example, has met relatively little success among minorities, especially black communities. Neither A.A. nor its sister programs Al-anon and Alateen for family members fully address all the issues now identified as critical to family recovery. For example, many female children from C.D. families have experienced sexual abuse. Self-help programs are not structured to offer the safe, professionally facilitated, therapeutic environment in which such powerful trauma can be healed. Thus, getting into a support group is crucial to recovery, but it is not the total answer.

4. Learn Intervention Skills

Often just taking the three Critical Actions described above will cause the C.D. person to accept help. When the disease is better understood, professional guidance is obtained, and the enabling stops, the C.D. person suddenly finds that his previous behavior is no longer being tolerated while help options are being presented in a more acceptable format. This combination of circumstances may serve to intervene.

But if the C.D. person is still in denial, you may want to learn more powerful ways to intervene. Your counselor can teach you how to use crisis as a focal point for intervention attempts. He or she can also refine your communications skills for use during the one-on-one intervention attempts that arise so often when living or working with an active C.D. person.

The counselor may advise a series of meetings at which the significant people in the C.D. person's life receive the general education, specific training, individual coaching, and co-dependency counseling necessary to prepare for a formal intervention attempt. These sessions may culminate in a gathering at which examples of the C.D. person's unacceptable alcohol- or other drug-related behavior are presented. The meeting is conducted in a nonjudgmental fashion and in an atmosphere of concern. The C.D. person is also told of the emotional impact his drinking and/or drugging has had on those who care. Help is then offered that he can accept with dignity.

An intervention planning meeting between yourself, a trained intervention counselor, and perhaps one or two of the other persons concerned about the C.D.'s problem can be very beneficial. With their input you can intelligently explore the potential for a formal intervention attempt upon the C.D. person. If such an effort seems appropriate, the counselor will help put together a detailed intervention plan. (See Chapter 8 for more details about intervention.)

5. Pursue the Goal of Family-Based Treatment

By now the actions taken should produce the courage and motivation to begin the search for treatment. Phone calls, visits, and other inquiries are necessary in order to find the right resource for your family's situation.

What Is Treatment?

The treatment of alcoholism and other drug dependencies today is the culmination of several decades of experiment, trial and error, and feedback from those treated. Programs today combine the best of psychotherapy, the twelve-step self-help programs, medicine, nutrition, and fitness plus an eclectic milieu of peripheral approaches such as relaxation training, assertiveness skills, occupational therapy, and so forth.

Treatment centers are like any other service. To be successful they must develop and maintain a core of satisfied "customers" speaking well of them in the community. In this case the satisfied "customers" are in the form of sober, happy, productive recovered alcoholics and other types of C.D. people. Treatment today is a big, highly competitive business. Thus, to keep and expand market share, these programs must work well now and keep getting better.

How Good Are Treatment Programs?

A reasonable and conservative estimate of the C.D. persons who enter a respected treatment program and achieve and maintain lifetime sobriety would be in the range of 50 percent to 60 percent. Keep in mind, however, that many others who relapse quickly recover and then stay sober for life. Hardly anybody ever undergoes treatment and reverts right back to his or her old ways. "If nothing else, it ruins their drinking" is often quipped.

When the family of a relapsing C.D. person has undergone treatment, learned to stop enabling, and is pursuing their own recovery, the C.D. person quickly realizes that no one will tolerate unacceptable behavior any longer.

There is no central source of data on the pros and cons or the successes and failures of various treatment approaches. Limited availability of official report cards notwithstanding, there are widely held beliefs about which treatment methods and practices work and which do not. In the absence of hard data, economics is often a useful way to wring out the truth of things. So, in seeking to define effective treatment, it is useful to look at the kind of treatment for which business and industry is willing to pay. Most companies of any size have come to realize that untreated C.D. is a major cause of attendance, performance, and behavior problems on the job. There are estimates as high as a hundred billion dollars a year in lost workplace productivity. Consequently, just about every large business and many small ones have established employee assistance programs through which to intervene and help C.D. employees. Such EAPs, as these help programs are called, continuously check out the treatment centers to which they refer C.D. employees and follow up on the results achieved. In this way companies review the way their health care monies are spent in an effort to control cost. So when deciding on a treatment program it may be a good idea to follow the lead of the employee assistance professionals.

Treatment Selection Guidelines

The following criteria, used by employee assistance program managers to identify quality treatment, may be of value in your quest:

- *Select the lowest-cost care commensurate with the needs of the client.* C.D. is the only illness in which it is customary to focus the best resources and highest cost care on those with the earliest stages of the disease. Conversely, as a victim experiences serious relapses and enters the later terminal stages, ever-cheaper, lower-quality, and less effective treatment is employed. Then when they get chronically devastated, it is customary to abandon them to die in the streets or under a bridge somewhere. In other words, the quality and duration of treatment is often determined by the insurance benefits available and not the clinical needs of the patient. This is like putting someone with high blood pressure and dangerous cholesterol levels in the intensive coronary care unit, then later—when he has a heart attack—sending him to a neighborhood clinic, and finally—when heart failure takes place—letting him die in the streets or perhaps in a jail cell.

Recommendation: If the C.D. person still has a primary career, a job, a family, and reasonable physical health, it is sensible to look into the relatively inexpensive and very effective outpatient programs now being offered. Or, if the professionals with whom you are working believe that inpatient care is advisable, ask them to consider a combination of inpatient/outpatient. However, in opting for these more economical programs, be sure the family component offered is intensive enough to meet the needs of the entire family.

- *Match treatment to socioeconomic status and special needs.* Years ago it was a common practice to treat C.D. people of all backgrounds and ages in the same programs, the idea being that they shared a common problem that responded to a universal solution. Experience has shown this to be an unwise approach. Adolescents, street-drug users, women, single women with young children, older citizens, gay persons, minorities, and certain professions such as clergy, physicians, and many other definable groups respond better to treatment programs built to meet their special needs.

Recommendation: Attend open A.A., Al-anon, or other support group meetings such as ACOA gatherings. Talk to people to whom you feel the C.D. person would relate and ask them for suggestions about treatment facilities. Then call, write, or visit these facilities and talk to a staff member. See enough and hear enough to decide whether the facility feels right for your family. Remember, like EAP managers, you're paying for services and have every right to shop.

- *Use only those programs with well-developed and proven family-oriented inpatient or outpatient treatment for those family and other concerned persons identified by the treatment staff as co-dependent.* These programs combine education with individual and group therapies. Heavy emphasis is placed on group therapy in which painful feelings can be processed. Some of the therapy may involve the C.D. person.

Recommendation: Arrange to speak to the director of the family treatment component. Describe your situation and feelings and ask what the program will do for you and other family members. See if the answer is responsive to your needs. You may not hear what you want to hear but what you need to hear. Listen less to your head than to your heart.

- *Be certain that the program includes a professionally directed, therapeutic aftercare component.* EAP managers place strong emphasis on the contribution to long-term recovery that results from professionally conducted aftercare.

Recommendation: Select a treatment program that insists on specific aftercare commitments from its graduating patients and aids them in connecting with the community-based resources needed to sustain recovery.

Measuring Success

On the surface it would seem that the proper measuring stick to rate various treatment centers would be to compare track records. The problem is that there are so many tracks. Furthermore, since most treatment outcome studies are prepared by the treatment facilities themselves, the numbers are difficult to validate. Nor is there even agreed-upon criteria for determining treatment success. Is it continued abstinence two years after treatment? Maybe. One ex-patient may have a relapse six months after treatment, which leads to real acceptance of his disease, and then may pursue sobriety and personal growth with great progress. Another may refuse to follow his aftercare commitments, fail to attend A.A., and generally be miserable to be around—but somehow manage not to drink. Which of the two should be counted as a success? Seemingly, abstinence alone is probably an inadequate indicator of the quality of recovery. Or a treatment program may boast of a high "still-sober-after-two-years" rate but have such a weak family program that the only one who is really getting well is the C.D. person. Surely that is not a quality program.

Another flaw in comparing recovery rates between treatment programs is that some may only count the patients who *completed* their program. The dropouts literally drop out of the statistics. Such a program may boast an 80 percent recovery rate without stating that perhaps half of its patients never complete the full treatment regimen.

To further complicate the situation, a truly excellent facility may sometimes therapeutically discharge uncooperative patients because their presence is contaminating the treatment of others. But if this facility measures its success rate against the number of patients who initially enter the program, it may compare poorly with a facility that only counted "graduates." Yet this facility may well have a program of greater integrity and be of more value to the patients who actually complete its program.

Trust Your Gut and the Wisdom of the Marketplace

Valid treatment outcome studies require expertise in double-blind studies and multivariate statistical analysis. Such skills are not readily available in C.D. treatment centers. Only recently, in the face of the managed care challenge, have sophisticated studies been launched. Early results show that treatment is effective and offers long term economic benefits to the nation. But the data needed to make a head to head comparison between individual treatment programs is not yet available.

So—is there no trustful data with which to compare treatment programs? We think not. Our suggestion is to pay attention to your intuitive reactions and also trust the wisdom of the marketplace. Staff personnel in quality treatment centers model wellness. They should be easy to talk with, have the right answers, make you feel comfortable, and give you a sense of hope. Until we start seeing consumer reports on C.D. treatment, a reliable alternative is to ask the people who should know: previous customers. When comparing cars or stereos, it's wise to consult an owner of the vehicle or unit you're considering. "Trust the man who owns one," a popular ad used to say. This timeworn advice is valid during these fluid times in the evolution of the C.D. treatment business. Success in the marketplace is a good indicator that the service provided is of high quality.

Why Treatment Instead of Just a Twelve-Step Program?

"We have borrowed the best from medicine, psychiatry, and religion." So said Bill Wilson, the very intelligent stockbroker who co-founded A.A. And he would be the first to agree that what they borrowed was the best of those fields as of the 1930s, when the book on which A.A. is based was written. Yet much has been learned about alcoholism since then. Fifty years of more enlightened examination of this national problem and tens of millions of dollars of research have brought us a long way. More is now known about the emotional damage, the family impact, and the physiology of alcoholism.

We live in a poly-drug society today within which major value shifts have occurred since the 1930s. Much of this new knowledge and cultural change confirms the miracle of A.A. and Al-anon. At the same time, a lot of it presents new and different opportunities for earlier intervention and more rapid and higher-quality recovery.

Combining the Best

The A.A. book *Twelve Steps and Twelve Traditions* outlines the principles upon which the Alcoholics Anonymous program has evolved. Al-anon, Narcotics Anonymous, Overeaters Anonymous, and others have all adopted these same principles in practice. if not officially. The forward to the "Twelve and Twelve"—as the book is affectionately called—states, "A.A.'s Twelve Steps are a group of principles...which enable the sufferer to become happy and whole." The key word here is *enable*—defined as "to provide the means to make possible."

The early members of A.A., many of whom are still living, never intended membership in A.A. to be the total means of an alcoholic's recovery efforts. In fact, some of them were instrumental in the development of formal treatment programs for the disease. They recognized that A.A. could provide the spiritual spark needed to light the lamp of recovery; that the Twelve Steps could show the way and thus enable. But for the sufferer to become "happily and usefully whole" he must call upon the "best that medicine, psychiatry, and religion" can offer. Thus today the Twelve Steps, first developed in Alcoholics Anonymous, are the cornerstone of quality recovery from pathological dependencies and still rightfully revered as the fundamental pathway.

The self-help programs spawned from A.A. are often the first place suffering people turn for help. Nonetheless, it is an observable fact that formal treatment can accelerate and improve the quality of recovery. The visible proof of the merits of combining treatment with the twelve-step programs can be seen and heard at twelve-step group meetings. It becomes quickly obvious who has been through treatment and who has not. Most treatment "graduates" demonstrate a clearer understanding of the biogenetic nature of their disease, wrestle less with vestiges of denial, and seem more comfortable with the idea of abstinence. Those who have undergone formal treatment are quite often more in touch with their feelings and in particular have learned how to deal with anger and fear in positive ways.

Probably the most distinguishing mark of those who have experienced treatment is their clearer grasp of the family aspects of the illness. On the other hand, those who undergo treatment but do not continue in a twelve-step program appear to be missing a valuable component in their lives. It is not that they can't stay sober and drug-free without A.A., because they often do. But they seem to lack the spiritual vitality, sense of purpose, and serenity that grows out of a life based on the principles embodied in the Twelve Steps. Our acquaintance with thousands of recovered persons has convinced us that the formula for accelerated recovery and optimum wellness is this: first-class family-based treatment, including a solid aftercare component, followed by "one day at a time" living built upon the long-respected Twelve Steps of Alcoholics Anonymous.

But Whatever Happens

If attempts to intervene fail or are impossible because of broken relationships, death, dollars, or distance and if treatment for the whole family is not possible, we encourage as many as possible of those impacted to seek co-dependency treatment for themselves. They need it, deserve it, and will pay a lifetime price in emotional pain without it.

6. Follow Through After Treatment

Some experts say that 20 percent of recovery takes place in treatment and most of the rest during the first two years afterwards, providing certain aftercare steps are taken. Of all the critical actions, following through with continued recovery efforts after treatment is perhaps the most crucial to long-term success.

Aftercare is usually structured through a formal commitment by the C.D. person and family to attend professionally facilitated weekly therapy meetings in which ex-patients and their families continue to work on chemical dependency and co-dependency issues. Aftercare combined with programs such as A.A., Al-anon, and Alateen is what assures sustained recovery.

Aftercare provides the environment in which to continue processing the emotional pain of the disease. It reinforces the new beginnings in damaged relationships and helps refine valuable skills for living, such as stress management, relaxation techniques, exercise programs, nutrition, communication skills, self-esteem building, and assertiveness.

Aftercare motivates C.D. patients through the difficult early stages of establishing their twelve-step program. It is not uncommon to hear untreated A.A. members still wrestling with these issues years after quitting drinking. Similarly, recovering co-dependent people, without the benefit of aftercare, may continue suffering for years and become disillusioned because they expected the C.D. person's sobriety alone to fix all their problems. The record is clear. Those who remain faithful to their aftercare contract seldom relapse. Those who don't, often do.

Are There Exceptions?

You may feel that all Six Critical Actions are not appropriate to your situation. Maybe, but consider carefully before eliminating. Intervention, in particular, may no longer be possible. Perhaps you and the C.D. person have divorced or are now too geographically or emotionally separated for intervention to be an option. The C.D. person may be imprisoned or even dead. The other members of the family may be too dysfunctional from their own experiences in a C.D. family to be of help in your quest for recovery. We hasten to add, however, that just about all co-dependent people feel that such is the case. Oftentimes it is simply a matter of "intervening on the interveners."

Whatever your situation, it is strongly suggested that you find a source of current information, get a professional assessment, join a self-help group, and at least seriously investigate professional help. Without help it is likely that your co-dependent past will haunt your relationships and efforts at personal growth all your life. But once the steps appropriate to your circumstances are identified, there are no shortcuts. The actions we've described are the decisions and actions that have led countless others to full recovery.

Only the Beginning

The Six Critical Actions only create a climate of opportunity in which those afflicted can again reach toward their own highest potential. Full recovery demands a full lifetime commitment and a whole-person approach. Chemical dependency and co-dependency are complex pathologies that impact the entire person: body, mind, emotions, and spirit. To fully recover from its ravaging years or even decades, victims must reestablish stewardship over their bodies, profoundly revise their thinking and thought processes, achieve higher levels of emotional maturity, and find sources of strength, hope, and purpose for their lives. This demands a lifetime of personal effort and program involvement aimed at continued spiritual development, the restoration of relationships, intellectual renewal, and self-esteem building.

Practical growth steps such as smoking cessation, weight control, physical fitness, marriage counseling, and financial planning are the hallmarks of those on a true recovery path. And experience has shown that the manifold components of recovery cannot be accomplished in isolation from each other. Praying the knees out of one's pants while perched complacently on one's posterior will not do the job. Neither will frantic efforts at therapy, self-help programs, and reading all the latest books and studies without developing a spiritual dimension to one's life. There is little true health in a "recovery" characterized by smoking, poor nutrition, toxic relationships, chronic stress, depression, and lack of purpose. If the whole person is not healed, the pain is just being shifted around.

Practical Steps With a Transcendent Payoff

The end result of accomplishing these actions transcends the sum of the individual steps involved. Those who have put real energy into these efforts report a weller-than-wellness. As is the case in many natural disasters, the rebuilding process frequently produces results far more beautiful and satisfying than the original. You will hear recovered C.D. and co-dependent people make statements such as, "I'm almost glad my family got sick so we could get to where we are now." Such an utterance is hard to believe when you are at the painful front end of the process. Still, many recovering persons feel certain that their illness has offered personal growth opportunities not available to their more "fortunate" peers.

At the Very Least

Whatever else you may decide to do, take the first two suggested critical actions: Get current information and get a professional assessment of your situation. This will, at the very least, get you pointed in the direction of further help. By the time you read this book, breakthrough knowledge may be available, more effective intervention concepts discovered, and new innovative treatment models developed. For these reasons we've tried to avoid absolute statements and dogmatic pronouncements about chemical dependency and co-dependency. There has been more learned about these maladies in the last ten years than the last ten thousand. No doubt that trend will continue. There do, however, appear to be two absolutes. Abstinence and twelve-step living will be the foundation of sustained recovery for the C.D. person. And in some cases co-dependency symptoms are too deeply imprinted to be remedied by self-help alone; there is a need for professional therapy or formal treatment. These two axioms should not be tampered with lightly. But beyond those bedrock concepts, the horizons of recovery will surely expand as knowledge grows. So, simply stated, once you find your way to competent help, trust the help you get.

5

Intervention Works

"Bottoming Out"

For years it was widely accepted that C.D. persons had to "hit bottom" before they would be receptive to help. The tragedy of this notion was that people were condemned to lose everything before they could hope to recover. In the early 1960s, Vernon Johnson, an Episcopal priest who was himself recovering from alcoholism, joined with a group of enlightened and influential Minnesotans to research ways of accelerating the C.D. person's entry into treatment. Their efforts showed that "bottoming out" was a subjective perception and not an objective condition. They found that a C.D. person hit bottom and agreed to accept help when it became clear that the consequences of drinking or drugging had become too painful to bear. It wasn't that conditions were not bad enough to warrant treatment but rather that the C.D. person was too deluded to accurately appraise his own plight.

Besides dispelling the bottoming-out myth, the Minnesota group's studies of voluntary entry versus court-directed treatment of C.D. persons also produced surprising results. They found that recovery rates were about the same whether patients entered treatment voluntarily or were coerced into it. Consequently, treatment with even a minimum of willingness brought excellent chances of recovery. Johnson recognized that it was the delusion of the C.D. persons combined with enabling behavior by concerned persons that was blinding them to the severity of their condition.

He and his associates developed techniques to stop this enabling and break through the delusion long enough for the C.D. person to accept help. This win/win, nonantagonistic, nonjudgmental approach has come to be known as the Johnson Institute model of intervention. Their pioneer work was summarized in Johnson's classic book, *I'll Quit Tomorrow*. This creative approach to getting C.D. people to accept help has evolved into a wide range of approaches and techniques.

Intervention is now used in many different forms to deal with C.D. cases, not only in individual families but in business and industry, the armed forces, professional sports leagues, and the medical, legal, and other professions. Yet all these methods embody three basic components: concern; the presentation to the C.D. of documented, specific, nonjudgmental data about his drinking and drugging behavior; and an offer of help options that can be accepted with dignity. Thousands of successful interventions, using variations of this model, have shattered the myth that C.D. persons must hit bottom and lose everything. There are now proven techniques that can dramatically accelerate the time at which a C.D. person will become willing to accept help. Those who claim otherwise—and you'll no doubt encounter some who will—are simply not aware of these historical facts. There is no longer any question—intervention works.

What Intervention Is

Intervention is a sustained process, not a single event. A process consisting of education, training, counseling, and attitude changes by which concerned people can help a C.D. person to see what most everyone else can already see: that alcohol and/or other drugs have begun to dominate and damage important areas of the victim's life.

The goal of intervention is to break through the wall of delusion surrounding the C.D. person long enough to get him or her to accept help. To repeat, intervention is a win-win, nonantagonistic effort done with an absence of judgment and packaged in concern. There is no labeling, generalizing, attacking, or moralizing. Sometimes, but not always, the intervention may be in the form of a confrontational meeting with the C.D. person. Often it is simply the natural consequences of raised awareness, attitude changes, and revised communication patterns on the part of those concerned.

What Intervention Is Not

Intervention is not a case of proving the C.D. person wrong and you right or getting him to admit to being an alcoholic or drug addict. Nor is intervention a conspiracy. From the very beginning of the process, communication within the C.D. family becomes more open and honest rather than less. Whenever possible, intervention is not based upon fear, coercion, or threat of consequences but derives its power primarily from love and concern. An intervention effort conducted by a properly trained and prepared individual or group has little danger of backfiring and making the situation worse.

Intervention, as some fear, is in no way a conspiritorial, desperate, last-ditch confrontation fraught with danger and marked by fear with an all-or-nothing aura. Rather, it is a well-planned, carefully executed, proven procedure with a very high probability of success.

Who Has the Right (and the power) to Intervene?

Folklore teaches us to "mind our own business." This is certainly a tempting position to take regarding someone else's drinking or drugging. Yet, when a pathology that surrounds itself with delusion is the "business" at hand, intervention becomes a lifesaving requirement. But who has the right to step into another person's life? Any one or combination of the following power bases qualifies someone to be an intervener.

1. Love and concern for the C.D. person.

2. The C.D. person's respect for you.

3. The possession of data concerning unacceptable drinking and/or drugging behavior.

4. Leverage or clout in the C.D. person's life.

Some potential interveners may offer all 4 strengths. Others a combination of several. A few may fit only one category. But anyone meeting any of these qualifications should be considered a potential intervener.

What Makes Intervention Work?

Most persons who have lived in a C.D. situation very long can honestly say, "I've tried to intervene every way I could. He just won't listen." What is different about what we are proposing? Our approaches are based on feedback from those upon who we have successfully intervened in the past. These now recovering C.D. victims consistently report the following about their mind set prior to the intervention. First, "I had no idea it was that bad." Second, "I had no idea I was hurting so many people so much." Third, "I really didn't believe anybody still cared." And finally, "I had no idea there was a way out with dignity." Any attempt to intervene needs to hook into these unspoken needs. The techniques recommended in this chapter are designed to tap into the energy that lies within that unrevealed pain and use it to fuel the recovery process.

Two Useful Metaphors

There are two ways to view intervention that seem to help potential participants grasp the conceptual foundation of this process. The first is the notion that intervention is a martial art. A martial art of interpersonal persuasion much like judo or karate are martial arts of personal combat. The martial arts master does not confront or try to overpower nor does he bear anger or malice toward his opponent. Rather, he uses the forces at work in the other person to his advantage. Likewise, the intervener uses the anger, fear, loneliness, and hopelessness experienced by the C.D. person as the force needed to initiate recovery. This is accomplished by structuring the intervention as a win-win, non-antagonistic, non-judgmental interaction that is packaged in love and concern yet touches the pain enough to gain acceptance of a dignified help option.

A second metaphor or conceptual framework that is helpful in understanding the dynamics of intervention is that it is a grief process. Most are familiar with the idea that those suffering a loss first experience shock, then anger, then attempt to bargain with their plight, and finally—if the process is allowed to play out, come to accept the loss. Human beings go through this cycle frequently, from discovering their favorite restaurant is out of the dish they anticipated, all the way to accepting the news that they have a terminal illness and are going to die. Intervention is an effort to move the C.D. person through shock and anger to accepting the loss of a great love of their life—chemical-induced euphoria. Those who have experienced an intervention describe how they first were shocked, then angered, attempted to bargain, and then finally accepted the help offered. Such feedback would support the notion that intervention works because it facilitates the grief process the C.D. person must go through in order to accept help.

The Fundamentals

The intervention process may culminate in the courtroom, the emergency room, the living room, the boss's office—anywhere that circumstances and events combine to break through the C.D. person's delusion. Interventions can be very brief. For example, Mother says to Son in emergency room after auto accident, "Alcohol did this. Will you accept treatment now?" Son, "Yes, Mom." End of intervention. Or it can involve years of effort by a family to get all the concerned others trained and prepared to conduct a formal intervention meeting with the C.D. person. Though interventions can take many forms, it is useful to divide them into three general categories:

1. *Crisis-based intervention.* The C.D. person is offered treatment under crisis circumstances while his denial is temporarily weakened as the result of an emergency situation: D.W.I. or other arrest, marriage breakup, job loss, auto accident, medical emergency, etc.

2. *The mini-intervention.* The boss, doctor, business associate, spouse, family member, or friend alone or in a small group confronts the C.D. person about his drinking and drugging and offers help

3. *Concerned group intervention.* This highly structured intervention attempt involves as many of the significant others in the C.D. person's life as can be recruited for the process.

Expect Contingencies

Because of the volatility of the disease and the number of variables involved, intervention attempts must include planning for contingencies. Contingencies are unexpected turns such as

1. Sudden crisis (D.W.I. or other arrests, job loss, injury, illness)

2. Changes of heart (either by the C D. person or those involved in the intervention)

3. Discovery by the C.D. person that an intervention effort is in progress. (As you will see, this is not a big problem and may even be desirable.)

4. Dramatic changes in the drinking or drugging pattern. (Someone thought to be just alcoholic is discovered to be using and dealing cocaine).

These kinds of contingencies do arise in the progress of intervention efforts. Consequently, those concerned persons involved will benefit from viewing their activities as a fluid and often rapidly changing process. You may start out with an eye toward employing one of the three approaches described above (crisis-based, mini-intervention, or concerned group). But as the scenario unfolds, the actual result may be a hybrid of all three concepts. For example, if a family begins preparing for a concerned group intervention and the C.D. person is suddenly hospitalized for a serious drinking-related accident, the effort immediately shifts in the direction of a crisis-based intervention. While experiencing the immediate shock of the accident, the C.D. person may agree to go to treatment but, after recovering from his injuries, renege on the commitment. Then several of the concerned group may jump in and employ mini- intervention skills, with their individual efforts saving the day.

Such a quick turn of events is quite common in the business of intervention. But whatever the turn of events, successful efforts in all three types are marked by the presence of concern, the absence of judgment, the presentation of specific data, the application of win-win communication techniques, and the offer of help options that can be accepted with dignity.

No Guarantees But Hopeful Probabilities

No intervention counselor can guarantee that the C.D. person will come to the intervention but there is almost always a way to get him there. There is no certainty that he will listen but most usually do. They might refuse help but in most cases they accept. Treatment might not work but it more often does. Relapse may occur but if so it will probably be short-lived and signal the last gasp of the disease before real recovery begins. Still it is natural, when you've lived in a negative environment so long, to expect the worst. Yet properly prepared intervention efforts work more often than not and nearly always improve the situation even when the hoped-for outcome is delayed. In our entire professional careers we have never had a client wish they hadn't attempted to intervene.

What About Violence?

Often those contemplating an intervention attempt are worried about the possibility of a violent or suicidal reaction by the C.D. person. If there is a history or threat of violence or suicidal intentions, <u>DO NOT ATTEMPT TO INTERVENE WITHOUT COMPETENT PROFESSIONAL HELP</u>. There is no national source of data about intervention attempts. So there may well have been incidents of violence and suicide. But in the broad range of interventions we have conducted and in the several hundred we have discussed with other intervention specialists, there have been no reports of either violence or postintervention suicide attempts. When interveners are coached and prepared properly, these efforts are characterized by love, concern, dignity, respect, and hopeful help options. Such is not the stuff of which violence is born. If, however, there is a history of violence, the propriety of attempting an intervention must be seriously examined. The first priority should be your own safety and recovery. Courageous counselors may be willing to attempt an intervention with such a person. However, they know how to take special precautions, such as being sure the C.D. person is not armed, positioning him between two people strong enough to physically restrain him if necessary, seating him in a low, soft, deep chair from which it is difficult to rise, and providing easy escape routes from the room for those likely to be a target of a violent response. We had to take such measures in the case of the man described earlier who had threatened to chop off his son's head on the butcher block. We would never have involved this young man without assuring his safety. That family, incidentally, underwent treatment, and father and son have begun to work out a trusting relationship.

It's also a wise procedure to seek advice from an attorney about restraining orders or commitment actions. Arrangements should also be made for safe places for the family to relocate if necessary. This all must sound scary, so let us restate: violent reactions seldom, if ever, occur. But certainly anxiety about such responses should be raised and discussed with your intervention counselor. He or she can put your fears at rest with clear and practical guidance. If there is a history of suicide threats or attempts, certainly caution is needed to be certain any intervention effort is structured to be as loving, supportive, and hopeful as possible People don't usually respond to an outpouring of love and concerned hope with self-destructive behavior. On the other hand, doing nothing and enabling them to continue to drink and drug certainly encourages a suicidal course. We have also never encountered violence during the course of an actual intervention. In one instance a young man verbally threatened us. Fortunately for us he was sitting between his uncle and his godfather, both of whom had been All-Pro linemen in the NFL. He was a rare and foolishly brave exception.

The following chapters describe each of the three general types of interventions, with real-life examples from our case files and suggestions on how to optimize—and if necessary, combine—these approaches.

6

The Crisis-Based
Intervention

Crises Are Also Opportunities

The lives of most C.D. persons eventually become one of crisis management. As the disease progresses and the C.D. person's behavior is more and more influenced by alcohol or other drugs, serious predicaments and ultimately severe crises usually unfold.

These incidents or circumstances can be fertile ground for intervention attempts. Most often these crisis-connected events are the consequences of actions while under the influence. But there is such a thing as a passive crisis as well—critical situations caused by what the C.D. person did *not* do: failing to get a promotion, not caring for his health, not paying the bills, or not meeting critical responsibilities as a spouse, parent, or citizen. In any case, crisis-based intervention is not a matter of "creating a crisis." C.D. people are quite capable of accomplishing that without assistance. Crisis-based intervention is an attempt to reinforce the adverse consequences of the crisis at a critical time and in an effective way. The object—as with all intervention efforts—is to break through the delusion long enough to get the C.D. person to accept help.

Case History—"Sharon the Terrible"

Sharon's parents came to us because their twenty-year-old daughter was in all kinds of trouble. She had written bad checks, received several D.W.I.'s, dropped out of college because of bad grades, and was running with a wild crowd. They had recently found drug paraphernalia in her room. Their one-on-one efforts to intervene were to no avail. Sharon denied she had a problem with alcohol and drugs and blamed her life problems on the poor example of her parents. They felt guilty, ashamed, and, most of all, powerless. The parents and others concerned about Sharon trained and prepared for a more structured and formal concerned group intervention. Early in the training, however, we suggested that if any crisis should suddenly occur in Sharon's life as a result of alcohol and drugs, a crisis-based intervention attempt should be made. Shortly thereafter, Sharon was seriously injured in a drinking-related automobile accident. We enlisted the help of the treating physician for data proving Sharon had been very drunk at the time of the accident and gathered facts from the arresting officer about her intoxicated behavior at the scene (she had staggered off drunkenly, even though bleeding and suffering from several broken bones and head injuries). Her mother, father, and a close friend participated in an intervention at her bedside in the hospital. Each in turn told her how much they cared about her and pointed out how alcohol was responsible for the accident and the pain it was causing Sharon, her family, and friends. They offered the opportunity to include treatment for her alcohol problem as part of total recovery from the accident. She accepted and, after her injuries were sufficiently healed, transferred to a C.D. treatment center. Sharon is sober and drug-free today.

Case History—"The Best Damn Defense Lawyer in the State"

On several occasions we have been asked to assist with interventions on "the best damn defense lawyer in the state." Since each time it was a different attorney, it would seem that C.D. defense lawyers certainly impress others with their skills. Clarence, this particular "best damn defense lawyer in the state," had been suddenly hospitalized for drinking-related health problems but was still sure that he "could handle it." Prior to the medical emergency, his wife had been preparing for a formal intervention involving a number of out-of-town friends and family members. This sudden hospitalization, however, provided a crisis-based intervention opportunity. After enlisting the treating physician, one of Clarence's law partners, and Clarence's father (himself no slouch with the scotch bottle), an intervention was done in the hospital room. The doctor stated that alcoholism was the primary cause of Clarence's secondary medical problems. That rare and courageous diagnosis, combined with the data presented by the spouse and law partner, broke through the delusion long enough for Clarence to accept transfer to a C.D. treatment center. He is sober today and the family much healthier after treatment. Of special note here is the impact an enlightened physician can have on the outcome of an intervention attempt.

Key Elements of Crisis-Based Intervention

The potency of crisis-based intervention stems from

1. Timing

2. The irrefutable nature of the crisis

3. The enlisting of powerful and objective witnesses

The intervention should be timed to take place while the C.D. person is recovering from the shock and initial trauma of whatever incident has occurred—arrest, injury, accident, broken relationship, etc.—and while still suffering the emotional consequences. In the case studies above, both C.D. persons were over the effects of anesthesia and free enough of severe pain to be lucid. But they were still scared, ashamed, and disgusted with themselves. Obviously, when a medical situation is involved, approval of the attending physician should be requested. The nature of these crisis situations is such that the evidence available is usually both objective and irrefutable and thus very difficult to resist: photos, video tapes, newspaper articles, police reports, injuries, or property damage to others, etc. The impact of evidence can be made even more powerful if the details are provided by an objective third party such as the arresting officer, attending physician, or eye witness. Because the C.D. person has such a defensive relationship with those close to him, it is often easier for him to believe information provided by someone outside the family system.

Cooperating With the Law

Several research studies suggest that some C.D. persons develop a drinking/drugging pattern that gets them in trouble with the law and some don't. And once a pattern of violence or intoxicated driving or stealing is established, it tends to continue and worsen. What this means is that allowing C.D. persons to pay the full consequences of their first brushes with the law is probably the most loving thing to do. Assisting them to "beat the rap" by providing high-powered attorneys, using political influence, or encouraging cover-ups may contribute to later and far more painful tragedy.

On the other hand, encounters with the law may offer two options for intervention. The first is passive: do nothing and permit the C.D. person to absorb the full impact of his lawbreaking behavior. This may mean a night in jail, finding and funding his own legal assistance, appearing in court alone, and facing the pain of incarceration, fines, and/or probation. This sounds cruel, but it is physical and emotional pain that fuels the recovery process. Thus, stepping in and insulating the C.D. person from the painful consequences of his intoxicated behavior may be denying him an important moment of truth as well as encouraging attitudes and behaviors with potential for dire future consequences. It's not easy to leave your kid, spouse, or sibling in jail. But very often that's the most loving thing to do.

The second option is to actively cooperate with law enforcement officers, prosecutors, and judicial officials. This might take the form of revealing the C.D. person's history of chemical dependency and asking them to offer the C.D. person the choice of treatment or prosecution. Many a C.D. person traces his recovery to such a forced choice. This kind of plea bargaining, however, needs to be approached with care and with the aid of a defense attorney experienced in such procedures. Judicial enlightenment about chemical dependency varies nationwide. It is probably accurate to assume that most judges today would rather see a C.D. person in a treatment bed than a jail cell, but that belief is not universal. So in these matters one should approach the idea of interfering in another person's legal destinies with care, discernment, and solid expert advice. But, given these cautions, we should not hesitate to exploit the potency of the law in what may be lifesaving circumstances.

What Really Is Up, Doc?

Often a medical crisis will enable a physician to intervene. Many such opportunities are lost because doctors will not risk confronting a patient's drinking or drug use unless they observe secondary symptoms like cirrhosis, gastritus, or needle infections. As discussed earlier, this reluctance may stem from the physician's own drinking or drug use, co-dependency, or lack of education and training about alcoholism and other chemical dependencies. But the most common reason physicians don't intervene more often is that they simply don't have enough data. When questioned about alcohol or drugs, C.D. patients almost always minimize or deny. So even when a problem is strongly suspected, the doctor is powerless unless some validating physical symptom is present.

Many M.D.'s are now trained to ask what are called the CAGE questions, a simple, easy-to-administer four-item test named for the symptoms it seeks to detect.

1. "Have you ever felt you should Cut down on your drinking?"

2. "Have people Annoyed you by criticizing your drinking?"

3. "Have you ever felt bad or Guilty about your drinking?"

4. "Have you ever had an Early morning drink to get rid of a hangover?"

One yes should raise suspicion. Two or more are indicators of a problem.

As a concerned friend or family member you can make the physician aware of the severity of the problem for his use in professional contacts with the C.D. person. This information can have a strong impact when discussed with the doctor, either in person or by phone, and then followed up by a letter describing your specific concerns and giving the doctor clearly stated permission to use the information.

Telling the Boss

Enlisting the C.D. person's employer in the intervention process may initially sound like economic suicide. "If I tell the boss, he'll lose his job" is a typical and valid apprehension. But of course if he doesn't quit drinking and/or drugging, he'll get fired anyway. No question about it, going to the boss is a tricky business. But it also might be just what's needed to push the C.D. person into help.

Here are a few ideas on this very sensitive subject. A less threatening starting place is to call (or have a confidant call) the employer and—without revealing identities—speak to the personnel manager or whoever acts in that capacity. Inquire about the organization's policy regarding employee alcohol or other drug problems and the availability of a formal employee assistance program. Should there be an official program, contact the program director—still anonymously—and find out how it works. If you become convinced that confiding in the program director (or one of the program staff to whom you may be referred) is a positive step, then take the risk. He or she can explain company policies, recommend help resources, clarify insurance benefits, and in some instances actually participate in the intervention effort. If there is no formal program or you just don't trust the response, at least ask the question—"What happens if one of your employees goes into treatment for alcohol or drug use?" The answer to that question can help you decide whether you want to involve anyone from the workplace.

What If He Is the Boss?

One of the most effective and commonly encountered defenses in C.D. people is overachievement on the job. "How can I be an alcoholic? I'm the best man in the outfit!" is a common utterance when C.D. persons are confronted. Since that is often true, C.D. people are frequently situated on lofty professional or corporate perches and not accountable to many others. Even so, there are usually business partners, professional peers, legal advisors, corporate physicians, and boards of directors who have power and influence over the C.D. person. When the C.D. person is the boss, such power brokers may well be your most forceful allies, especially if the C.D. person's behavior is an economic threat to them. Everybody is accountable to somebody.

When to Involve the Workplace

There is no clear-cut guide as to whether and when to enlist help from the boss, co-workers, the company doctor, or the employee assistance program in the intervention process. But when an alcohol- or drug- related crisis has either become known at work or is affecting job performance, the secret is already out. So you might as well pursue the help that may lie in the hands of those at work who still care. This can get complicated, because supervisors and co-workers can also be enablers. Just like family members, they may have been covering up, lying, and making excuses for the C.D. person. They too can be reluctant to confront someone else's drinking or drug use because of their own. But if a real crisis occurs that will affect job performance—arrest, unacceptable absenteeism, serious injury, public embarrassment, professional licensing problems, damage to corporate reputation, or product or consumer liability—the organization is already involved. Therefore, you might as well enlist its help to intervene. Your alcohol and drug abuse counselor, personal attorney, and Al-anon sponsor/group members can be of assistance in making these decisions.

Semper Paratus

The next two chapters cover the two most common forms of intervention: the mini-intervention and the concerned group. But as you begin pursuing the skills needed for those kinds of approaches, a crisis may erupt. So, as you gather the forces and seek the counseling and training needed for a more formal and structured intervention effort, be ready to act quickly and decisively in an unexpected emergency. Don't worry about "doing it right." Just get to the C.D. person, tell him you care, point out what has happened because of drinking and/or drugging, and ask if he'd be willing to accept some help. Assure the C.D. that you know he is not bad, stupid, or crazy but that the present situation makes it mighty obvious that he has a diseased relationship with alcohol or drugs—and that help is available. Remind him of friends or public figures he admires who have undergone similar treatment. Emphasize that now—while the pain of the present crisis is fresh in his mind—is the time to decide to end the pain for himself and those who care. Will it help? More people probably enter help under these circumstances than any other. When the D.A. is breathing down their necks, the doctor is staring at them over the still-damp X-rays, or the boss is offering them one more chance, C.D. persons often experience instant enlightenment. As one recovered sage once said, "I didn't have a spiritual awakening. I had a rude awakening." Crisis-based interventions are very powerful and should be attempted whenever circumstances offer an opportunity.

7

The Mini-Intervention

It's Tough

One concerned person alone confronting a C.D. person is the most tried and least successful way to intervene. These mini-intervention efforts certainly don't fail for lack of concern or effort. But the underlying dynamics of these confrontations doom most such attempts. Unless the confronting person has special training and preparation, the conversation usually degenerates into generalities and accusations such as "You've turned into a drunk and you're ruining our marriage." To which the C.D. person replies with a full array of defensive and manipulative skills. By the time the change is over, the confronter often feels guilty for having raised the subject and is convinced that a lot of the drinking or drugging is his or her fault. These highly charged and often argumentative and judgmental encounters can be refined and made useful, however, if certain ground rules are followed and a few simple skills practiced.

The mini-intervention approach has an important place in the overall intervention scheme. For, although one such confrontation by itself is seldom effective, there often is a positive and cumulative result when conducted on a frequent and recurring basis. The C.D. person's delusion and denial can be gradually undermined when many of those who care about him stop enabling, break the no-talk rules, and consistently hold him accountable for his behavior under the influence.

Safety First—Yours!

When there is a history or threat of physical violence, any intervention effort should be approached with great caution and in certain cases avoided. *Your personal safety and that of your family and friends is the first priority.* Remember, C.D. persons are capable of acts under the influence of the chemical that grossly violate their sober values. This not infrequently includes violent acts against loved ones. If physical harm is a concern, get competent professional advice before attempting intervention. *If violence occurs, get out...get protection...get legal advice.* You can do that by temporarily fleeing to a safe place (the home of a relative or friend or a community shelter), reporting the incident to the police, and discussing the situation with an attorney. Keep in mind that you didn't cause the abuse and you can't fix it. If you can't afford a lawyer, contact the legal aid society. Sadly, there is a lot of family violence these days. Overworked police can sometimes get a bit apathetic about these domestic situations. At the same time, being physically battered literally beats down your ability to reach out for help. This combination of police overload and victim reluctance can be deadly. We urge as powerfully as we can: *if someone is physically hurting you, CRY FOR HELP UNTIL YOU GET IT!!!* It is unwise to return to an abusive C.D. person until he has gotten help and a professional advises that it is safe to renew the relationship. These self-protection actions may sound scary at a time when you are already quite fearful. Nonetheless, there is no benefit from keeping yourself or loved ones in harm's way in an attempt to "save" the C.D. person. On the contrary, many C.D. people have found their way to treatment and recovery by way of the shock of loved ones leaving and the police arriving. Put yourself on top of your own priority list.

But If It's Safe

When physical harm is not a threat, every drinking or drugging bout can be an opportunity for mini-intervention. Such a confrontation might sound something like this: "Shirley, I am very concerned about you. Last night when I came home, you seemed to be asleep on the couch in the clothes you'd worn to work. When I tried to awaken you, I could smell alcohol on your breath, and you didn't respond when I tried to talk to you. A drink had been spilled on the floor, and the stub of a joint was in the ashtray. Both the kids were in their beds crying. Joey told me you sent them to their room after picking them up at the nursery at 5:30. He said you promised them dinner in a little while. It was 10:00 and they still hadn't eaten. The baby had spread the contents of her dirty diaper all over her clothes and face and had pulled the nipple off her bottle and spilled it all over the mess. Joey kept repeating through his tears, 'Mommy must be dead, she won't wake up. Mommy must be dead, she won't wake up.' He was terrified, and the baby was purple-faced from hours of screaming. I was angry, scared, and disgusted. Shirley, I know how much you love the kids and that you would never behave this way if you hadn't been drinking and smoking pot. Please, get some help."

Notice that the above statement is very specific, contains no labels or moral judgments, and yet holds the C.D. person responsible for her behavior and its emotional impact on others.

Developing a Core Message

Mini-interventions seem frightening because past experience has taught us to expect anger, denial, and all the other defenses and manipulations that accompany this disease. The result is often to wish we had not raised the subject, or even leaves us feeling that the whole mess is our fault. Take a lesson from the politicians. Candidates and office holders today hire media consultants to teach them how to keep interviews focused on their agenda and not that of the interviewer; they develop what is termed a core message. Questions asked or arguments raised receive a brief response and then they bridge to their core message. You can apply the same skill to your mini-intervention attempts. Your core message should sound something like this:

"Joe, I'm very concerned about you. Last night I saw you gulping drinks at the boss's dinner party. Later, you told that awful joke about the bullfighter. Nobody laughed. They just stared in disbelief. I heard your boss mutter, 'There goes the office drunk again. We're going to have to do something about him.' I know how much your job means to you, Joe. There is a program here in town that can help us with the way alcohol is affecting our lives. All I have to do is call and set up an appointment for an assessment. Will you go with me?"

When Joe responds, "My boss is an old prude. I was just having a good time," or some other alibi or excuse, don't get hooked into an argument. Bridge to your core message.

"Maybe he is. Still, I am very concerned and I know you wouldn't have embarrassed yourself if you hadn't been drinking. You value your job too much. There is a program here in town etc., etc., etc."

You can avoid argument and maintain win-win dynamics with this technique. So compose and mentally rehearse your core message. The content will vary from time to time but the outline is the same: concern—a description of the drinking/drugging behavior—there is help—let's go. Having a well rehearsed core message is the key to effective mini-intervention attempts. This technique takes much of the fear out of confronting the C.D. person with his chemically induced behavior. It also keeps the message of hope and help in the forefront of your relationship.

Timing

The C.D. person will be most receptive to these intervention efforts during the "morning after"—when sober or at least less under the influence and yet suffering a hangover, remorse, or fear of the consequences of recent chemically induced behavior. Physical and emotional pain is almost always what motivates the C.D. person to accept help. These one-on-one scenes can be a powerful means to bring that pain into the consciousness of the victim. Individually, such attempts will seldom penetrate the C.D. person's well-developed defenses. But when done with love and concern as each opportunity presents itself, these efforts can have a cumulative impact on the delusion and denial surrounding the disease. Finally, remember that not saying anything to C.D. persons regarding their aberrant behavior enables them to stay blinded by delusion and allows the disease to progress. And as this progression advances, intervention becomes more and more difficult. So the time to act is yesterday. If you don't act soon, there literally may be no tomorrow.

Peer Intervention Programs

If the one about whom you are concerned is a licensed professional, some powerful assistance may be available to you. Most professions—physicians, attorneys, dentists, pharmacists, nurses, veterinarians, airline pilots, and others—have what are called impaired professional or peer assistance programs. The strength of these activities varies from occupation to occupation and state to state. The best of them employ well trained volunteer interventionists from the profession who carry the clout of possible license suspension if the C.D. person refuses to accept treatment. Call the state association for the profession in question and ask to speak to the person who manages their peer assistance program. Remain anonymous until you feel comfortable with the help they offer. Assistance can range from a briefing on the profession's policies when a C.D. member undergoes treatment all the way to aiding in the organizing and conduct of the intervention itself. Our work includes conducting training courses for prospective interveners in these peer assistance programs in many parts of the country. We know first hand that many of them are well organized and offer invaluable help. If this applies, be sure to check it out.

On the Job

Mini-interventions are especially useful and effective in the work setting. The implied threat of adverse job action if help is not accepted can have a powerful impact. If you are reading this book because you're the employer, supervisor, or manager of a once-valued employee whose attendance, performance, or behavior on the job is deteriorating, C.D. or co-dependency is the likely culprit. Is it appropriate to intervene? You bet. What employees do off the job is none of your business. But attendance, performance, and behavior at work is your business. On that basis you have a right to intervene. First, check with the personnel office to see whether the company has an organized employee assistance program. If so, call the program coordinator and follow his or her advice. If there is no established program, you may wish to attempt to intervene yourself.

When you do, don't try to diagnose the problem. Stick to documented examples of attendance, performance, and/or behavior problems. Don't judge, moralize, label, or argue. Simply state the case and offer help options. If challenged, use concern as your justification for intervening.

Developing the Necessary Skills

Several years ago we developed a device to help keep these on-the-job interventions on track. It's called the REACH outline. It has proven helpful in staying organized and taking the fear out of workplace and other one-on-one confrontations.

Many managers and supervisors to whom we have taught this REACH approach reported the outline to be very useful. Keep in mind that an employee cannot usually be forced to accept treatment. But it can be made clear that if things don't change for the better, there will be consequences to their continued unacceptable attendance, performance, or behavior.

R — eason   "The reason for this meeting is..."

E — valuation   State the specific attendance, performance, and/or behavior problems.

A — lternatives "As your supervisor, here are my alternatives..." (Spell out the specific help that is available and the company policies regarding insurance coverage, time off work, etc.) Then point out what the company policy will be if the unacceptable attendance, performance, and behavior does not improve within a specific time period.

C — oncern   Emphasize that concern for the person is a primary motive for this confrontation.

H — ope   Point out the reasons for the employee to be hopeful that help does work and all can be well.

Mini-intervention attempts can be made more effective by the acquisition of certain attitudes and communication skills. These abilities are also embodied in the more elaborate and structured concerned group intervention described in the next chapter. If you can master the techniques demanded by this approach, you have automatically learned the skills needed for all three. Consequently, we recommend that anyone faced with the possibility of an intervention refer to procedures and skills covered in detail in Chapter 8.

8

The Concerned Group
Intervention

Love Does Conquer All

Love and concern are the most powerful forces in any intervention attempt. And the love and concern of many is even more powerful. Consequently, a group of family, friends, co-workers, and professional peers who care about the C.D. person collectively possess the greatest potential for successful intervention. Such an approach is called a concerned group intervention. Typically it is a very structured effort involving considerable preparation and training. Concerned group interventions have been successful when led by one of the significant participants. However, the likelihood of success is enhanced when the effort is conducted under the guidance of a specially qualified professional. The concerned group intervention may be defined as follows: *a meeting with a C.D. person in which as many significant others as possible, after careful preparation, present specific but nonjudgmental examples of behavior-under-the-influence that conflict with the C.D. person's values, report the pain it has caused them; and offer options that the C.D. person can accept with dignity.*

There is no official, national intervention scorekeeper. However, our professional contact with intervention counselors around the country indicates that efforts of this type have at least a 70 percent probability of ending with the C.D. person agreeing to enter treatment, either immediately or within a few days. As of this writing, we have personally facilitated nearly 500 such attempts and over 90 percent of the C.D. persons took the help offered. In the situations that "didn't work," either important people in the C.D. person's life could not or would not participate, the data presented were not powerful enough, or certain "concerned" persons sabotaged the effort because—for financial, business, or personal reasons—they did not want the C.D. person to get well. Perhaps more notable than the few failures are the many concerned groups who never needed to hold the formal intervention. The changes they made in their relationship with the C.D. person as a result of preparing for the intervention resulted in circumstances that led him to accept help. Getting ready for the intervention shows that the best way to change someone else's behavior is to begin by changing your own.

Finding Power

Feeling powerless is a logical state of affairs for a C.D. family. Believing that you've tried everything possible and yet seeing all efforts fail produces a sense of futility. Consequently, desperation rather than enlightenment drives most C.D. families to seek "outside" help. This is ironic because the power to intervene really lies "inside" the system of family and friends that surrounds the C.D. person. It is the emotional pain suffered by those who love the C.D. person that fuels the intervention process. The C.D. person has learned to control the feelings of those around him and manipulate their behavior. As long as this power is granted, little can be done to change the situation. But by breaking the no-talk rules, confronting the unacceptable behaviors, taking back control of your own feelings, and getting help for yourselves, the spark of intervention can be lit. The key point is that the power to intervene is internal to the concerned group rather than some magic external force brought to bear by a counselor. The intervention process simply converts the negative emotional energy in the C.D. family and friends into a positive force that drives the healing process. It's you who has the raw power! All that is needed is guidance on how to channel and use it.

A Proven Formula

Over the years we have modified and refined our particular formula for the concerned group intervention into a rather rigid series of steps which, when followed, produced a very high record of success. To the extent that it becomes necessary to change or depart from this proven approach, the likelihood of the C.D. person accepting help will be lessened. The intervention process, as we define it, involves three phases of activity: planning and coordinating, training and preparation, and intervention and follow-through. Accordingly, we will describe each of these phases and pass on suggestions learned from our experiences in real-life interventions.

Phase One: Planning and Coordinating

Find a Competent Counselor

You'll need trained help in dealing with a chemically dependent family member, friend, employee, or co-worker. *Act. Do it now!* Call a local alcohol or drug program or agency and ask about intervention counselors and programs. If that's too scary, *right now* call someone to whom you've turned in the past: physician, counselor, attorney, clergy person, etc. Don't ask them to help you intervene, if they could have, they already would have. Just ask them to steer you to someone or someplace that might understand intervention. When you do make contact with a potential intervention counselor, ask whether he or she is trained and experienced with the Johnson Institute model of intervention. Professionals with the proper training will be familiar with this term. Take the time to find an intervention counselor experienced with this model. It works.

The best and most successful intervention counselors have a unique combination of skills and background. First of all, they have current knowledge about chemical dependency and how it affects individuals and families. The intervention counselor must be able to penetrate the manipulation, controlling, and intimidation and see instead a diseased person full of emotional pain and desperately in need of help. At the same time, the counselor must be aware that the wall of defensive behavior, delusion, and denial surrounding the C.D. person must be breached or he may die—certainly spiritually and often physically.

Beyond just understanding this illness and the plight of its victims, the intervention counselor must possess the charisma and leadership skills required to corral as many as a dozen or more concerned people, all of whom are to some extent suffering co-dependency symptoms. To mold such a confluence of frequently opposed agendas into a unified, trained, and motivated intervention group is a high-order challenge. So the intervention counselor must be educator, therapist, coach, and, to a large extent, salesperson—salesperson because a high level of persuasive communication skills on the part of the counselor can be of great value during the closing moments of an intervention. Sometimes, when the data presented don't quite break through the C.D. person's delusion, a respectful, nonantagonistic, win/win dialogue between the counselor and the C.D. person can overcome objections and save the day. When you seek out professional intervention assistance, look for experience, emotional maturity, and a track record of successful interventions.

Arrange a Professional Intervention Planning Conference

Before involving many others in the process, one or two of the primary concerned persons should meet with the intervention counselor to sort out the problem, decide on courses of action, identify potential interveners, and plan the intervention effort. At this meeting one of the interveners is usually appointed as the single point of contact for all future communications and coordination concerning the intervention. Keep attendance at this gathering down to two or three key players—usually the person who initiated the idea and one other trusted concerned person. The purpose is to break the no-talk rules, gain an accurate picture of the situation, identify all potential interveners, develop the strategies and schedules needed to get everyone trained and prepared, decide on a treatment program, and select at least a tentative time and place for the actual intervention.

Recruit and Motivate Interveners

Under the guidance of the counselor, potential interveners are contacted and enlisted to participate in the intervention process. The core of this group is usually family members and close friends, but may include ex-spouses, disliked in-laws, "fragile" family members, young children, distant relatives, long-lost friends, and others who may be difficult to recruit but nonetheless represent potent interveners. This step is not easy. Chemically dependent families are often geographically and emotionally separated. Because of their own co-dependency, some family members or friends may be unwilling or unable to participate. So frequently it is necessary to "intervene on the interveners"—that is, design strategies to gain the support of key persons who are resistant. Some may just need a bit of reassurance and encouragement from the intervention counselor. Others will respond after receiving more current information. But some may require tough confrontation to break through their own denial. Such challenges in pulling together an intervention are the rule, not the exception. Families seldom march into the counselor's office arm-in-arm, possessed with unity of purpose and high motivation saying, "Murphy family reporting for intervention duty." In reality, most families considering intervention are divided, scared, confused, and full of doubt. Assistance will be needed to meld them into a cohesive and effective intervention team. Experienced intervention counselors know how to do this. We are reminded of a politician's wife who was so "devoted" that the other concerned persons were afraid to involve her in the intervention effort. Because she was sensitive to her husband's political aspirations, her friends were worried she would blow the whistle. The strategy employed was for two of them to invite her for breakfast at a restaurant near the hotel where the intervention group was to train and prepare. At the breakfast, she was invited "to a meeting of friends discussing her husband's political future." She accepted. At the meeting the concerned persons told her that he had no political future unless his alcoholism was arrested. Since they were his primary fund-raisers, she listened, stayed, and played a crucial role in the intervention. This is what is meant by intervening on the interveners.

What About the Kids?

Consistently, we've observed children to have strong impact in an intervention. Yet the natural and understandable desire of older family members is to protect the kids. But that is much like trying to protect them from a storm by pretending it isn't out there. The children have heard the thunder and seen the lightning of this family disturbance and know much more about what is going on than adults suspect or wish to admit. More importantly, kids are feeling the emotional pain and need help as much as anyone in the family system. They need to talk about these sights and sounds, and the intervention is a good place to start. Follow the advice on this matter of the professional with whom you are working. But we have seen young children powerfully impact the C.D. person with a therapeutic result for the youngsters as well. For example, a six-year-old daughter revealed how her alcoholic father kept a pan next to his chair in which to throw up. After doing so, he would make her empty it. Kids need to talk about these awful realities. When unable to, they will turn them painfully inward and carry the damage into adulthood.

Phase Two: Training and Preparation

Attend an Education Program

The identified and recruited intervention participants need to attend an education program that provides an update on chemical dependency, its impact on families, and the principles of intervention. Public education about intervention is now found in almost any major community. Often these programs are presented as a free service by agencies such as the local council on alcoholism and drug abuse. Many treatment centers also sponsor community education on these subjects. Programs that present mock interventions or include films or video tapes portraying intervention scenes are especially valuable. Check the public service announcements in the local newspaper, call the council on alcoholism and drug abuse, or query the treatment centers usually listed in the Yellow Pages under "Alcoholism Information and Treatment Centers."

Get Help for Co-Dependency

Intervention training often gets interveners in touch with their own co-dependency. Participants suffering from the pains of co-dependency are strongly encouraged, at the very least, to seek help from a support group such as Al-anon, Adult Children of Alcoholics, Tough Love Parents, etc. Since just about everyone who has an emotional bond with a C.D. person suffers from some co-dependency, it's a good idea for all participants to get an evaluation from the counselor as to the propriety of seeking therapy for co-dependency.

Untreated co-dependent people can sabotage the intervention. They bring with them defensive behaviors; the controlling, the attention-getting tactics, the inappropriate humor, or the silence of fear. If these issues are not being dealt with in venues separate from the intervention, then valuable time and energy will be wasted during intervention, preparation. Intervention facilitators must help participants break through their own delusion and denial in order to recall the C.D.'s unacceptable behavior. That is more easily accomplished if the participants are already in a "safe" system and getting the help they need for their own pain and defenses. If you have lived around a C.D. person for any length of time at any time in your life, you will benefit from help and you deserve it.

Break the No-Talk Rules

It is essential to create an atmosphere of openness, trust, and honesty within the intervention group. This may require free discussion of previously taboo events and subjects and the putting aside of long-standing differences. C.D. people, by virtue of chemically induced behavior and sophisticated defense systems, will often perpetrate an array of intrigues, secret alliances,triangles (sexual and otherwise), bizarre incidents, and other "delicate" situations. Not surfacing and processing such data early can lead to unexpected surprises that may sabotage the intervention effort and/or the concealment of valuable information. Family members are often reluctant to discuss these sensitive matters, believing they are the only ones who know. This is seldom the case, but these extreme examples of behavior-in-conflict-with-values make for the most powerful kinds of intervention statements.

For the C.D. person to see the severity of his condition, he must experience the emotional consequences of his worst drinking and/or drugging behaviors. To touch that pain demands breaking the no-talk rules and presenting the truth, no matter how uncomfortable that may be.

A classic case in our files involves a woman's sexual indiscretion. During the phase of intervention training in which the concerned persons were writing their statements, a male friend of the family came to us privately. He described how, in the course of a pool party at his home, the woman being intervened upon had gotten very drunk and seduced him behind the cabana. The friend had himself been intoxicated enough to temporarily put aside the fact that he was supposed to be her husband's best friend. To his credit, however, he was willing to break the no-talk rules and bring up this incident, but he feared it would embarrass the husband and children. A while later, the woman's thirteen-year-old son furtively approached us, relating the same incident. It seems he was spending the night with the party host's son and witnessed Mom's indiscretion from a balcony above the pool. The young man felt sure his mother would never do such a thing sober and wanted to tell her this in the intervention—except he didn't want to hurt his father. By now you have probably guessed who appeared next: Dad. But he, of course, wanted to protect the son and his friend. This tale demonstrates that, if one person is brave enough to come forward with an incident in which the C.D. person grossly violated his own values while under the influence, others will corroborate and give permission to use it. This kind of powerful specific data is vital to breaking through the deadly delusion that surrounds the C.D. person.

Write Intervention Statements

The concerned group will be coached on how to compose two or three very specific, hard-hitting but nonjudgmental written statements that point out powerful examples of the C.D. person's unacceptable drinking and/or drugging behavior. The use of written rather than extemporaneous intervention statements is strongly recommended. Unscripted interventions tend to quickly degenerate into win-lose, antagonistic, argumentative battles. It takes a while to come up with effective intervention statements. One older woman came to our information program several times. She told us that her drinking husband never did anything "bad." She couldn't grasp the notion that it was what he wasn't doing that was "bad." He was no longer husband, father, lover, friend; he just quietly drank. We ran into her months later. She told us through tear-filled eyes, "He finally did something bad. One night he died."

If you have trouble recalling incidents, think about ruined holidays, birthdays, anniversaries, kid's important school or sports functions, dangerous driving behavior, broken promises, blackouts, sexual impotency, physical and emotional abuse, missed work, passing out, throwing up, staying out all night, losing the car, or failure to perform as a spouse, parent, citizen, friend, worker. In other words, things the C.D. person did in ways he really didn't want to or things he really wanted to do but failed to do. At first such incidents may be difficult to remember. Talk with the others about your history with the C.D. person. Break the no-talk rules, and eventually hard-hitting statements will emerge. Write them down in the following format:

Intervention Statement Outline

1. *Concern:* State your love and/or concern for the C.D. person.

2. *Incident:* Describe in specific detail an incident in which the C.D. person did something under the influence that seriously violated his own values. Give dates, times, places, graphic portrayals, sounds, smells, expressions—exactly what happened.

3. *Evidence:* Provide proof that chemicals were involved in the incident, such as "I saw you drink three double scotches before we left the house. You then had a double martini before dinner and two glasses of wine with your meal, followed by two brandies."

4. *Feelings:* Describe how being a witness or participant in the incident made you feel—sad, terrified, sick to your stomach, angry, hurt, discounted, unloved, disappointed.

5. *Concern:* Close with another statement of concern.

The following statements have been used in various actual interventions:

> I love you, John. Last Friday at 4 p.m, you called from the office and said you wanted to take me out for dinner and to be ready at 6 p.m. I dressed in the blue suit you said you liked so much and looked forward to the evening as I waited for you to arrive. I waited and waited, and finally at 11 p.m. I went to bed, not knowing what had happened and feeling disappointed, angry, and very scared. At 3 a.m. I heard banging on the front door and someone rattling the doorknob. I got up just in time to see you fall into the living room and grab at the couch for support. You stared at me with your eyes like slits and your jaw clenched, and thundered through slurred speech, "What the hell are you staring at?" I could smell the alcohol across the room and saw the red, glazed eyes. You pushed past me and

sprawled onto the bed, fully clothed. I felt frightened, angry, and very alone.

When I approached you the next morning about what had happened, you did not recall anything and said, "You made that up. It wasn't that bad." I am very scared and feel so powerless. I am so concerned.

Mom, I love you a lot. Last month my friends came over for my birthday. We were in my room listening to records when you walked into the room dressed in your slip. You started dancing around the room to the music and slurred, "Aren't we having fun, fun, fun?" I could smell the alcohol on your breath and watched with dread as you whirled unsteadily around the room. I was so embarrassed. I didn't know what to do. My feet seemed glued to the floor. My friends scampered out of the house, laughing as they ran. I wanted to die. I wish I had my sober mom back.

Mom, I love you. Last Wednesday you said you would pick me up from school and I waited and waited for over an hour and you didn't come. I decided I had better walk home, and when I got there I found you on your bed, eyes half open, smelling of alcohol, clothes disheveled. I tried to wake you but you didn't wake up. You had threatened to kill yourself before, and this time I was afraid you had. I kept crying, "Mom, I love you. Mom, I love you," till your eyes opened wide and I knew you were alive. Please get help, Mom. I love you.

Jack, I care about you. We have no physical relationship anymore. Friday night I tried to set up a romantic evening. I fixed a candlelight dinner and arranged for the children to be at the movie. You came home in a good mood, smiling and happy, and held me as though you really cared. We had dinner and I played some of our favorite music. You insisted on having more and more wine, and as you drank, you changed. You talked over and over about what a son of a bitch your boss was and stopped paying any attention to me. I tried to get you to dance with me and you said, "You're too old to dance. You don't know any of the new dances like the girls at the club do." I was so hurt. I went into the kitchen and cried. Later on, you said you wanted me to make love to you. By then you smelled bad and were slurring your words and staggering. When we went to bed, you couldn't make love, Jack. You were unable to. You were impotent, Jack. I care about you so much.

I am terribly worried about you, Jim. When you were younger, you were always reading about ships and the sea. So often you would talk about going to Annapolis and becoming a naval officer. During your first two years in high school your grades were tops and you wrote our congressman about an appointment to the Academy. Beginning last semester your grades dropped, your good friends Bob and Dave stopped coming around, and you began to skip studying and to stay out late. Last week, while doing the laundry, your mother found marijuana remnants in your jeans pockets. Then Saturday night you bumped your car into the garage door and were weaving as you came up the walk. You had trouble getting your key in the door. I opened it and could smell alcohol on your breath. You said in a high-pitched voice, "Hi, Pop. How the f _ _ _ are you?" You fell into my arms and I had to help you to bed. The next day you couldn't remember where you'd been or the scene at the door. I see alcohol and drugs destroying your dream, and I feel sad, scared, and powerless. We've found a program that can help you. Please accept the help we offer.

Note the absence of judgment, moralizing, labeling, and generalities. The idea is to create a win/win, nonantagonistic, concerned, and loving atmosphere. If the intervention effort feels conspiratorial, accusative, or otherwise negative, the statements should be refined and revised until the net impact of listening to all the statements seems loving and nonjudgmental.

Concerned Group Work Sessions

Preparing for a formal intervention will require attendance at working meetings conducted by the intervention counselor(s) during which participants refine their draft statements, coordinate schedules, assign responsibilities, and rehearse. Get together as many times as needed to be certain each participant's statements are as potent and well composed as possible. It is helpful to view the situation this way: If all the statements were put in a hat and the C.D. person were to draw just one, would that single statement have the power to intervene? Such is an impossible goal, but it is a good target.

Follow the suggestions of the intervention counselor for edits, changes, and word choices; his or her experience is the best guide. Keep working on and refining the statements, but don't waste time and money arguing with the counselor. Intervention is not an exact science nor entirely an intuitive art, and you'll find that the counselor's professional experience is usually the best guide. Considerable time and effort is required to write, revise, edit, and fine-tune intervention statements. But once this work is done, leave well enough alone. Excessive revision and rehearsing will bring on staleness and rob the process of emotional power.

Gather for a Final Preparation Meeting

In this final session the intervention statements are critiqued one last time. The group then role-plays the intervention. This gives the participants an opportunity to feel the power of their combined statements, which removes some of the fear and apprehension. The practice session also assists the intervention counselor(s) in determining the sequence in which participants should read their statements, where they should sit in relation to each other and to the C.D. person, and other logistics. Subjects to be discussed at this meeting might include making treatment arrangements, escorting the C.D. person to the treatment facility, packing his bag, arranging for time off work, caring for the cats and dogs, or any other obstacles that might surface. The date, time, and place of the intervention attempt are determined along with logistics such as where participants will park and who will invite—and perhaps escort—the C.D. person to the meeting. Any remaining doubts, concerns, and "what ifs" are resolved. It is our custom to end this final gathering by having all join hands in a circle and then praying or meditating—whatever is your preference—in order to instill a sense of closure and unity.

Once we encountered a rather cynical power-broker type during an intervention on a very powerful political figure. Upon completion of the final preparation meeting, we led this joining of hands. From the look on his face, he obviously viewed this ritual as foolish and unnecessary. The touch-and-go but eventually successful intervention involved a group of fifteen family members, friends, and political allies and one very tough and highly resistant C.D. politician. Afterward, the cynic came to us and said, "When you had us join hands together last night I felt silly and questioned the need for such a device with mature people. But today, when it looked as if things were going badly, I remembered the feeling of being all together in this effort and it gave me great strength." Moral: trust the counselor. He or she may know you and the situation better than you think.

Deal With the What Ifs

Last-minute doubts, apprehensions, and fears of those preparing for a formal intervention attempt need to be resolved. What if...he won't show up...arrives under the influence...flees after seeing the group...gets angry or violent...breaks down in tears...argues...refuses help...cuts them off financially? Won't he lose his job...be embarrassed publicly...hate us for doing this...feel that we ganged up and conspired...seek revenge? Isn't this disloyal, unfair, downright sneaky? The answers to these concerns and many other such "what ifs" could fill a book. In general, the response to all these questions is contained in the key words of the definition for a concerned group intervention: *A meeting of concerned persons with a chemically dependent person at which specific nonjudgmental examples of drinking—or drugging-related behavior—which was in conflict with his own values—is presented in an atmosphere of concern, after which help options are offered that the C.D. person can accept with dignity.* Such a confrontation is a loving act. By its very nature a professionally facilitated concerned group intervention should produce a calm, nonthreatening, business-like scene. It is an "everybody wins" proposition in which the C.D. person receives a great deal of love and concern—only his behavior is attacked.

The data presented simply prove how an otherwise good, intelligent, sane human being is doing a lot of self-defeating things that cause an enormous amount of pain in himself and those he professes to love. There is no judging, labeling, personal attacking, anger, or other provocative behavior. Throughout a properly conducted intervention, the C.D. person's dignity is respected and his worth affirmed. If properly trained, participants will realize they are part of a life-saving endeavor. Furthermore, if the participants have joined a support group or sought other help for their codependency issues, they will have heard many of these "what if" situations discussed by fellow recovering family members who have already been involved in an intervention.

Trust the Professional(s)

Intervention counselors should have reassuring answers to most of these concerns. If the one you employ doesn't, get somebody else. Trained professionals will have strategies for getting the C.D. person to come to the meeting. They will know how to arrange the room, seat the people, engender a willingness on the part of the C.D. person to listen, determine the sequence in which statements are presented, handle objections raised by the C.D., prevent or deal with violence, and so on. Find a good intervention counselor and then trust the one you find.

What If He Won't Come to the Meeting?

He always does, but just about everyone preparing for an intervention worries about this possibility. A proven approach is as follows: Identify the person within the intervention group who has the most positive or least antagonistic relationship with the C.D.

person. Have that designated messenger call the C.D. person and issue an invitation that sounds something like, "I need to talk to you about matters involving you that concern the entire family. Would you please meet with me at (intervention location/ date/ time)?" If the C.D. person asks for details, the messenger remains vague but does not lie. The response might be: "It's a confidential matter that I'd rather not discuss on the phone, but it is something very important and I really need your participation. Please come!" Of course, the C.D. person will suspect something is up, especially if many of those concerned have recently accelerated and strengthened their mini-intervention attempts. And that's O.K. It is not necessary for the intervention to come as a total surprise in order to be effective. What those who have been intervened upon tell us later is that, yes, they knew something was going on but realized it would be difficult to avoid the meeting. Besides, they were curious and, in addition, felt confident of being able to handle whatever it was all about. After all, they had been manipulating and controlling this bunch for years. Why should this be any different?

What If He Flees?

Won't the C.D. person turn around and leave when he sees the concerned group? It's only happened to us twice. Once the C.D. person walked out and went into treatment on his own a few days later. Another time we went after the person and convinced her to return. However, to head off this contingency, we now designate someone in the group to go after the C.D. person should he attempt to leave. The person explains that this is a gathering of people who love him and simply want to discuss some matters of concern. Having such a contingency plan is reassuring to those involved, but here is no absolute guarantee that the C.D. person will return and listen.

Phase Three: The Intervention Phase

This Is It!

This is the actual meeting with the C.D. person at which the statements are read and help is offered. If the C.D. person accepts, he is taken directly from the intervention site to the treatment facility where arrangements have been made. Here is what it is like.

Typical Intervention Scene

The C.D. person is escorted into the room. The concerned persons are seated in a loose circle, with empty seats available for the C.D. person and the escort. Everybody is scared stiff, including any rational intervention counselor. As they enter the circle, a respected member of the group, who may be the escort, introduces the C.D. person to the intervention counselor, who shows the C.D. person a prearranged seat.

As the escort takes a seat, he or she closes the circle, thus psychologically bringing the C.D. person into the group and symbolically but not physically blocking his exit. The C.D. person looks surprised and usually snaps an angry comment such as, "What's this all about?" The lead intervention counselor responds with a preamble sounding something like this: "Hello, Charlie (or Shirley or whoever). My name is John O'Neill. This is my associate (if there is one). We work with families, and your family and friends came to us a while back because they were concerned about things that were happening in their lives that involve you. Our suggestion was to write down those concerns on a piece of paper so they can express them precisely and with love. They've done that, and so I'd like to ask that you listen to what they have to say. Then you can respond however you see fit. Would you be willing to listen to what they have to say?"

In the vast majority of cases the C.D. person agrees to listen, although sometimes with some snide remark for good measure. The counselor then points to the first intervener, who loudly, clearly, sincerely, and with feeling reads all of his or her statements. Anger is discouraged at the intervention. It should be temporarily put on hold to be dealt with later in treatment. But expressing all other feelings is strongly encouraged. There appears to be a correlation between the amount of tears shed and the impact of the statements. If the C.D. person starts to argue, the intervener stops reading. It takes two to argue, so everyone just remains silent. When the C.D. person quiets down, the intervener continues. One by one, each person reads all of his or her statements. In some cases, the C.D. person has argued with the first few statements, but realizing no one was willing to fight, sat back and listened. Occasionally, a C.D. person has tried to confront others in the group about their own drinking or drugging. We quickly reemphasized that the purpose of the gathering was to share concerns about him, the chemical use of others could be discussed at another time. Sooner or later one of the statements really hits hard emotionally. Perhaps it described a serious event during a blackout or an act that grossly violated his values. The statements of young children in particular often have a very powerful impact. Unless the C.D. person has lost the capacity to feel, this specific but nonjudgmental data will begin to evoke an emotional response. At first it may take a trained observer to discern the impact; a change in breathing rate, downward eye movements, dry-throated swallowing, but often these minimal reactions will build into tears and even sobbing. It is important not to rescue the C.D. person from his pain at this critical moment. Grant him the privilege of, at least on this occasion, paying the emotional price for his drinking or other drugging behavior. It is this pain that fuels the willingness to accept help, so let it work.

When all the participants have presented their statements, the intervention counselor will probably allow a brief period of silence to let the power of the moment run its course. Then he or she will close with a statement such as this: "(Name of C.D. person), your family and friends believe that none of the things they have told you about would have ever happened had it not been for alcohol (or other drugs). They have cared enough about you to learn more about how this chemical affects individuals and families. They know now that some people are so constituted genetically that, if they experiment very long with mood-altering chemicals, episodes of loss of control—such as have been described here—will occur. They also know now that this loss of control happened not because they were bad, stupid, or crazy but because they have an illness. Part of this illness is that those who have it can't see that they've got it. That's why they held this meeting—to tell you as lovingly as possible just how serious your situation has become and how much pain it is causing you and those who love you. They wanted you to see what they have seen. They have found a program here in town (or wherever) that treats this illness and have made reservations for you to enter that program. Would you accept that help?"

Where Do We Go From Here?

From here the intervention can go in several directions. In over half of those that we have facilitated, the C.D. person's response was a variation of "I had no idea things were so bad, that I was hurting so many people so much, and really didn't believe anybody still cared. What do you want me to do?" It is noteworthy that in most of these cases, the family of the C.D. person had predicted that the C.D. person would be angry and negative and refuse help. Many C.D. persons, of course, do not immediately leap at the opportunity for help. Very often the denial will still be extreme and quite vocal. That is why it is important to retain a counselor with the courage, maturity, and skills needed to deal with any emotional barrage from the C.D. person—be it anger, tears, or fears—and then calmly, one by one, put to rest the C.D. person's objections and arguments.

What If He Says No?

During the course of intervention training, the concerned persons will be asked to ponder the question: "What will you do if the C.D. person says no? Will you continue to enable as you have in the past? Are you going to seek or continue to participate in help for yourself? Are you going to set any limits as to how much, if any, drinking- or drugging-related behavior you will accept? Will a "no" affect your future dealings about sex, driving, socializing, or even the continuance of your relationship to him as parent, child, spouse, boss, friend, or neighbor?"

Each participant is asked to be prepared to "recontract" his relationship with the C.D. person if he turns down the offer of help. This step has seldom been necessary in our intervention work. But it has been a very important step for the concerned persons in order to remove the fear of a negative response. At the same time, this "recontracting" requirement helps the concerned persons become more aware of ways in which they are enabling and identifies behaviors they will no longer tolerate. The content of the recontracting statement must be based on what you honestly will or will not do. The counselor can suggest options, but only you can decide. Avoid empty threats. You have probably been threatening throughout this disease and taken no follow-up action. As a consequence, you may have become unbelievable. Now is the time to say what you mean and mean what you say. Here are some examples:

"Mom, Dad says I don't have to ride in the car with you from school when you've been drinking. I'll have my teacher call a cab for me. And if she asks why, I'll tell her the truth."

"Son, if you can't find it in your heart to accept the help offered, I want you to move out of the house before this weekend. There will be no more money. You are on your own. Remember we love you and the help is always there."

"Honey, I'm sorry you won't go to treatment. I intend to get the help that I need to recover from the way your disease has harmed me. From now on I will not call the boss and make excuses for you. If you don't do the chores around the house, they will be left undone. And I insist that there be no physical contact between us when you are under the influence."

"Since you will not accept help, I am leaving with the children and filing for divorce."

Remember, these recontracting statements will rarely if ever have to be employed. But it is important that each participant answer for himself or herself this question: "What will I do if he says no?"

Family Power or Professional Skill?

Most of the interventions we have facilitated required a good deal of adroitly managed dialogue between us and the C.D. person to finally gain his willingness to accept treatment. The skill here is for the counselor to convert the C.D. person's objections and denials into questions to be answered or issues to be discussed rather than differences to be argued about. Under such circumstances, it may seem that the counselor "talked" the C.D. person into treatment. Such is not exactly the case. What does happen is that the emotion-charged presentation of the concerned group's statements and the outpouring of love create an atmosphere in which such persuasions become possible. This mix of concerned-person power and counselor skills merges into the magic that makes this kind of intervention so often successful.

Will It Work?

Emphatically yes! The odds are favorably high provided proven methods are followed. If your counselor is competent, if all the significant others in the C.D. person's life participate, if each of them is properly trained and prepared, if the statements they present are specific and powerful yet packaged in love and concern, and if the help options offered can be accepted with dignity, then there is more than an 80 percent probability that the C.D. person will agree to the help suggested. More importantly, when the above conditions are present, the system of family, friends, and co-workers surrounding the C.D. person has changed in many positive ways. The C.D. person will have to make changes to fit into this healthier system. This is another reason for saying that intervention is a process and not an event. The C.D. person may refuse help in the immediate moment of the intervention. But if those who love him have gotten help for their own co-dependency, broken the no-talk rules, and stopped the enabling, then the process keeps pressuring the C.D. person to see what's really happening and eventually opt for help.

The "What If" Commitment

Not to be confused with the "what if" concerns discussed earlier, the "what if" commitment is a last-ditch effort to achieve some positive results when the C.D. person adamantly refuses treatment. The C.D. person may take the position that "Yes, there is a problem, but I can handle it—I'll quit drinking/drugging on my own (or with the help of A.A., N.A., or other self-help programs)." The intervention counselor will, of course, try to show him how difficult it is to quit without help and even may advise against withdrawal from alcohol or other drugs without close medical supervision. But when every effort to coax the C.D. person into accepting treatment fails and it seems fruitless to go on, the counselor will close out the proceedings by saying something like the following: "I know you mean what you say about quitting (or cutting back), but most people who have experienced the kind of consequences of their drinking/drugging that have been described here find it impossible to return to controlled use or to quit without help." To which the C.D. person will predictably reply, "Well, I know that I can!" At which time the counselor will counter with, "What if you can't? Would you then accept treatment?" The idea is to get the C.D. person to agree that, if he cannot quit on his own, he will immediately enter treatment. Because the C.D. person is so sure that he can stop, he will usually agree. The counselor will then attempt to reinforce and elevate the strength of the commitment: "So you are making this commitment to your family and friends—that if you return to (or can't control) your drinking/drugging, you give your solemn word to immediately enter treatment. Is that correct?" The idea here is to effect another intervention in advance. If the C.D. person does experience further problems—and without a recovery program they just about always do—those who participated in the intervention remind him of his promise and hold him to it.

When the Attempt Fails

Sometimes there is not a happy ending. Usually when the C.D. person's feeling life, or affect as the psychologists call it, is shut down. Touching the pain is what powers the concerned-person intervention. When he can't get in touch with his own pain or the pain suffered by others, what is said has little impact. We recall the case of a five-year-old in tears climbing onto the lap of her father and begging him to "go get well at the hospital" and receiving not a twinge of emotional response. Even when such letdowns occur, it's not the end of the world. Whatever happens it is certainly the beginning of a new life. No more no-talk rules or pretending everything is alright or accepting the unacceptable. You're getting the help to recover, whatever the C.D. person chooses to do. And it isn't over. This is a process and not just a single event. The forces set loose at the intervention will continue to put pressure on the C.D. person to accept help. The ball is now in his court to stay. Even when intervention doesn't work—it sticks...it keeps working.

Loose Ends

Although chemical dependency is a universal disease, it unfolds uniquely in each victim's family. So, too, each intervention will have its own special challenges that may demand innovation and improvisation to overcome. In addition to the two more common outcomes just described, there are infinite variations: the C.D. person might agree to go if someone else in the group who also has a problem will enter treatment as well. (That happened to us once.) Some of the supposed "concerned persons" may turn out to be selling drugs to the C.D. person. (That has happened a couple of times.) The C.D. person whom everyone described as a pussycat will become violently angry, while another, thought to be awesomely threatening, will break down in tears and leap for the help offered. (Those kinds of unexpected reactions happen frequently.) One of the interveners who never shows emotion will break down, and this will have a profoundly penetrating effect on the C.D. person's delusion. (This is also a frequent occurrence, usually involving either a very tough guy or a child who never felt safe enough before to really speak of his or her pain.) C.D. persons have interrupted part way through the gathering and agreed to accept help. Others have refused vigorously, become very angry, and stayed that way for several days following, spouting all manner of windy threats, and then quietly entered the recommended treatment center unassisted.

In summary, the concerned group intervention process is highly effective when the group is properly educated and prepared and the counselor is experienced and skilled. Each effort is unique and exciting with potential for both failure and joy. But none of them we have observed has ever failed to produce more positive results than negative consequences. At the very least, the intervention experience gives the concerned persons a taste of wellness and from that there is no turning back.

Intervening on Other Problems

We are frequently asked about the use of the concerned group approach for other kinds of problems, such as overeating, compulsive gambling, or workaholism. Our knowledge and experience is with chemical dependency. We do know of cases, however, where this approach has been employed successfully to motivate into help those suffering from other kinds of compulsive behaviors. Our suggestion in these cases would be to get professional assistance from someone who has experience using this type of intervention and who also possesses a background in dealing with the particular problem involved.

Follow-Through

There are some steps that should be taken after an intervention attempt to be certain no unfinished business remains. First, if the attempt is successful, the written intervention statements should be saved for possible use in treatment. Either the intervention counselor or one of the interveners should collect them, have the authors write on them that they give permission for the statements to be read again during the treatment process, and inform the treatment center intake staff that an intervention did take place and that the statements were preserved. The data contained therein can be very useful if the C.D. person remains in a state of heavy denial after program entry, a not-uncommon occurrence. Secondly, the concerned persons should gather with the counselor for a "de-briefing." In this meeting participants are encouraged to discuss any questions about upcoming family treatment or any issues left over from the intervention. This is also a chance to process any unresolved feelings experienced as a result of their involvement: fear; anger toward the C.D. person, the counselor, or other participants; joy, relief, or the freedom to feel out loud and reestablish emotional equilibrium. Thirdly, each concerned person needs to recommit to pursue his or her own recovery from co-dependency regardless of the treatment outcome of the C.D. person. And, finally, we recommend that participants take especially good care of themselves physically for a few days following the intervention. This is a very emotionally and physically draining endeavor. It's a good idea to be kind to yourselves—after all, you deserve it. You may have just saved someone's life.

It Always Makes Things Better

Absolute statements—"always," "never," "without a doubt," "every," etc.—are words and phrases that can be argumentative and polarizing. This is especially true when discussing problems as emotion-packed as chemical dependency and co-dependency. So it is with some forethought that we head this paragraph "It Always Makes Things Better." Yet properly conducted intervention preparation is a process that usually stops the enabling, gets some of the concerned persons into help for their co-dependency, and moves family dynamics in a positive direction. This means that, even if the C.D. person initially refuses help, the system in which it was O.K. for him to drink, drug, and behave in inappropriate ways no longer exists. Thus, intervention *always* makes things better, even if the C.D. reacts negatively. There is another important dynamic operating as well. As shown earlier in the discussion of co-dependency, when someone in a family develops a negative condition such as C.D., the rest of the family take on negative survival roles to keep the family system in balance. But this works in the other direction, too. When some of the family members begin to recover from co-dependency, the others—including the C.D. person—must change to accommodate this new wellness. So it is accurate to say that a properly orchestrated intervention effort is *always* successful.

Intervention—A Wrap-Up

Intervention, be it crisis-based, one-on-one, or the concerned group approach, is simply an effort to love the person behind the disease enough to help him see what he is unable to see. All intervention attempts involve concern, specific data, and the offering of help options the C.D. person can accept with dignity. Each type of intervention works best if the statements used are concise, specific, and nonjudgmental. When the interveners are properly trained and prepared, the effort is neither conspiratorial, judgmental, or antagonistic. Rather, it is a genuine act of love, based on well-proven methods and carried out with respect. In some ways, intervention is to chemical dependency as CPR is to cardiovascular disease—an emergency lifesaving procedure but one best conducted by those properly trained and prepared.

Part Three

Understanding
the Problem

9

The Chemical Love Affair

The Deadly Romance

How could someone we love and respect become a slave to alcohol or other drugs? Just as relationships with a C.D. person are a compelling and painful love story, the tales told by victims of chemical dependency are sagas of agonizing love affairs. Recovered C.D. victims universally relate how they were strongly attracted, very early, to the "high" received from mood-altering chemicals. They seemed to quickly develop an especially deep, primitive love relationship with chemically induced euphoria. This special affinity sooner or later led them into orchestrating moods and solving problems with alcohol and drugs *instead of maturing emotionally and refining adult coping skills.* Under those circumstances, alcohol and/or drugs quickly became a "best friend." Other best friends, spouses, children, and co-workers found themselves isolated and even feeling inadequate and guilty because the C.D. person preferred alcohol and drugs to them.

The Eye of the Beholder

Recovered persons describe how alcohol and drugs began to take a paramount role in their lives. They were not *choosing to abuse.* On the contrary, they discovered that they could no longer keep promises to themselves about when, how much, and with what consequences they would drink or drug. It seemed that they had lost the ability to relate to chemically induced euphoria with any predictable consistency. More and more their behavior was influenced by the presence of the chemical. They found themselves doing things they didn't want to do and not doing things they knew they were supposed to do. Loss of control over alcohol and/ or other drugs occurred more frequently with more serious consequences. Their loved ones found themselves confused by this behavior, and they too began to feel powerless. Nothing seemed to help, no matter what they tried or how they reacted.

"I'll Take a Double"

C.D. people consistently report developing a tolerance for the chemical very early in their experience. This "hollow leg" phenomenon demanded an increase in dosage—gulping drinks, drinking doubles, drinking before going drinking, mixing booze and pot or booze and pills or cocaine and heroin —in order to continue to reach the same high. Because of this increasing tolerance, the C.D. person remained conscious longer, even though chemical levels in the brain were very high. Behavior under the influence of these high levels often became very bizarre, sometimes grossly violating his values. Family members and friends watched in disbelief and felt more powerless, guilty, and afraid.

They've Changed!

Chemical use at these higher dosages and its associated negative behavior hurt. It caused the C.D. person a great deal of emotional pain—shame, guilt, fear, remorse, self-directed anger, loneliness, and self-hatred. This reservoir of pain grew and began to influence the C.D. person's attitude toward himself, life, and of course those around him. Pain made the world seem a negative place and the people in it very threatening. In order to deal with this pain, the C.D. victim developed an array of defensive behaviors: blame, denial, hostility, aggression, charm, overachievement, withdrawal. These defenses worked temporarily to get people off his back but caused long-term problems in relationships. By now, those who cared about the C.D. person were probably at the receiving end of a great deal of unpredictable and unacceptable behavior. Thus the C.D. person began to drive away those who cared the most. He seemed to have changed into a different person. In fact, what had really taken place is that he had literally *become* his defenses.

And They Lied!

It's still not very acceptable to be a drunk or a drug addict in our society. And most C.D. people know that deep down inside they are good, intelligent, sane people. They couldn't possibly be alcoholics or addicts. After all, folklore had taught them all their lives that persons like themselves don't get that way. As a consequence, they lied to themselves and others to protect their own self-worth. The C.D. persons reported how they minimized, excused, and alibied away their unacceptable drinking and drugging behavior to maintain a level of self-esteem. Either it wasn't as bad as others said, there was a perfectly good explanation, or it would be different next time. This rationalization was simply a knee-jerk psychological reaction on the part of the C.D. persons to protect their own self-image, much in the way people will lie to themselves about baldness, wrinkles, and weight gain. Only the consequences of this self-deceit involved more than vanity; it could have been deadly.

Stuffing

It hurts to mess up, to violate one's own rules of behavior, to break promises to oneself. Yet that is exactly what the C.D. persons said they did over and over in the pursuit of a fatal love affair with chemical euphoria. To escape this emotional pain, the C.D. persons learned to repress unpleasant memories of unacceptable alcohol-and/or drug-related behavior. By quickly stuffing these painful memories in the deeper, less accessible areas of the memory, the C.D. persons were able to escape the shame, guilt, and remorse that closer examination would bring. Unfortunately, this repression deprived the C.D. persons of data that could have helped them see the severity of their condition, and widened the gap between what they remembered versus what those around them actually saw.

Blackouts

As though trying to contribute to this delusion, the chemical itself often caused a form of temporary amnesia called a blackout. In a blackout, the C.D. persons were able to retrieve the memory data necessary to function in the here and now: how to write a check, drive a car, fly an airplane, or even remove a brain tumor. But they temporarily stopped storing long-term memories. There are documented cases of airline pilots not remembering flights and surgeons not recalling operations. Sometimes the blacked-out C.D. persons appeared intoxicated, but on other occasions they may have had enough eyedrops in their eyes, mouthwash on their breath, caffeine in their system, antacids in their stomach, and booze or drugs in their blood to appear and act sober. Yet they were not storing long-term memory data.

One frightening aspect of blackouts is that C.D. persons may not behave in accordance with their values while blacked out. We have seen estimates asserting that over half of the inmates in

United States prisons report not remembering the crime that put them there.

It Was Great!

The irony of the memory breakdowns that deluded the C.D. persons is that, while rationalization, repression, and blackouts prevented them from recalling many drinking- or drugging-related events, they vividly remembered how good they felt. Vernon E. Johnson, founder of the renowned Johnson Institute in Minneapolis, terms this phenomenon "euphoric recall." Apparently human memory of events takes place in the higher, or cognitive, part of our brain, an area that alcohol and drugs tend to inactivate in the early stages of intoxication. But because the deeper-feeling parts of our brain take longer to "short out" by chemicals, the C.D. persons experienced intense recollections of their chemical euphoria. The net result is that they minimized, alibied, excused, twisted, distorted, repressed, and sometimes completely forgot many of their embarrassing behaviors while clearly remembering the euphoria. Meanwhile, friends and family watched in horror and clearly recalled the staggering, word-slurring, emotional abuse, foolhardy risks, insults, or erratic driving that may have actually occurred.

Delusion and Denial

These classic responses of rationalization to protect self-worth, repression to escape emotional consequences, and blackouts causing chemically induced memory losses, and the overriding memory of the euphoric payoff formed a thick wall of delusion surrounding the C.D. persons and blinded them to the impact on themselves and those they loved. This delusion was part of their pathology and the reason few victims spontaneously recover. It may have happened, but you don't often hear of an alcoholic getting up one morning and saying, "I realize I have a problem and have been acting in defensive and bizarre ways, so I think I'll go to an A.A. meeting and get some help." This rarely occurs, because the C.D. person is thoroughly but sincerely deluded.

Put It All Together

That's the story related by one recovered C.D. after another. The circumstances, melodramas and predicaments may vary, but the basic tale can be summarized as follows: A special attraction to the chemical high, followed by a growing tolerance for the chemical, led C.D.-prone persons to loss of control over its use.

This inability to consistently predict the consequences once they drank or drugged led to repeated incidents of conduct under the influence which violated their own value systems. Such unacceptable conduct, incidentally, may have been passive rather than active—not doing the things expected of them as spouses, children, employees, students, or friends. This kind of behavior caused an increasing level of emotional pain. To ease this pain, the C.D. persons took on an array of defensive behaviors. Because it was not O.K. to get this disease, they lied to themselves in order to shore up their weakening self-worth. Then a series of memory breakdowns and quirks combined to surround the whole process in a seemingly impenetrable wall of delusion. And thus we have, in the words of Vernon Johnson, "a primary, progressive, chronic, and terminal disease." It is primary because it must be treated first before any other problems—legal, marital, financial, health, family, or professional—can be dealt with permanently; progressive because all the symptoms described almost always get worse and seldom get better unless intervened upon from the outside; chronic because there is no specific cure, only the means to arrest it; and, finally, fatal because people die from this malady by the thousands.

How Bad Is It?

Chemical dependency is usually acknowledged to be the nation's number three health problem after heart disease and cancer. But if we consider the number of deaths due to alcohol- and drug-related accidents, suicides, family violence, and crime, the problem becomes even more serious. Then suppose we add the number of death certificates which, out of supposed kindness toward the family, state some other "natural" cause instead of chronic alcoholism or drug addiction. And what about including the cancer deaths related to the heavy smoking associated with alcohol and drug use? And then there is the fact that C.D. people are seldom concerned with physical fitness or nutrition and probably experience an inordinate share of early cardiovascular-related deaths. We could go on, but isn't this enough to suggest that C.D. may, in fact, be the greatest cause of premature death in this country? *This is a fatal disease.*

Beyond Controversy

So we are dealing with life-or-death matters. Far too often this disease has a tragic and unnecessary fatal conclusion. Even when physical death is deferred, spiritual death occurs—in the sense that the victim stops pursuing his true potential and fails to achieve once-important dreams, goals, and aspirations. We therefore suggest that—because the very life of a loved one may be at stake—intellectual controversy or extended dialogue about the causes of this condition is a luxury ill afforded.

The fact is that millions of recovered C.D. people could tell the tale we just related. The vast majority of them were obviously otherwise good, intelligent, sane people. They simply could not relate to alcohol or other drugs in any consistently positive way. When those who loved them found the courage to take the critical actions described earlier in this book, intervention and treatment was usually successful. But when nothing happened "from the outside" to interrupt the progress of the disease, spiritual and often physical death was the result.

The next chapter will cover some of the contemporary thought about why people get hooked on alcohol and drugs in the way just described. Some discussion of causes seems to be a necessary step for those trying to cope with C.D. But, as we ponder the reasons why, it's a good idea to keep in mind that this is not just a behavioral or social problem we are facing—it is an often fatal disease.

10

A Respected Consensus

Through the Information Barrier

What causes some people who use alcohol or other drugs to develop the chemical love affair while others escape? The answer is buried in a mass of clouded, confused, and controversial scientific opinion. And the picture is further muddied by the incredible amount of folklore on the subject. Everyone has an opinion, even though most of the information is out of date and gets in the way of rather than aids recovery. Not only is much of our traditional information inaccurate, but there is a great deal of misunderstanding among professionals about the disease as well.

Controversy about C.D.—its causes and treatment—abounds. Intellectualizing can delay action while accomplishing little. Wanting to understand can be tempting because it is easier and less risky to read, think, and talk about the problem than to do something about it. It is not necessary to be an in-depth expert about C.D. in order to intervene upon it. More than likely you have already discovered that this disease cannot be outsmarted. Nor can you reason with the C.D. person about his condition or educate yourself over its impact. In all kinds of ways, chemical dependency is a disease responding much better to common-sense action than high-blown theories. Consequently, this chapter is near the back of the book and presents only a brief overview of basics about the nature of C.D. Our limited purpose is to provide enough information to counter obsolete ideas, understand the major components of the disease, and recognize quality help. But we encourage you to put minimal energy into trying to figure it out and concentrate on actions leading to recovery.

The Consensus

The research picture is now clear enough to know with certainty which beliefs are helping people recover and which are not. Here is one that works. The official program of the 1987 International Congress for Alcoholism and Drug Abuse Counselors held in London stated as its purpose:

> To underscore the basic truth that alcoholism and other drug addictions are biogenetic medical/physical primary diseases that are diagnosable and highly responsive to treatment delivered by trained multidisciplinary specialists in a primary disease, non-drug, 12-step compatible and abstinence-based recovery treatment program.

Such a statement sums up quite well the present mainstream thinking about C.D.: that it is a diagnosable and treatable disease, pure and simple. Since this gathering is attended by the professionals who treat the disease day in and day out around the world, the statement also endorses just which intervention and treatment approaches are achieving success. Our personal belief is that sometime in the future someone will walk off a stage with a Nobel Prize for proving the above description of C.D. to be scientific fact.

An Official Definition

The following is the current definition of alcoholism as approved by the boards of directors of The National Council on Alcoholism and Drug Dependence (February 3, 1990) and of the American Society of Addiction Medicine (February 25, 1990).

Definition of Alcoholism

Alcoholism is a **primary**, chronic **disease** with genetic, psychosocial, and environmental factors influencing its development and manifestations. **The disease is often progressive and fatal**. It is characterized by continuous or periodic: **impaired control** over drinking, **preoccupation** with the drug alcohol, use of alcohol despite **adverse consequences**, and distortions in thinking, mostly notably **denial**.

- **Primary** refers to the nature of alcoholism as a disease entity in addition to and separate from other pathophysiologic states which may be associated with it. "Primary" suggests that alcoholism, as an addiction, is not a symptom of an underlying disease state.

- **Disease** means an involuntary disability. It represents the sum of the abnormal phenomena displayed by a group of individuals. These phenomena are associated with a specified common set of characteristics by which these individuals differ from the norm, and which places them at a disadvantage.

- Often **progressive** and **fatal** means that the disease persists over time and that physical, emotional, and social changes are often cumulative and may progress as drinking continues. Alcoholism causes premature death through overdose, organic complications involving the brain, liver, heart and many other organs, and by contributing to suicide, homocide, motor vehicle crashes, and other traumatic events.

- **Impaired control** means that the inability to limit alcohol use or to consistently limit on any drinking occasion the duration of the episode, the quantity consumed, and/or the behavorial consequences of drinking.

- **Preoccupation** in association with alcohol use indicates excessive, focused attention given to the drug, its effects, and/or its use. The relative value thus assigned to alcohol by the individual often leads to a diversion of energies away from important life concerns.

- **Adverse consequences** are alcohol-related problems or impairments in such areas as: physical health (e.g., alcohol withdrawal syndromes, liver disease, gastritis, anemia, neurological disorders); psychological, functioning (e.g., impairments in cognition, changes in mood and behavior); interpersonal functioning (e.g., marital problems and child abuse, impaired social relationships); occupational functioning (e.g., scholastic or job problems); and legal, financial, or spiritual problems.

- **Denial** is used not only in the psychoanalytic sense of a single psychological defense mechanism disavowing the significance of events, but more broadly to include a range of psychological maneuvers designed to reduce awareness of the fact that alcohol use is the cause of an individual's problems rather than a solution to those problems. Denial becomes an integral part of the disease and a major obstacle to recovery.

It seems clear that regardless of the ongoing debate, as a practical matter the notion that C.D. is a bona fide disease with a strong genetic component is widely accepted and dominates treatment approaches, insurance coverages, and the laws of the land. *Medical and scientific opinion is not divided on the basic concept that C.D. is a disease process in every sense of the word.* The fact that C.D. is a pathology is no longer questioned by specialists in field or those current in their understanding of the research, although there is continuing research and scientific debate about the specific biochemistry.

Why the Controversy?

Why don't we have clear public consensus on this issue of so much importance to many Americans? There appear to be four major reasons for the continued existence of official confusion, denial, hesitancy, and controversy:

1. Low research priorities

2. The emotional impact of the disease on many of those from whom we might ordinarily expect answers

3. The confusion caused by headline-seeking dissenters

4. The conflicts brought on by our own alcohol and drug experience

Research

Part of this national delusion and conflicting dialogue can be blamed on lack of long-term research. As a nation we spend a billion dollars a year on cancer research and half a billion on heart investigation, both deserving efforts, but only 200 million looking into alcoholism, about the same as dental research. And it is not gum disease that is bloodying our streets and highways. Thus, as in most complex but underresearched diseases, there is no single study at which to point that proves the cause(s) and cure(s) of chemical dependency.

Emotional Impact

The research, prevention, and treatment arena is often charged with emotion because many scientists, physicians, psychologists, politicians, educators, and other such influential persons have been personally impacted by living with a victim of C.D. Consequently, studies of C.D. that support the notion of an inherited disease process sometimes fall not just on deaf ears but on powerful prejudices and ragged emotions as well. Respected researchers have more difficulty getting papers and studies on the subject of chemical dependency published in professional journals than on other health care subjects. This is most likely because chemical dependency is seldom just an academic issue. Very few people receive new information about this disease with scholarly objectivity.

Contrast

Consider this: A few years ago, when physicians, politicians, science writers, and newspaper editors picked up research that posed a then tenuous link between dietary cholesterol and heart disease, they were quick to accept and anxious to spread the news to their patients, constituents, or readers. They responded likewise a little later, when a connection between lack of fiber in the diet and certain cancers was first suspected. As a result, these ideas have become part of our popular medical folklore in less than one generation. This conversion has occurred in spite of the fact that there was, and to some extent still is, controversy about the studies that produced these conclusions. Yet research at least equal in scope and validity that points toward C.D. as a genetically transmitted biochemical disease meets awesome resistance. Why? It's as though each disease had the same size wagonload of scientific proof. Yet, when the wagons are pushed up the hill of public resistance, the C.D. wagon keeps rolling back down.

Invisible Barriers

Part of the reason lies in the fact that at least 25 percent of those physicians, scientists, politicians, writers, and newspaper editors (and we might add computer programmers, bus drivers, bricklayers, mechanics, clerks, etc.) who make official pronouncements or generate new folklore are suffering from the effects of living with a C.D. person. They can no more be objective about C.D. than they could be indifferent to a horse that repeatedly kicks them. So an invisible barrier of pain and prejudice seems to block and distort efforts to gain professional and public acceptance of new information. Add to that the fact that perhaps 85 percent of the C.D. victims are in denial and not advocating for causes and cures, while nearly all of the victims of cancer, AIDS, heart disease, etc., are clamoring for more research.

Headline Seekers

Another element in the confusion about C.D. stems from economics. Dissenters from the mainstream make money. For researchers or writers in the human behavior field, the fastest way to get squeezed between the sports scores and the obituaries is to restate that alcoholism and other chemical dependencies are treatable diseases and that the treatment must be based on total abstinence. But to make minor headlines, just claim to have taught a handful of "alcoholics" how to be social drinkers again. Controversy sells! Certainly the writings of the respected researchers and pioneers in this field do get published. However, adding more proof to an existing precept doesn't make for best sellers. On the other hand, articles based on one or another of these "cures" or controversial notions about C.D. sell, and since authors seldom work in the mainstream of C.D. research or treatment, their theories don't have to pass the scrutiny of informed peers. So these "You too can learn to drink safely" notions fall upon an eager audience.

For just about every chemically dependent person wants to hear that there is an easy cure or, better yet, a way to regain control. And what family member or friend of a C.D. person wouldn't like to believe that all the C.D. person has to do is learn to control his drinking. Or that the right combination of vitamins and exercise will cure the problem. In magazine articles and talk show appearances, professional guests from medicine, psychiatry, psychology, and science who are neither expert nor experienced or respected in the C.D. field will sometimes talk of C.D. as secondary to childhood rearing, depression, schizophrenia, homosexuality, excess heterosexuality, vitamin deficiency, Vietnam battle experiences—and the list goes on and on.

Some talk of alcoholics returning to controlled social drinking by way of behavior modification techniques or of drug addicts responding to treatment by another drug. Others claim success employing techniques tested and discarded years ago as ineffective by the respected treatment programs. Sadly, these behavior modification, nutritional, physical fitness, or other easier, softer remedies contribute to the false assumption that there is a solution for C.D. based on ways other than total abstinence and major life changes. Worse yet, they perpetuate those harmful myths in our society.

All of this flies in the face of what surely must be the largest and most ineffective folk medicine experiment ever conducted: trying to control chemical dependencies by means other than abstinence. Millions have tried it, and it simply doesn't work often enough to be considered as a valid alternative. The whole idea is illogical—trying to control loss of control by controlling it. To the credit of the broadcast industry and the responsible periodicals, we do occasionally hear and read from the real authorities in the intervention and treatment field; respected M.D.'s, clergy, and innovative therapists. Their experience and track records make them worthy of attention in better understanding this disease. But be warned, the confusion caused by come-lately headline seekers and pop psychologists can be disconcerting and, more importantly, can cause delays. Our advice is to trust the veteran treatment professionals who can point to real-life families who have recovered as a result of their work. As the back country Hunter said to his bragging associate, "Show me your coon-skins!"

Why Not Controlled Drinking?

The most frequent excursion of the controversy peddlers is the notion of teaching alcoholics to again be social drinkers. Their argument usually goes something like this: By labeling alcoholism as a disease and making abstinence the only acceptable treatment outcome, the door is closed on efforts to develop therapies aimed at controlled drinking. They then cite controversial studies supposedly proving that at least a small percentage of alcoholics can be taught how to return to normal drinking. Now, the validity of these studies can be argued for days. But doing so misses the point: *Why would society want to consider the ability to drink or drug normally as an important life skill, let alone a desired therapeutic outcome?* There is not a single positive human activity that can be performed better under the influence of mood-altering substances. We've known a couple of authors who insisted they could create only while under the influence. But after treatment they admitted that not only were they as creative now but they also meet their deadlines. There are literally millions of recovered and abstaining C.D. persons whose lives bear testimony to the preferability of a chemical-free lifestyle. They can sing, dance, tell jokes, be creative, make love, act spontaneously, and be happy, joyous, and free without the aid of chemicals.

All mood-alterers are physically toxic and cause the user to temporarily become something other than his authentic self. Alcohol, in particular, has an entrenched role in many of our cultural rituals that we are not trying to challenge. *What we emphatically attack, however, is the idea that there is any legitimate clinical need to attempt to restore mastery of these substances in someone whose life has once been severely disrupted by their use.* If asparagus or sweet potatoes or oysters cause problems in people's lives, they simply quit eating them and go about their business. To our knowledge, the concept of controlled drinking as a treatment outcome for diagnosed alcoholics has never been seriously proposed by any respected professional with extensive experience in the treatment of chemical dependency. So our suggestion is, in your personal war on drugs, stay away from the armchair generals and get your advice from the combat veterans. We are not suggesting canceling the first amendment. But the time-worn advice "Keep it simple and insist on proof" is still valid.

Our Own Experience

A major component in our national reluctance to deal with C.D. as the disease it is stems from our own life experiences with alcohol and drugs. Most of us have experimented with at least alcohol and perhaps other prescribed or even illegal drugs. Many of us even abused those chemicals while at college, in the service, away for the summer, or at other times. We quickly learned that abusing booze and other drugs led to physical, behavioral, and emotional consequences. Normal people will not pay that price for a chemical high, so they modified their use with willpower and reason. Since they could do that, it seemed quite logical that others could as well.

When observing someone who can't control his chemical use, it *seems* that C.D. is a behavioral issue or, at best, secondary to some other problem in the victim's life. These conclusions are simple, logical, and dead wrong. Yet, sadly, some of those who cling to these beliefs are the very professionals who are supposed to be making objective judgments about other people's loss of control. Avoiding professionals with such a belief is crucial when you look for help.

The Dilemma

There is so much prejudice, emotional reaction, and misleading information that chemical dependency will most likely not be universally recognized as a treatable disease until there is not just sufficient but also overwhelming scientific evidence to support that contention. But low national priority, limited budgets, and emotions within the scientific community, combined with the conflicting messages from our own alcohol/drug use, are delaying much needed research and discounting the value of the work already done. For all these reasons our folklore clings, with awesome stubbornness, to the idea that C.D. occurs in people because of underlying lack of willpower, ignorance, or mental illness—in spite of the fact that common sense and experience show otherwise.

Common Sense to the Rescue—Sort of

Common sense, backed by validated experience, can be a useful guide when there is conflicting scientific opinion on a subject. Now that we have given controversy its due, let's see what common sense tempered by the experience of others can tell us about understanding chemical dependency.

Are They Bad? Stupid? Crazy?

To begin with, it can be readily observed that our persistent myths continue to fill prisons, cemeteries, and mental institutions with good, intelligent, sane yet chemically dependent people. As many as 85 percent of those in United States prisons are there for alcohol or other drug-related crimes. A state attorney general recently told us that every person executed in that state since the reinstatement of the death penalty had either been chemically dependent or been raised in a C.D. family. This is not to suggest that the gates of the prisons be opened and all the C.D. people released. In fact, part of the intervention process is convincing C.D. persons that they will be held accountable for their behavior under the influence, and many of these criminals are not chemically dependent but simply chose to abuse alcohol and drugs. What we are suggesting, however, is that the prisons, mental institutions, and cemeteries would be far less crowded if we, as a society, better understood how to prevent, recognize, intervene in, and treat this disease. It is obvious that people don't become chemically dependent because they are bad, because too many good people are afflicted. Look at President Ford's wife, Betty. We've met and talked to her, and she's one of the "goodest" women you'd ever want to meet. Yet she underwent treatment for alcohol and other drug dependency in 1978.

It is likewise clear that C.D. does not strike victims because they are stupid or ignorant. Physicians probably have the highest average l.Q. of any major profession. Their education also makes them very knowledgeable about how drugs affect the body, yet there are an estimated 22,000 alcoholic M.D.'s. It is certainly not because "they don't know better."

Another prevalent but erroneous notion is that C.D. people are just folks who have somehow been knocked off of their psychological horse and are just drinking in order to find the courage to get back in the saddle. Many psychiatrists, psychologists, and social workers practicing today were educated to believe—and still believe—the premise that people become chemically dependent because of some underlying psychiatric or emotional disorder. Such an idea is attractive because it implies that the cause of the drinking or drugging can be found and remedied, permitting a return to normal alcohol and/or other drug use. This persistent myth is appealing but doesn't hold up to the evidence. Most treatment programs administer psychological tests and do a psychiatric evaluation when a patient is admitted. The procedures used are well validated and, if administered to the population at large, will show that 10 to 15 percent of the people walking the streets are suffering from an emotional or psychiatric illness warranting treatment. But when these same tests are given, after detoxification, to those entering treatment for alcoholism or other forms of C.D., about the same percentage test psychologically abnormal, as in the population at large. A review of the current research literature on this subject of "dual diagnosis" or "co-morbidity" produces no consensus. What is generally believed, however, is that C.D. is not caused by underlying mental illness and therefore cannot be cured through the use of medications or therapies specific to such problems. In fact, even when there are secondary psychiatric problems, little can be done to help the mental illness until the primary disease of chemical dependency is arrested.

First Families—No Exception

President Reagan described his father's alcoholic drinking. As mentioned, former First Lady Betty Ford is a happily recovered victim of chemically dependency. Former president Jimmy Carter's brother Billy made headlines with his publicly scandalous alcoholic behavior. Unfortunately, his later recovery received far less publicity. Jacquelyn Kennedy's father and Eleanor Roosevelt's father both apparently drank alcoholically, and the list goes on. It does not seem that any of these First Family members were immoral, stupid, or mentally ill. They just found out in a very publicly visible fashion that their brain chemistry couldn't successfully deal with mood-alterers.

Even the Warriors Fell

Military history from Alexander the Great through Ulysses S. Grant and on into today is resplendent with men of extraordinary bravery, brilliance, and leadership who couldn't hold their liquor and nearly died trying. Look at lists of all-star team rosters, MVPs, hall of famers, literary prize winners, Academy Award winners, Medal of Honor recipients, famous painters and composers, and noted politicians. You will find a noteworthy share of courageous, tough, high-functioning, brilliant, morally sound people totally devastated by this disease. Even baronial American industrial dynasties like the Fords and Firestones have fallen victim as well. It seems that C.D. is a most democratic malady, striking anywhere the right genes have found residence without regard to power, intelligence, talent, wealth, ability, or strength of character.

Facts We Do Know

In spite of research deficiencies, much has been learned to improve our understanding of this malady.

- One study of 200 Harvard University graduates over a forty-five-year period demonstrated that the only common factor in the 13 percent who became alcoholic was a family history of alcoholism.

- Respected studies done in Scandinavia and the United States show that identical twin offspring of alcoholics have similar higher alcoholism rates.

- Adoption studies show that children separated from alcoholic parents and raised in non-alcoholic families retain their three to four times greater probability of becoming alcoholic, while children separated from non-alcoholic parents and raised in alcoholic families demonstrate no greater risk than if they had stayed in the non-alcoholic family.

- Certain ethnic groups like Scandinavians, Irish, and Native Americans have very high alcoholism rates, while others, such as Orientals, Arabs, and Jews, have very low rates. Studies among these high- and low-susceptibility groups imply that changes in the environment have little effect on C.D. rates. For example, when Japanese move from Tokyo to New York City, they don't grow to like or tolerate martinis any better.

- It has also been shown that a high percentage of male offspring of male alcoholics have certain distinctly different brain-wave patterns and may metabolize alcohol differently than normal children—from the very first drink. These same findings have now been found in daughters of alcoholics.

- At present there is a $25 million consortium involving six university research centers investigating the genetics of alcoholism. Tissue samples from 600 alcoholic family members are being analysed in a search for genetic clues. This bodes well for the real possibility of a test for genetic predisposition in the future.

Thus, the research tracks with the common-sense observation that alcoholism runs in certain ethnic groups and concentrates in certain families. All this points to a strong genetic component. Because of these many indications, it is quite true to say that most respected scientists in the C.D. field today believe that a primary contributing cause of C.D. to be an inherited predisposition in some people to interact with alcohol and other mood-alterers differently than "normal" people, and in a way that sooner or later leads to loss of control over the use of those substances. Certainly, this phenomenon has consistently been confirmed in tens and perhaps hundreds of thousands of persons who have been observed in treatment over the years. This "wrong way" of interacting with chemicals seems to lead these "prewired" ones to an instinctual rather than a cognitive relationship with alcohol and other drugs. That is, they seem to connect with the chemical at a deeper and more primitive level in the brain than normal people. Once that deeper connection is made, those prone to chemical dependency are no longer able to control their use of alcohol or other mood-alterers with willpower and reason.

At least five neurotransmitters in the brain are being studied as possible sites of this aberrant brain chemistry interaction with alcohol and other mood-altering chemicals. But whatever the precise locus in the brain may prove to be, the tragic life histories of millions of suffering people over tens of thousands of years support the fact that this loss of control is permanent. Once this condition occurs, the only way C.D. people are able to survive is to abstain from all mood-altering chemicals.

Other Factors

To be sure, this disease does not occur in isolation from social and historical context. Certainly legal advertising and illegal pushing, peer pressures, drug-abusing tendencies in our society, and the increased potency of today's street drugs all contribute to the growing numbers of people suffering from C.D. Nonetheless, the weight of studies, research, statistical data, scientific observation, actual cases, expert opinion, and common sense leaves little doubt that C.D. is a medical/biological dysfunction with a genetic component. It seems clear that some people have a special affinity for the effect of alcohol and other mood-alterers and that this evolves into a pathology—a pathology that meets the classic medical definition of a disease in every way. C.D. has an etiology, a classic list of specific symptoms, a progression, and a treatment. Look at enough cases and you cannot help but be convinced that it is not a moral issue, a condition caused by stupid choices, or the symptom of a psychological problem. *It is a disease.*

Much work is being done to unravel the precise neurochemistry of C.D. Medical treatments such as craving blockers, relapse prevention, and ways to repair organ damage are under development, but with our present state of understanding, the only way to treat this disease is through abstinence and major life changes. Clinical observation and follow-up of thousands of recovering C.D. persons shows that most needed therapeutic help to learn to live happily and productively without alcohol and/or other drugs. Family members are also powerfully affected emotionally and behaviorally by living with a C.D. person; they deserve and require help as well. Coming to believe these realities is fundamental to overcoming this disease in yourself or someone you care about.

11

Alcohol and Other Drugs Today

Good News!

Is your situation part of a worsening national alcohol and drug disaster? The media and the politicians would have us believe that it's chemical warfare out there, with the chemicals winning. Well, they aren't—and that's a fact! Certainly major challenges face the criminal justice system because of the crime and violence associated with the distribution and selling of illegal drugs. There is an urgent need to get a research, prevention, and law enforcement jump on the next round of "wonder drugs" that we didn't get on crack or cocaine. And it is true that almost half of us admit to knowing a cocaine addict and that one out of three Americans reports trying to deal with an alcohol problem in someone they love. So yes, there is little doubt that drinking and drugging is a significant national problem or that it's big business—some legal, some illegal. One beer company alone spends over half a billion dollars a year promoting its products. Nobody has any idea how much is spent "marketing" illicit drugs. To be sure, there is plenty of bad news. Yet there is much good news as well. In fact, now and then there should be a headline that reads "Alcohol and Drug Situation Improving" because it is.

Surprise Statistics

Abuse of all categories of drugs has decreased sharply since the epidemic levels of the 1970s. For example, the number of Americans who used cocaine was down from twelve million in 1985 to eight million in 1988. And the trend is continuing into the 90s. Current marijuana use among 12- to 17-year-olds is at the lowest level in ten years. A recent government-sponsored survey of high school seniors shows a marked change in attitudes toward drug use. Four out of five seniors are now convinced that frequent marijuana use poses "great risk". Seven out of ten feel that any cocaine use is dangerous. Over the last twelve years, consumption of wine in the United States went up very slightly, but beer has leveled off and distilled spirits—hard liquor—has gone down 25 percent. That's a major social change.

For all these reasons there is reason for guarded optimism in the prevention, intervention, and treatment of alcohol and drug dependencies. There is exciting, breakthrough research being done that improves our understanding. Powerful new family, workplace, and community intervention techniques are getting results. Excellent treatment programs and effective counseling are now available in just about every community. The cost of such care is coming

down. As a consequence, alcoholics and other chemically dependent people are now being intervened upon earlier, being treated
more effectively, and achieving long-term sobriety at a higher rate.
This success means less pain, grief, and expense for families,
friends, employers, the country—all of us. So, on balance, the news
is good.

The Stars Are Coming Out

Highly visible spheres of influence such as the armed forces,
the professional sports leagues, the motion picture and television
industry, and countless companies, large and small, have launched
aggressive prevention, intervention, and assistance programs. Betty
Ford, Elizabeth Taylor, and the host of other celebrities and athletes
who have bravely gone public with their C.D. treatment have sof-
tened much of the stigma. Their courageous revelations have given
permission and inspired others still suffering to seek help. Just seeing the media reports about these celebrity "coming out parties"
has caused many health professionals to rethink their role and update their knowledge and skill. The public now knows that this is
a disease that can strike anyone.

A condition many thought only existed in back alleys and
under bridges is now being recognized in the country clubs, board
rooms, churches, and kitchens of the nation. Because of this des-
tigmatization, more people are reaching out for help sooner. Thus,
consumer demand for quality care has put pressure on the health
service industry, and it has responded. At the same time, a multi-
tude of self-help groups, spinoffs from the model of the highly respected and long-successful Alcoholics Anonymous program, are
providing remarkably effective and absolutely free folk therapy for
the whole gamut of addictive/compulsive behaviors. All this is
part of a cultural shift away from negative drinking and drugging
lifestyles that were once admired but are beginning to be frowned
upon. So even though the adverse impact of alcohol and drugs is
still significant, it is accurate to say that times are hopeful because
use patterns are changing in positive ways and because enlightenment, encouragement, and help for alcohol and other drug problems are all around.

Illegal Drugs Are Scary

In spite of all this good news, when someone we love gets involved in the illegal drug scene, there is often a special sense of fear and bewilderment not experienced when the drug is alcohol. The situation is more frightening perhaps because there are so many unknowns. Alarms are intuitively triggered because you correctly sense that a higher percentage of those who do try these other drugs become addicted. Probably 80 percent of a population could use alcohol all of their lives without becoming alcoholic. Nearly anyone, however, who experiments for very long with the likes of cocaine, heroin, amphetamines, tranquilizers, or their analogs can become pathologically dependent. The research hints that just about everyone has "receptors" in the brain for these kinds of drugs. Thus, a good deal of the confusion about the drug scene derives from the fact that, although far more people use alcohol than all other mood-altering chemicals combined, only a relatively small percentage will become pathologically dependent or alcoholic.

On the other hand, far fewer people are using drugs other than alcohol, but a higher percentage become dependent. Then, too, in the past, except for legally prescribed mood-alterers, it's been tough and expensive to get "drugs." Illegal drugs had to penetrate the borders and defy law enforcement efforts before invading our cities. Or a physician had to be corrupted into writing illegal prescriptions. All those factors restricted availability and added to the risk and cost. But nowadays there are new generations of cheaper, more powerful, and sometimes even temporarily legal "designer" drugs being manufactured in garage and basement laboratories. And inhalant substances such as glue, paint, gasoline, and solvents are available through retail outlets selling them for their intended lawful purposes. For most people this all seems foreign and confusing.

It can be kept simple. If someone you love is messing up his or her life, it really matters little which drug is involved. Whether legal or illegal, drunk, snorted, shot up with a needle, or smoked in a pipe, all these substances wind up in the bloodstream. From there they are carried to the part of the brain that controls feelings, moods, and instincts. When the imprint takes place at a deeper and more primitive level than it does in "normal" people, a dependency develops. If the drug is alcohol, such dependency is called alcoholism. Other drug"isms" develop the same way.

No one yet knows how to reverse the process and enable those who have once lost control to regain it. Abstinence is the only way the alcoholic or otherwise chemically dependent person can keep from pulling the loss-of-control trigger on himself. In addition, once a person crosses the invisible line separating controlled use from the loss of control, there seems to be no turning back, *regardless of the chemical involved*. Literally millions of alcoholics over the centuries have found that they cannot safely use any other mood-alterer, either. The same cross-dependency phenomenon occurs in persons once addicted to cocaine, narcotics, tranquilizers, and so forth. From then on, chemical highs from any substance legal or illegal, including alcohol, seem to trigger loss of control as well.

Although the chemistry and pathology involved in this cross-dependency is still not entirely clear, the real-life consequences are quite obvious. There seems little doubt that, once the primitive brain falls in love with chemically induced euphoria, it can no longer consistently discriminate the source of that feeling. Or as an ex-drunk once said, "The cucumber has crossed an invisible line to picklehood and there is no turning back."

False Alarms

Because there is so much alarm about illegal drug abuse, many of us do tune out until it hits home. The media have emphasized heroin junkies and street gangs roaming the cities, young professionals snorting coke on the job, amphetamine-crazed truck drivers endangering the highways, and the school kids literally going to pot. There are shocking tales of pro ballplayers dropping dead in the prime of their youth, rock stars falling off concert stages in comas, and movie stars trying to bring carry-on bags full of illicit substances through customs. We are warned, at every turn, how this ever-more treacherous drug scene is an awesome threat to our homes, families, and respected ways of life. After a while, it is easy to tune out—to leave the problem to the police, the government, and the other war-on-drugs warriors.

A War Against the Wrong Enemy

The so-called war on drugs is an especially sensitive issue among those who battle this disease on a daily basis through prevention, intervention, and treatment. We certainly believe there is a drug crisis and that extraordinary measures are in order. But most of us, and we believe we can speak here for most in our profession, are convinced that the present goals and priorities miss the mark. Generally, the following criticisms are voiced:

1. Alcohol, the most used, abused, and costly drug, is seldom if ever mentioned in the war on drugs in spite of the fact that three hundred people a day die from alcohol, while five die from crack or cocaine. (Studies have also shown that many death certificates cover up links to alcoholism.)

2. Approximately 80 percent of the drugs are consumed by 20 percent of the users—those who have become dependent. Yet the funding emphasis is on interdiction and law enforcement instead of prevention, intervention, and treatment.

3. Potentially catastrophic realities are being ignored. For example, AIDS is rapidly shifting from a gay disease to an addict disease. (Nearly half of the IV drug users in New York and New Jersey now test HIV-positive.) It costs the health care system $400,000 to treat a terminally ill AIDS patient. That same addict could be intervened upon before he or she got to the needle-using stage and treated at the prestigious Betty Ford Center for less than $12,000. *Yet funding for treatment was cut by two-thirds during the Reagan-Bush-era war on drugs.*

4. Prevention programs continue to emphasize naive concepts, while placing little emphasis on the entry-level drug, alcohol, or helping young people to assess their biogenetic potential for C.D.

5. Research funding priorities are way out of line in relation to the severity of the problem.

Consider This Hypothesis

At any given time over the last three decades the number of persons willing to experiment with illegal drugs has remained relatively constant. An educated estimate would place that potential market at around fifty million people. Each succeeding generation was marketed by their contemporary crop of drug dealers with whatever the wonder drug of the time happened to be. Gradually, as the substance was exposed as toxic, addictive, and often deadly, the experimenters stop using it. So the customer base shrank to the small percentage (perhaps 15 to 20 percent) who had become dependent on that drug and couldn't quit. That's not enough to sustain an "industry," so the dealers moved on to other market niches and offered newer, more glamorous "products." Thus historically there were the hippies of the sixties and seventies with marijuana, the yuppies of the seventies and eighties with cocaine, and now the "yuckies" (young urban crack/cocaine kids) of the eighties and nineties.

Today's war on drugs is more sensational because of the enormous sums of money involved and the violent crime associated with the distribution system. Yet the basic dynamics involved are still the same: As the drug's harmful effects are integrated into street folklore, the experimenters wise up and quit, leaving only the tragic chemically dependent victims as consumers. Thus demand goes down. The accompanying drop in prices combined with modest gains in law enforcement drives the dealers temporarily out of business. And once again it appears that the current war on drugs is over and the good guys won. Then another generation grows into the market niche and from around the corner comes another "harmless, nonaddictive, no-side-effects pleasure potion" complete with new and even more vicious drug lords. And the battle begins anew.

The Numbers

A further look at some numbers may help clarify the order of battle in the war on drugs. As noted earlier, statistics about alcohol and drug use vary widely, are contested by differing factions, and are based on controversial definitions. Nonetheless, a conservative interpretation of the data shows that approximately 90 percent of Americans have tried alcohol, while only about 10 percent report having experimented with other drugs. According to an ABC News poll, 66 percent of those asked admit to frequent alcohol use, while only 4 percent own up to recurring illicit drug use. Now, as we said, those accosted on the street by pollsters inquiring about their illegal drug use might well be less than honest. Still, it's probably fair to say that the drunks far outnumber the dope fiends on Main Street. Perhaps more important is the fact that *at least one hundred and fifty thousand die annually from alcohol-related deaths* versus about four thousand from illicit drugs. There are probably no more than eight million "drug addicts" in the United States, while there may be more than twenty million alcoholics.

Why Focus on Alcohol?

More people use alcohol than other drugs, and more become dependent on alcohol than all other drugs combined. Alcohol causes far more crime and social problems. The damage caused by alcohol in the home, on the street, and in the workplace costs far more than that caused by other drugs. This is essentially true in all age groups, cultural niches, and geographical locations. So alcohol is our number one drug problem. *Alcohol is also the historical and traditional fountainhead of the folklore surrounding all other mood-altering drug use.* Belief that intoxication is a desirable state of affairs is an alcohol-based tradition. The notion that chemically altering your mood improves social intercourse emanates from alcohol history. The concept of relieving stress chemically is an alcohol heritage. The idea that joy and celebration are enhanced by mild—or not so mild—inebriation and all the rituals that go with it is an alcohol myth. And the message that says anybody can drink safely if they just use common sense and good judgment—if they are "responsible drinkers," as one whiskey ad urges—is the greatest alcohol myth of all.

What Can Be Done?

We are not trying to pour out anybody's sippin' whiskey. But the alcohol industry must be convinced, coerced, or, if necessary, sued and legislated into changing its marketing strategies. At present, the industry follows the course of least marketing resistance. It sells to the 20 percent of the drinkers who consume 80 percent of the alcohol. Unfortunately, many of that 20 percent are the suffering alcoholics. The following steps would be a beginning remedy to that situation:

1. Stop all alcohol advertising in places accessible to children. (By the age of eighteen the average kid has seen 100,000 beer commercials on television.)

2. Provide clear warning labels on all products advising users of the potential physical harm and addictive properties of the contents.

3. Subsidize national education programs that warn the public of the precursors and early warning signs of alcoholism.

4. Stop all lobbying activities aimed at preventing passage of stricter laws concerning the public use of alcohol—i.e., drinking at parks, beaches, sports events, and community festivals; while operating vehicles or traveling on airplanes; when gatherings include young people; and so forth.

This would be no more than temporary hardship to the alcohol manufacturers. Unlike the awesome health consequences facing the cigarette industry, many people can safely use alcohol. All the beer and liquor makers have to do to be socially responsible is to refocus their merchandising toward those who can safely use their products, adequately warn those who can't, and stop fighting efforts to protect the public safety. Such actions regarding alcohol use would go a long way toward changing national attitudes about the entire role of mood-alterers. It will no doubt take generations, but we must destroy the myth that properly functioning human minds and emotions can be improved by mood-altering chemicals—that a booze high or other drug-induced high is "better" than natural harmony and serenity—that alcohol-triggered feelings of camaraderie are better than real-life brotherhood and genuine heart-felt love—that celebration is enhanced through sedation...and the insane notion that toxic, addictive, empty-calorie intoxicants are desirable fare for intelligent people.

Back to the War

So yes, there needs to be a war on drugs. But the enemy needs to be more clearly defined and the forces concentrated on the right targets. Education and prevention need to focus on changing national attitudes about the whole idea of intoxication as a positive experience—with appropriate emphasis on Drug Number One: alcohol, and on clear warnings of the disease potential lurking in experimental drug use. Peer-based programs work best. Young people don't listen to experts. They listen to other kids who make sense. Intervention and treatment must be at least as available as the drugs are. That means neighborhood-based programs that speak to the cultural needs of the people they are trying to help. There are many successful models of such programs. They are cheap, effective, easy to start up, and essentially self-sustaining.

Remember the concept: 20 percent of the users consume 80 percent of the drugs, and those users are the ones suffering from C.D. Shift the funding from interdiction and law enforcement to intervention and treatment and you destroy most of the market. *That's how to win the war on drugs cost-effectively.* Finally, the law enforcement effort needs reorganization. The present scattered "war effort" violates the very principles of war. There is no clear mission statement, obvious commander-in-chief, coordinating staff, centralized command and control system, concentration of force, or sustained application of power. It's an overpublicized and under-funded nightmare of an operation unworthy of the first-class organizations tasked to perform its ill-defined and misdirected skirmishes.

A Research-Based War on Drugs

Science is now positioned to provide the answer to the truly age-old questions: "Who is abusing on purpose?" and "Who has a disease of impaired control?"

Research technology breakthroughs now make it likely that science will pinpoint the precise neurochemistry of alcoholism and related addictive diseases in the near future. These breakthroughs will allow clear differentiation between willful alcohol and other drug abuse and pathological alcohol or other drug dependencies.

Researchers already are in agreement about where in the brain the drugs of addiction operate. Science is also convinced that genetics play a significant role in determining who will become addicted. The genetic, neurochemical and biological research technologies and skills needed to probe and explore the mechanisms of alcoholism and other drug dependencies are now available. Exploiting those medical research developments can lead to objective medical diagnostic tests, discovery of genetic markers for addictive disease, non-addictive specific relapse prevention medicines, and even direct medical treatments to intervene and arrest the disease. As this unfolds, we can expect more and more involvement by mainstream medicine in the intervention and treatment of addictive diseases.

As a consequence of this "medicalization" of addictive disease treatment, the alcohol and related diseases should be considered as bona fide *medical* pathologies in the conceptualization of any national health care system, and medical research into basic causes and more specific treatments should have a high priority.

There is no doubt that addictions are a major public health challenge. Researchers are providing mounting evidence that today's psychosocial treatment modes work well enough to more than justify their costs. Even without the treatment breakthroughs described here, it is clear that treating addictions early saves the larger cost—cirrhosis, heart disease, cancer, or AIDS—that often result from untreated addictions.

Raising the priority for research to the same level as law enforcement, prevention, and treatment promises new approaches that can bring about enormous savings in health care, criminal justice, and social programs. These payoffs, combined with the increased national productivity to be gained, present a cost-to-benefit ratio rarely seen in the public policy arena.

There is no greater health care bargain than today's alcoholism and related disease treatment, and no more promising opportunity for dramatic savings in lives, property, and tax dollars than to support a major, research-based war to end the addiction epidemic.

Summary

There is many a battle yet to be fought, but the defense in the war on drugs is catching up with the offense. There is strong positive change moving across our land. The message is getting around that drugs are out and reality is in. Truly enlightened changes in government policies, personal lifestyles, and individual attitudes about alcohol and drug use are rounding the corner into full view. For all these reasons we believe that alcohol and drugs in America are matters of major concern but should rightfully be seen through a hopeful framework.

On balance, the picture can be summed up as follows: Alcohol and other legal and illegal drug abuse and dependency are very serious national problems, but the threat is not growing at the rate the headlines would seem to indicate. With strong central leadership, clear guidelines, and concentration of force, the war on drugs can be won.

Alcohol is still by far the most widespread and damaging drug of abuse, but a higher percentage of those who use drugs other than alcohol become dependent. These alcohol or other drug dependencies are observed to have specific genetic, biological, and psychological components, and have been defined as a treatable disease called chemical dependency. These C.D. persons constitute the primary market for alcohol and other drugs. Therefore, the major focus of the war on drugs needs to be on the prevention or early intervention and treatment of these victims. This and research to find real causes and true remedies is far less expensive than waiting for the disease to progress and paying the cost of crime, violence, imprisonment, welfare families, AIDS, etc.

When somebody you care about becomes a victim of C.D., the situation can be confusing and painful. Yet there is no justification for panic, but lots of reasons for hope, both as a nation facing a serious health and social problem and as individuals confronting an alcohol or other drug problem in someone we love. In today's more enlightened climate, there is effective, professional, and affordable help out there. It is possible, through intervention and treatment, to get the C.D. person to accept recovery as a logical, attractive, lofty choice. Treatment brings an array of positive payoffs into the lives of C.D. persons and their families. What all this means to you is that it will be easier to deal with a loved one's problem in an era where intoxication is more frowned upon, drugs are no longer "in," and quality help is all around.

Part Four

Finding the Resources

12

When You Can't Afford Help

The Money Issue

Quality in counseling and treatment, like quality elsewhere, costs money. Concern about the financing of recovery tends to reduce itself to four key questions: Are professional chemical and co-dependency treatment programs really necessary? Are they worth the price? Can you afford them? What if there is little money and limited or no insurance?

Is This Really Necessary?

We think the answer is yes. The debate usually centers around the efficacy of A.A. and other twelve-step programs versus formal treatment. Yet if you observe the recovery scene for decades, as we have, it is evident that there is no conflict between the two approaches. Each plays an important role, and they mutually reenforce each other. The ideal is to integrate both and derive the synergistic effect that results. As described earlier, this essentially biogenetic disease begins with powerlessness over alcohol and other mood-altering chemicals. But with this powerlessness unfolds an awesomely complex array of symptoms: physical illnesses, emotional problems, legal entanglements, marital strife, financial messes, sexual dysfunctions, troubled children, workplace frictions, damaged self-esteem, family communication breakdowns, and more. It is simply impossible to confront all these issues clearly and deal with them in a timely and lasting manner without special therapies conducted in a therapeutic atmosphere.

You can conquer the powerlessness with the help of a twelve-step program and then peck away at these secondary problems with self-help efforts, occasional individual counseling sessions, and years of "working on your program." But there is no real substitute for the Big Three: an intensive and structured treatment experience, professionally facilitated aftercare, and sustained lifetime participation in a twelve-step program. That's the best of all possible combinations.

People do achieve a measure of recovery without special assistance. A.A. and the other twelve-step programs have proven eminently successful in helping chemically dependent and codependent people overcome compulsions, clear away the wreckage of the past, and raise the victim's life to a higher spiritual plane. It is for these results that involvement in a twelve-step program is recognized as a core element in just about all respected treatment programs. But twelve-step programs are not designed to aggressively batter down and eliminate vestiges of delusion and denial;

screen for medical and psychological symptoms; aggressively confront defensive behaviors; dig into and process deeply buried emotional pain; sort out and mend the aftermath of painful family issues; provide current education about the disease; counsel regarding sexual dysfunctions, smoking, weight control, nutrition, and finances; offer physical and/or occupational rehabilitation; or teach specific skills for adult living such as communication, assertiveness, relaxation, and grieving. First-rate treatment centers address all those aspects of the disease and more.

On the other hand, those who just undergo treatment but forgo twelve-step involvement afterward seem to have a higher relapse rate. So is twelve-step program involvement necessary to recovery? Absolutely! if you want quality recovery and the odds against relapse on your side. Is treatment necessary? Positively! if you want to deal with all the issues and all the pain. It is enlightening to attend a twelve-step group meeting and observe the quality of recovery in those who have experienced treatment and those who have not. There are certainly notable exceptions, but for the most part the untreated will be viewed as successfully dealing with the pain, while the treated have successfully put most of it behind them. Both are success stories, but, as you will observe, all success is not equal. Treatment does pay off. It is worth the cost.

Is the Price Fair?

Even in this era of frightening increases in medical costs, the price of C.D.-related treatment has consistently been decreasing. There are three main reasons: First, experience has shown that unless the patient lacks a work or family support system or is suffering from serious medical or psychiatric problems, treatment may not need to be conducted in expensive hospital-based inpatient facilities. The trend has been toward less costly nonmedical and, wherever possible, outpatient settings. Second, because of increased awareness about intervention, C.D. victims are accepting help at earlier stages of the disease when treatment seems to be more effective. And third, competition is driving cost down almost everywhere. The medical director of one national treatment organization recently told us that in one region of the country they had been forced to reduce their fees by nearly two-thirds to meet the competition. The marketplace offers a variety of C.D. and co-dependency programs—which makes the cost highly competitive. So shop carefully, and you will pay only a fair price for quality treatment.

Will My Insurance Pay?

God only knows! In this era of managed care, HMOs, Medicare, and state and federal regulations or lack thereof, insurance coverage for chemical and co-dependency treatment is a very cloudy picture. In our state, for example, a few years ago the insurance authority ruled that health insurance companies *must* offer its client organizations coverage for alcoholism and other chemical dependencies. The intent was to encourage universal payment for these illnesses in order to motivate more victims to seek early help. (A number of studies had shown that in the long run this saves insurance costs: it's cheaper to treat early alcoholism now than terminal secondary illnesses later.) Up until that ruling, most insurance companies in the state had been paying for C.D. treatment under the nonspecific category of mental or nervous disorders. But after the new ruling went into effect, many organizations, *including many state government agencies*, when offered the specific coverage, refused it. During this same confusing era, some federal government agencies, for a period of time, stopped offering to their employees most coverage for these diseases. These particular glitches have been remedied now.

On the other hand, the Supreme Court once ruled that the Veterans Administration could deny benefit extensions to C.D. veterans. So there seem to be cycles of enlightenment, then retrenchment, regarding insurance coverage. Thus, third-party payment is often a confusing picture. Certain health insurance policies specify alcoholism and related disease benefits, while others clearly exclude or limit coverage. Some providers make no mention of these maladies, yet in fact pay for most treatment costs. As a general rule, the majority of health insurance programs will pay 80 percent of the fees charged by properly credentialed treatment facilities. Yet so-called managed care often brokers treatment choices based on cost reduction rather than appropriate patient-treatment matching.

Coverage seems to go through these confusing cycles, so we recommend taking your policy in hand and visiting the admissions office of a local treatment center. Ask them to check out the coverage. They will be pleased to do so since they would like to get your future business.

HMOs

There are many outstanding health maintenance organizations (HMOs) providing quality medical care at an attractive cost. We have, however, encountered some HMOs that do not have trained C.D. and co-dependency specialists on their staffs. Consequently, C.D. members or their families stand a good chance of falling into the traps described in Chapter 3. If you belong to one of these organizations, you may want to check out the help it offers for alcoholism or other drug dependencies. And find out if there is any provision for counseling/treatment of co-dependency. Should the program be found lacking, you may want to switch to another form of health care protection before seeking help. Otherwise there is the potential for getting inappropriate or ineffective remedies from the HMO while at the same time establishing a preexisting condition that could prevent reimbursement—at least for a waiting period—from any subsequent coverage you might acquire.

What About Special Programs?

As C.D. treatment has developed, it has become clear that certain populations do better in programs designed to meet their special needs. Certainly adolescents need treatment separate from adults. Gays and lesbians seem to do best in treatment programs specifically designed for homosexuals. Women-only programs or those offering special tracks for females claim greater recovery rates. Special issues pertinent to these select populations can best be addressed in the safety of others experiencing those same problems. One powerful example of these needs stems from the shockingly high rate of sexual abuse in chemically dependent women. That subject is better dealt with in a program sensitive to that issue.

There are many so-called Impaired Professional Programs aimed at M.D.'s, attorneys, dentists, pharmacists, veterinarians, nurses, etc. A number of these centers have outstanding treatment models, highly trained staffs, and hard-earned national reputations. Some, however, simply use the impaired professional aegis as a marketing ploy.

If you are considering such a choice, check out the reputation of the facility with the appropriate professional organization (Medical Society, Dental Association, Bar Association, etc.).

There are arguments for and against special programs. One side says "Don't make the C.D. professional special. Their ego is already in the way of recovery." Others make the case that physicians, attorneys, and other professionals do have unique challenges to recovery and deserve and require customized mized approaches. Our experience shows that physicians, clergy, and attorneys do better in programs tailored to the sensitivities of those vocations. Most M.D., clergy, or lawyer treatment models involve longer-term in-patient care and more closely supervised aftercare. Those approaches seem to pay off in higher quality recovery. As for other C.D. professionals, we suggest taking advice of recovered C.D. people from that particular career. Again, consult with the appropriate professional association for advice.

We Can't Afford It!

Frequently, suffering family members lament: "This intervention and treatment sounds great, but we don't have that kind of money and there is no insurance." The choices may be difficult, but the cost of intervention and treatment must be weighed against the penalties for delay. Economic disaster goes hand in hand with chemical dependency. D.W.I. fines and legal fees; auto accidents; lawsuits; divorces; illness and injury; job loss or damage to professional credentials and reputation; money wasted on booze, drugs, and associated carousing; gambling; and poor business decisions can produce a terrible dollar toll. In a year and half or so the typical alcoholic can spend as much on booze as the cost of treatment. And we've encountered cocaine users who snort away that much in a month. So, compared with the expense of allowing the disease to continue, treatment is a very cost-effective choice. This may mean selling the family jewels, giving up the annual vacation trip, or going into debt. It's still probably worth it. For without help, the resources of a C.D. family dwindle away with the progress of the disease. The corny old salesman's adage applies in a very real sense. "You can't afford not to buy treatment."

But If You Truly Can't Afford It

Suppose help is honestly beyond financial reach. There are still options. It may take a bit of street-smarts and some hard work, but it is possible to accomplish all the help actions we've written about by using low-cost or no-cost-to-you resources. Consider this analogy: People with lots of money can go to a single department or grocery store and buy everything they need in one stop—within reason—without regard for price. Not being similarly blessed financially, you may find it necessary to watch for sales, clip coupons, buy different products at different stores to get the best values, and just generally put more energy and shrewdness into your clothing or grocery shopping. Using the same approach, it's possible to fill your recovery bag with all the needed services. Here are some ideas:

- Try to negotiate affordable fees. Some helping professionals and treatment centers charge sliding-scale fees based on ability to pay.

- Check with the best counselors and programs to see whether you can make some kind of payment arrangement. A facility with empty beds to fill may consider some kind of extremely long-term payment plan. Some health care organizations today even accept credit cards.

- Ask local private treatment centers if they have any free or reduced-cost bed spaces allocated for those in need.

And be sure to take advantage of the many free services available in your area:

- The local Council on Alcoholism and Drug Abuse may offer free information programs on alcohol, other drugs, and on intervention for families. This local council may even provide no-cost intervention counseling. They sometimes offer out-patient treatment as well. If not, the council can probably steer you to a treatment center that presents low-cost or no-cost community information programs and intervention assistance.

- Investigate tax- or donation-supported programs for which your family may quality (V.A., state hospital, fraternal organizations, local mental health agencies, etc.). Many of these programs are excellent and employ some of the most competent and dedicated professionals in the field.

- Call the United Way office and ask for the names of any C.D.-related services funded by the agency.

- Contact your community Council of Churches and see whether there may be members of the clergy in your town who are trained in intervention and C.D. counseling.

- Join a self-help program like A.A., Al-anon, Alateen, Narcotics Anonymous, Co-Dependents Anonymous, or Adult Children of Alcoholics. They are nearly always available, and there are no dues or fees for membership. The people you meet there will help you find additional affordable help.

- Go to the library and browse through the many excellent books on alcoholism and other drug problems. The librarian can help you locate them.

- Write the state alcoholism authority. Your local council on alcoholism and drug abuse can provide the address. There may even be a local office. This state authority is responsible for channeling millions of dollars in state and federal aid into education, research, and direct care. Ask them for help.

- Consult the list of resources in the back of this book for additional leads that may be helpful.

The point is, don't give up. You may be poor or perhaps just temporarily broke, but you are not without imagination and common sense. So put to work the same savvy and resourcefulness that you use when shopping for food and clothing and services. Shop around until you pull together the resources needed to help your family. Keep in mind the hopeful fact that the helping community in the field of chemical dependency is replete with those who have also suffered from this disease. Though they may be "professionals" who make their living assisting others, most of them won't let you down just because you're broke. If you reach out, somehow, someway, someone will take your hand.

13

Finding Courage and Support

The News Is Good

In this book we've tried to restore hope, give useful perspectives, and suggest proven paths and guidelines. Chemical dependencies are awful things, and living with a victim is a most disturbing experience. But the trends are positive. National awareness abounds.

Use and abuse seems to be leveling off. Getting high is no longer an "in" thing to do. With less and less cultural tolerance of intoxicated behavior, the victims of C.D. are beginning to stand out. That means earlier intervention and therefore less damage to victims and families. More professionally based help is available. Competition for the treatment of this "new" disease is lowering the cost of care. Realization by the insurance industry of the cost benefits derived from providing better coverage for these illnesses is helping families to pay for quality treatment. The challenge of managed care is resolving itself through better cooperation and communications between providers and insurers. Organizations such as the National Treatment Consortium are taking the actions needed to bring together employers, insurers, and treatment providers.

Practical early intervention methods have proven very effective. Recent excellent, well-validated studies show that treatment does bring about full recovery in most cases. And an impressive array of community-based help resources and self-help programs is available just about everywhere. So there is every reason to feel positive and be hopeful. On balance the news is good. The help is out there and it does work.

Afraid and Alone

The apparent hopelessness of chemical dependency and co-dependency steals away the todays of our lives. Because the present is so painful, thoughts and energies project into the future with fear and anxiety or dwell on the past with guilt and remorse. Yet, in order to take positive steps with these diseases, it is vital to operate in the here and now—where choices can be made that will lead to wellness. Making those choices takes courage and support. C.D. families give up their power of choice as they learn how to survive in an atmosphere of fear and isolation. Survival may ease the pain temporarily, but it is not recovery. To really break free from this trap takes choices. And to make those choices you will need new sources of courage and support.

There is a modern-day fable about a big-city policeman who encountered a sad-faced alcoholic on a shadowy street corner. The pitiful man was on his knees, slowly circling a lamppost. His frightened face was just inches away from the post, and he was beating on it with both fists. Over and over he cried, "Help me! Please help me!" The policeman tapped him gently on the shoulder with his club and asked, "What's wrong?" "I'm walled in," was the pathetic reply. Such is the feeling that paralyzes the C.D. family—a sense of hopelessness, powerlessness, and isolation. Yet, just as with the sad fellow in the fable, all that's needed is to turn outward to find sources of courage and support.

The First Stop

Carl Jung, the revered pioneer of modern psychiatry, once said that after midlife all problems are fundamentally spiritual. He might well have made the same observation about chemical dependency and co-dependency. Recovery from these maladies is essentially a spiritual task. Keep in mind here that spirituality is not necessarily "religionality," although many do find a formal religion to be the most accessible path to a spiritual dimension in their lives. However, for many others, the experience of living in a C.D. situation has brought spiritual despair. It is toward them, in particular, that these next few words about spirituality are aimed.

By spirituality we mean tuning into and connecting with the power sources that reside in the universe outside ourselves—nature, other people, the collective wisdom of the ages, and the love, truth, justice, and beauty that surround us. Some choose to call that power God. What to call this "power greater than ourselves" is optional. The fact that we need such power to recover isn't optional. Communion with this sense of beingness may translate into a belief in a personal, good, and loving God— and it may not. But however we may choose to connect, connect we must. We live in a little box of space and time and possess only limited control over even that small domain. Yet there is a whole universe of circumstances and events that make up our lives over which we have no apparent control. We must either see this larger domain as chaos rushing toward nothingness or as an elegant mystery gradually revealing its rhyme and reason. Opting for chaos dooms us to a life of despair, self-pity, and, worst of all, inaction. The ultimate symptom of C.D. and co-dependency is spiritual darkness. Recovery from these diseases demands the light of faith in the fundamental goodness and order of the visible world, an abiding acceptance of the notion that pain is not the way things are supposed to be, that suffering is an aberration, and that not actualizing into the person you were meant to be is—beyond all else—unnatural.

Transcendence

What has happened to the victims of these diseases is that they have stopped becoming what they were meant to be. Recovery from chemical dependency and co-dependency means getting back on schedule and on course toward becoming our very best possible selves. This means more than just breaking addictions or modifying behavior. It is coming to believe that our role in this universe is to grow into the unique creatures we were meant to be. Achieving such rebirth and renewal requires more than simply repairing the separate broken parts of us. There isn't enough time in a human life to fix piece by piece all of the emotional, behavioral, financial, legal, marital, family, health, and professional damages caused by these diseases. Healing must therefore be holistic and transcendent if it is to be rapid enough to justify the pursuit. Most of those who have recovered and whose lives are marked by freedom, serenity, and joy have found it necessary and practical to seek powers greater than themselves. They started by believing in believing. Soon that one-too-many believings faded away and faith banished fear. Maybe faith in God but, if not, then at least faith in the possibilities of life and the potential and worth of self. That's the magic: recovery believed in is recovery begun.

A Proven Pathway

Millions of C.D. people have found a practical pathway to spirituality in the Twelve Steps of Alcoholics Anonymous. A.A. is the unchallenged fountainhead from which has flowed our stubborn national acceptance of alcoholism as a treatable disease. Scott Peck, author of the immensely popular *The Road Less Traveled*, ranks A.A. among the three most important innovations of this century, along with television and the jet airplane. And deservedly so. He does this because the entire concept of self-help began with A.A. A.A. has saved more individual alcoholic lives and families than everything else ever tried combined. The famous Twelve Steps upon which the program is based has been adapted successfully as a remedy for just about every compulsive behavior known. There is little doubt that the treatment of alcoholism would still be in the Dark Ages were it not for the work of influential alcoholics who first found sobriety through this magnificent program. Marty Mann, author of *New Primer on Alcoholism* and the late founding president of the National Council on Alcoholism, herself recovered in A.A., states: "NCA was founded in 1944 in an atmosphere of total darkness. The public attitude was compounded of ignorance, fear, prejudice and hostility and the public attitude included most professionals. Almost nothing was being done about alcoholism except by alcoholics themselves."

A.A. at Work

Early employee assistance programs in major corporations such as Du Pont, Eastman Kodak, Standard Oil, and Consolidated Edison were simply based on referring employees with drinking problems to A.A. There was no other help available. In many cases these EAPs, as they later came to be known, were started and managed by employees who had found their own recovery in Alcoholics Anonymous. Most early treatment programs were simply medically supervised detoxification followed by introduction to this program.

Respected treatment centers to this day use the Twelve Steps and involve the patient in A.A. as the core of their program models. The Twelve-Step programs can be the bedrock of continued growth. And the gateway to adding a spiritual dimension to life.

Gather With the Strong

As you pursue intervention and recovery for your family, there will be no shortage of doubters, doomsayers, and providers of conflicting advice. Almost everyone around you will have had some experience with C.D. people—most of it painful and reflective of inaccurate information about the disease. Thus, it is important to rally around those who can offer encouragement, helpful input, and emotional support. You'll need friends to call when there is crisis or doubt, or when you want to share feelings and test out ideas. Support groups such as Al-anon, Alateen, Tough Love Parents, and Adult Children of Alcoholics are a readily accessible place to connect with such friends.

If self-help is not enough for you, then seek out a good professional therapy group to meet your needs. Perhaps a church in the community may be enlightened about C.D., offering an opportunity to meet people who are dealing with these same problems. But, by whatever means, it's crucial to find those from whom you can derive courage and strength. Co-dependency undermines the choice-making apparatus, so you will need encouragement to take the steps required. Living with a C.D. person's defensive behavior brings paralyzing guilt and fear. Thus breaking out of that trap is difficult without prompting and urging from concerned others. Most find that they need coaches, cheerleaders, and fellow team members to help them get moving. If you reach out to make these contacts, they will happen. As the Buddhists say, "When the student is ready, the teacher appears."

The Strength of Many

Chemical dependency and co-dependency can make their victims feel isolated and alone, as if these events and this pain were unique and never happened to anyone else. It has. In ten thousand years of Western culture probably no tragedy, even the frightening wars and plagues, has caused more pain. All around you—at work, in your neighborhood, and at church—are those who have recovered and those still suffering. Far from alone, you are standing in the midst of an enormous resource of recovery experience and shared pain. All you need to do is reach out...ask...step forward...seek and you really shall find. Your strength will be multiplied. Wellness can begin for you and your family right now. Use the guidelines suggested and find the help you need. And when the magic of intervention, treatment, and spiritual living has turned your pain to joy, look to those still suffering and do what you can to perpetuate the gift. Help the others still suffering to get help.

Resources

Organizations

The status of helpful resources for problems relating to alcohol and other drugs is ever-changing. Organizations and services evolve under the impact of media emphasis, level of public concern, health insurance trends, legislative changes, availability of funds, and a host of other variables. The following organizations have demonstrated a measure of staying power. Nonetheless, you may experience an occasional returned letter or disconnected telephone. Don't be discouraged. Try another, and you will no doubt eventually connect with the help needed.

A.A. World Service (Alcoholics Anonymous)
P.O. Box 459, Grand Central Station
New York, NY 10163
(212) 870-3400

Al-Anon/Alateen/Adult Child Family Groups
Headquarters
P.O. Box 862, Midtown Station
New York, NY 10018-0862
(800) 344-2666

A.A., Al-Anon, and Alateen are usually listed in the telephone directory. Call for meeting schedules and literature, or to talk to a member.

American Society of Addiction Medicine, Inc.
5225 Wisconsin Ave. NW, #409
Washington, DC 20015
(202) 244-8948

Many of the following national organizations may have local chapters in your community. Check the business pages in the telephone directory.

National Black Alcoholism & Addictions Council
1629 K St. NW, Suite 802
Washington, DC 20006
(202) 296-2696

National Clearinghouse for Alcohol and Drug Information (NCADI)
P.O. Box 2345
Rockville, MD 20847-2345
(301) 468-2600, (800) 729-6686

National Council on Alcoholism and Drug Dependency (NCADD)
12 West 21st St., 8th Fl.
New York, NY 10010
(212) 206-6770, (800) NCA-CALL

Council on Alcoholism/Drug Abuse
Listed in local telephone directory.

State Commission on Alcoholism/Drug Abuse
District offices are listed in local telephone directory.

Cocaine Hotline
1-800-COCAINE

Narcotics Anonymous
(818) 780-3951

Books

Alcoholics Anonymous. New York, NY: A.A. World Services, 1976.
The famous "Big Book" upon which A.A. and other twelve-step programs are based.

Twelve Steps and Twelve Traditions. New York, NY: A.A. World Services, 1953.
A timeless articulation of the foundational principles of the A.A. program.

The Dilemma of the Alcoholic Marriage. New York, NY: Al-Anon Family Group, 1981.
The official Al-Anon book about alcoholism, communication, and marriage.

Johnson, Vernon. *I'll Quit Tomorrow.* New York, NY: Harper & Row, 1973.
An explanation of the progressive disease of chemical dependency and ways to intervene, by the pioneer of the family intervention technique.

Mann, Marty. *New Primer on Alcoholism.* New York: Holt, Rinehart and Winston, 1950.

Classic by a pioneering woman founder of the National Council of Alcoholism.

Peck, M. Scott. *The Road Less Traveled*. New York, NY: Simon and Schuster, 1983.
Longtime best-seller about truth, reality, mature love, and successful living in the contemporary world.

Perkins, William Mack, and Nancy McMurtrie-Perkins. *Raising Drug-Free Kids in a Drug-Filled World*. Center City, MN: Hazelden, 1986.
Proven prevention guidelines for parents by two nationally recognized chemical dependency counselors.

Powell, John. *Fully Human, Fully Alive*. Niles, IL: Argus Communications, 1976.
Uplifting reflections on human worth, positive living, the significance of individuals, and the spiritual meaning of life.

Satir, Virginia. *Peoplemaking*. Palo Alto, CA: Behavior Books, 1972.
Thoughts about family systems and how they work by the revered originator of many of today's family therapy approaches.

Satir, Virginia. *Self-Esteem*. Palo Alto, CA: Science and Behavior Books, 1975.
A wonderful little book with profound meaning. A gift to yourself.

Woititz, J. *Adult Children of Alcoholics*. Pompano Beach, FL: Health Communications, 1983.
Describes self-defeating behaviors that are common to adult children of alcoholics and suggests what to do about them.

York, Phyllis, David York, and Ted Wachtel. *Toughlove*. Garden City, NY: Doubleday, 1982.
Help for parents dealing with rebellious adolescents.

For the Professional

NIAAA Dept. of Health and Human Services Public Health Service, Alcohol Drug Abuse & Mental Health Administration. *Alcohol Alert*. Rockville, MD 20857.

NIAAA Superintendent of Documents, US Government Printing Office. *Alcohol Health and Research World*. Washington, DC 20402. (202) 783-3238.

Quarterly.

Manisses Communication Group. *Alcoholism & Drug Abuse Week.* 3
    Govenor St., Providence, RI 02906-0357. (401) 831-6020.
Weekly on insurance, treatment, and legislative issues.

Index

Other New Harbinger Self-Help Titles

Redefining Mr. Right, $11.95

Dying of Embarrassment: Help for Social Anxiety and Social Phobia, $11.95

The Depression Workbook: Living With Depression and Manic Depression, $13.95

Risk-Taking for Personal Growth: A Step-by-Step Workbook, $11.95

The Marriage Bed: Renewing Love, Friendship, Trust, and Romance, $11.95

Focal Group Psychotherapy: For Mental Health Professionals, $44.95

Hot Water Therapy: How to Save Your Back, Neck & Shoulders in 10 Minutes a Day $11.95

Older & Wiser: A Workbook for Coping With Aging, $12.95

Prisoners of Belief: Exposing & Changing Beliefs that Control Your Life, $10.95

Be Sick Well: A Healthy Approach to Chronic Illness, $11.95

Men & Grief: A Guide for Men Surviving the Death of a Loved One., $11.95

When the Bough Breaks: A Guide for Parents of Sexually Abused Childern, $11.95

Love Addiction: A Guide to Emotional Independence, $11.95

When Once Is Not Enough: Help for Obsessive Compulsives, $11.95

The New Three Minute Meditator, $9.95

Getting to Sleep, $10.95

The Relaxation & Stress Reduction Workbook, 3rd Edition, $13.95

Leader's Guide to the Relaxation & Stress Reduction Workbook, $19.95

Beyond Grief: A Guide for Recovering from the Death of a Loved One, $10.95

Thoughts & Feelings: The Art of Cognitive Stress Intervention, $13.95

Messages: The Communication Skills Book, $12.95

The Divorce Book, $11.95

Hypnosis for Change: A Manual of Proven Techniques, 2nd Edition, $12.95

The Deadly Diet: Recovering from Anorexia & Bulimia, $11.95

Self-Esteem, $12.95

Chronic Pain Control Workbook, $13.95

Rekindling Desire: Bringing Your Sexual Relationship Back to Life, $12.95

Life Without Fear: Anxiety and Its Cure, $10.95

Visualization for Change, $12.95

Guideposts to Meaning: Discovering What Really Matters, $11.95

Videotape: Clinical Hypnosis for Stress & Anxiety Reduction, $24.95

Starting Out Right: Essential Parenting Skills for Your Child's First Seven Years, $12.95

Big Kids: A Parent's Guide to Weight Control for Children, $11.95

My Parent's Keeper: Adult Children of the Emotionally Disturbed, $11.95

When Anger Hurts, $12.95

Free of the Shadows: Recovering from Sexual Violence, $12.95

Resolving Conflict With Others and Within Yourself, $12.95

Lifetime Weight Control, $11.95

The Anxiety & Phobia Workbook, $13.95

Love and Renewal: A Couple's Guide to Commitment, $12.95

The Habit Control Workbook, $12.95

Call **toll free, 1-800-748-6273**, to order books. Have your Visa or Mastercard number ready.

Or send a check for the titles you want to New Harbinger Publications, 5674 Shattuck Avenue, Oakland, CA 94609. Include $2.00 for the first book and 50¢ for each additional book, to cover shipping and handling. (California residents please include appropriate sales tax.) Allow four to six weeks for delivery.

Prices subject to change without notice.